Escape from the Taliban

Escape from the Taliban

One Woman's Experiences in Afghanistan

Bashir Sakhawarz

First published in Great Britain in 2023 by
Pen & Sword History
An imprint of
Pen & Sword Books Ltd
Yorkshire - Philadelphia

Copyright © Bashir Sakhawarz, 2023

ISBN 978 1 39904 240 6

The right of Bashir Sakhawarz to be identified as the Author of this work has been asserted by him in accordance with the Copyright, Designs and Patents Act 1988.

A CIP catalogue record for this book is available from the British Library

All rights reserved. No part of this book may be reproduced or transmitted in any form or by any means, electronic or mechanical including photocopying, recording or by any information storage and retrieval system, without permission from the Publisher in writing.

Typeset in INDIA by IMPEC eSolutions
Printed and bound in the UK by CPI Group (UK) Ltd, Croydon, CR0 4YY

Pen & Sword Books Ltd. incorporates the Imprints of Pen & Sword Archaeology, Atlas, Aviation, Battleground, Discovery, Family History, History, Maritime, Military, Naval, Politics, Railways, Select, Transport, True Crime, Fiction, Frontline Books, Leo Cooper, Praetorian Press, Seaforth Publishing, Wharncliffe, White Owl and After the Battle.

For a complete list of Pen & Sword titles please contact
PEN & SWORD BOOKS LIMITED
47 Church Street, Barnsley, South Yorkshire S70 2AS, United Kingdom
E-mail: enquiries@pen-and-sword.co.uk
Website: www.pen-and-sword.co.uk

or

PEN AND SWORD BOOKS
1950 Lawrence Rd, Havertown, PA 19083, USA
E-mail: Uspen-and-sword@casematepublishers.com
Website: www.penandswordbooks.com

For my family: Romana, Sama and Pedraam

Contents

Acknowledgements viii

Chapter 1	Flying on the roof of an aeroplane	1
Chapter 2	Great loss	17
Chapter 3	Too little, too much	28
Chapter 4	*The Truth about the Saur Revolution*	45
Chapter 5	War was the only project	58
Chapter 6	Life and death	70
Chapter 7	Russians on the streets	85
Chapter 8	How to forget these days?	99
Chapter 9	Shaky days	109
Chapter 10	The most un-Islamic Islamic Groups	116
Chapter 11	It was yours, now it is mine	119
Chapter 12	The tunnel	146
Chapter 13	At the mercy of Adai	164
Chapter 14	Going to Pakistan	178
Chapter 15	Searching for Shah Mahmud: Part 1	193
Chapter 16	Searching for Shah Mahmud: Part 2	205
Chapter 17	Living with Shah Mahmud	214
Chapter 18	Without Kabir	222
Chapter 19	Searching for work	227
Chapter 20	Almost six years later	235
Chapter 21	Fremont, Freedom, California	243
Chapter 22	Children's success and demand	252

Acknowledgements

This book would have not come to existence without inspiration from Nagina Azizi and enormous support from Ivan Kent, a talented author.

I also thank my publishing team Tara Moran, Harriet Fielding and Diane Wordsworth.

Chapter 1

Flying on the roof of an aeroplane

I was woken by a desperate hammering on the door of our hotel room. I checked my watch. It was a little after ten, the bright sunshine outside barely leaking around the curtains. I leapt out of bed and ran to open the door, observing that my daughter Fariba was undisturbed by the noise and thinking that young people seem able to sleep through anything, even a noise like exploding bombs.

Khalil, my cousin, faced me through the doorway. He looked frightened. His first words were: "Salaam, cousin. I need to talk with you. Now!"

For a moment I stared at him, speechless. Then my brain began to work again. "Let me dress. I'll come down and meet you in the restaurant."

I went immediately to the bathroom and splashed water on my face. I was worried but did not want to wake my daughter. We had been to dinner the previous night at the house of my future daughter-in-law's family. Shahla was my son Haseeb's fiancée and although I would have preferred an early night it would have seemed rude to drag Fariba and Haseeb back to the hotel, so we had stayed talking together with Shahla and her family until near midnight. What could possibly have happened to make Khalil so worried? Had something happened to Shahla or her family? I dressed as quickly as I could and rushed downstairs to find Khalil.

My first words were: "What is it, Khalil? What is the trouble? Is the family okay?"

"Family are fine but I have bad news and I am worried for you."

"What is the matter?" I asked. "You are killing me with such talk." I waved my right hand and pulled his elbow across the table towards me. "Please explain."

"The presidential palace is in the hands of the Taliban and President Ashraf Ghani has fled the country."

"Is this some kind of bad joke?" I asked.

"I wish it was," he replied.

His news was impossible to believe. Just around midnight we had returned to the Parwan Hotel through a very quiet Kabul. If anything had happened during the night I would surely have heard it since I am a very light sleeper and even a single shot wakes me. My experience of previous struggles for power in Kabul told me that the end was always terrifying with the sound of gunshot and explosions. I had witnessed such horrific events at least six times in the past, all bloody and explosive.

Khalil explained that the Taliban in their pickup trucks, the type of vehicle they used to transport soldiers, had entered Kabul overnight. There had been no resistance. They surrounded the Arg, the presidential palace, where the guards panicked and fled rather than face the brutality of the Taliban. Finding himself in such a perilous situation, President Ghani had been flown out of Kabul in a helicopter.

"How do you know about this?" I asked incredulously.

"My neighbour works as a chef in the Arg. He told me this morning and I came immediately to tell you."

"Oh God! I don't believe it," I protested.

"There is no time!"

"Time for what?" I was beginning to panic.

"You must wake up the children and we should go straight to the airport to see if you can fly back to America."

"But Haseeb went with his father last night and he is still with him. I can't go without Haseeb! Besides, we aren't booked to fly until next week."

"You don't need a ticket," Khalil exclaimed. "Just pray that you can find a place in one of those army planes. Everyone who has papers showing a US connection is running towards the airport now. The US Army will allow those people to get in."

"I can't go, Khalil – not without Haseeb," I insisted. I felt desperate and powerless.

Khalil was almost shouting at me. "You don't see the situation clearly, Deeba! It's a disaster. Haseeb is a man now. He worked with the US forces on the front line in the past. I can arrange for him to walk to the Pakistani border. From Pakistan he will be able to fly to America."

"Can't I do the same?"

"Deeba! You are not young any more. It is five days walking at night to the Pakistani border. You'd have to cross rivers and mountains… and you know how the Taliban treats women."

"But let's try to take Haseeb," I insisted.

Khalil was adamant. "It takes hours to go to your husband's place – you don't have time."

To dare once is brave but to dare twice is madness. I escaped from the hands of and also ran away from an abusive husband who kept beating me many years ago. Now, in August 2021, I was back in Kabul and at risk of being captured again. Maybe I am mad, but loving one's children makes a mother mad.

At home in California, in April 2021, Haseeb told me of his intention to become engaged to Shahla, a beautiful 21-year-old girl from Kabul he had met while he was working as an interpreter for the US Army in 2017. Haseeb said he would go alone for his engagement, but I would not hear of that. Haseeb had also been planning to bring his father, my abusive husband Kabir, to California. I would have to face Kabir sooner or later and so I would not let him steal from me a mother's right to be at her son's betrothal.

That April was the same month that President Joe Biden announced the total withdrawal of the US Army from Afghanistan. At the time I thought he was just threatening. I did not believe that he would do it. I thought the threat was to make President Ghani get rid of corruption in the Afghan National Army and to use the army more effectively. Who, I asked myself, was going to throw away twenty years of costly effort resulting in so many American casualties? Nevertheless, I was worried and found it increasingly difficult to sleep sometimes. I could not understand why Biden made such a statement, especially if it was not just a threat. Was this some kind of strategy to win the hearts of the Americans who voted for him, those who thought they did not have to sacrifice their lives in Afghanistan?

I had always followed the progress of events in Afghanistan, partly because it was my home, partly because of my son's direct involvement as an interpreter with US forces, and also because of my son's intention to bring his father to America but especially now, because I wanted to meet the family of my son's intended bride and to be present at his betrothal in Afghanistan. I knew that the Taliban were fighting fiercely to occupy more and more of Afghanistan, but they were only managing to control some villages and more rural districts. Afghan forces did recapture these places but then, losing them again, had to retake them once more. Our Afghan army and its western allies kept the Taliban out of key provinces and cities and there was no fighting around Kabul, where I would go to meet Shahla and her family. I decided straightaway that I would go with him because I had never heard of any engagement being conducted without the presence of the mothers – this is very important for an Afghan woman. Seeing my determination and knowing about Afghan traditions, he agreed, whereupon my daughter Fariba insisted on accompanying us.

I was delighted to be back once more in my country and, seeing how peaceful Kabul appeared, I had the illusion that there could be no fighting anywhere in the whole country. In this joyful frame of mind, I began going around to the houses of Shahla's parents and the rest of our family and friends to distribute the presents I brought with me from California.

My primary mission was to arrange the engagement of my son and his fiancée. My secondary mission was to help my husband get to the US because that is what my children asked me to do. Even though it meant having to face the man who had brutally tortured me, I accepted the task because, for me, children come first. My time in California was a time of self-discovery. As a result, I am much stronger now and know he can never treat me like that again. In California I have only a small apartment, which I use with my children. I will accept that Kabir may share the apartment with us. He may share Haseeb's room or sleep on the sofa, but I will never permit him to sleep in my bed with me. It was Haseeb's wish that his father should come to America and he was the one who found a lawyer to make the case for Kabir to do so.

Four years ago, when Haseeb told me that he wanted to go to Afghanistan to work as an interpreter for the US Army fighting the Taliban, I cried and begged him not to go.

He is a very strongminded young man. "I don't want you to work in Jack in the Box for pity money, damaging your back," he said while busy packing his suitcase. "Besides, it is my duty to help my people by stopping the Taliban. You know what they do to the women, the country and the rest of our people."

"At least you could've told me in advance," I said, tears in my eyes as I helped him pack.

"Mother, I kept it secret deliberately. If I gave you a warning, you would have hidden my passport, asked my uncles to help you and stopped me going."

He was right, I would have tried to stop him. I am a mother and have seen too many mothers lose their sons. But I am also proud of him for having done what he believed to be right. Thus, four years later, I was back in my country and delighted to be able to organise Haseeb's engagement to Shahla. She is a pretty girl who, when I went to meet her at her family home in Maiwand, Kabul, kissed my hands and called me Mother. I want to be like a mother to her when she comes to Freemont, California, and shall try my best to fill the vacuum she will feel when separated from her family. Of course, Haseeb's love will also help and I shall make sure that Haseeb never forgets to love Shahla. Historically, a woman in our country is called *mazlum*, victim. Just by being born a woman you are a victim. I wanted to tell Shahla that she was not *mazlum* and show her the beauty of freedom, away from pressures of family and her own people. I wanted to show her what I have discovered in the west to help her realise her own values.

I was accompanied on this journey by Fariba, my younger daughter, who had recently graduated from a US university where she had read Development Studies in order one day to participate in rebuilding her own country. Just two years older than Shahla, she is an independent girl with no plans to get married. I am sure Shahla will learn a lot from her too. *Shahla* in Persian, my own language, means beautiful eyes and I am sure she had seen only war and trouble with her beautiful eyes. Like Haseeb she is a war child and this common ground should cement their love. The challenges in California will not be as great as those in Kabul, where she witnessed her school friend disfigured on her way to school by a Taliban terrorist throwing acid in her face. Shahla told me how a bomb that exploded in the market where she was shopping killed four brothers in their shop whose mother not only lost all her sons but had to put up with her husband marrying another young wife to start a new family and to have sons again because without a son society believes the name of the family will disappear. I am proud that my two daughters have done very well with their education. Much better than my sons.

My hopes for a better future for my family were in danger that morning. Khalil was undoubtedly right that Haseeb could walk to freedom. When he was working for the US Army, he had walked for days from one side of the country to the other. He told me that he had even crossed the border into Pakistan chasing Taliban terrorists. But that did not help me or Fariba. I was angry with Khalil because in our communications he had kept secret details of the full extent of the Taliban's progress. He, like me, thought the Afghan Army was the biggest in the region and, supported by NATO, would ensure that the Taliban would never be able to capture Kabul. Like me he had believed that the US government had warned the Taliban that they would be punished if ever they tried to invade again. All I had seen on US media tended to support Khalil's optimistic statements. Nevertheless, the speed of the Taliban's progress had been astonishing. In July I could not have imagined that in just one month they would capture city after city but, least of all, that Kabul could fall so easily and so quickly. We had all assumed that the Americans with their unparalleled military strength and the best intelligence in the world would prevent such a disaster.

I woke Fariba but, like me a little earlier, she thought the news was a cruel joke. It took some time for her to accept what it meant for us all. We packed our clothes in a great rush, mixing clean with unclean, and then hurried down to join Khalil.

"What is all this?" Khalil asked immediately, pointing at our suitcases. "Leave them with the receptionist. I'll pick them up later. Pray there'll be space for you and Fariba on the American plane. Just bring a small handbag and make sure you've got your passport and papers."

I had been thinking of a normal flight with seats but he made me realise that we would be lucky even to get into a big army plane, probably crammed in, sitting on the floor or even standing. He rushed us outside onto the street. I noticed how quiet it was. A car passed occasionally. The day before that street had been full of traffic. We waited for a long time. No taxi appeared. We walked to the nearest taxi stand but found it empty. After what seemed an age, a very old taxi appeared. The driver asked for four times the usual fare. We did not argue.

Vast numbers of people of all ages were walking towards the airport. About a kilometre away from it the road was blocked by such a mass of people that it seemed as if the whole country was on the move. Fear was on everybody's face – fear of the terror of the Taliban. Small children were carried on their fathers' backs. Some children were wailing under the hot sun. When it became impossible to go further, we had to abandon the taxi and continue on foot. Hemmed-in by the crowd and lacking protection from the hot sun we were sweating and my asthma kicked in. It was only then that I remembered that in the rush to leave the hotel room I had left my inhaler behind. Beside suffering from asthma, I was also extremely thirsty. But there was nothing I could do about it. Normally I remembered to take a bottle of water with me before a flight, but the panic and hurry made me forget that too.

A woman next to me tripped and fell. Others stepped on her body. I did not see her get up. I could not go to help her because the crush was pushing us on. Khalil kept shouting, telling us we must stick together because it would be impossible to find each other later. I checked on Fariba to see how she was doing and realised that, because of her youth and strength, she was in much better shape than I.

That final kilometre took a very long time until, finally, the sheer wall of people stopped us from moving forward. We were in the middle of chaos. The crowd surged across the once pretty lawn and flowers in front of the terminal, destroying it all. English soldiers tried to bring order, standing on top of concrete walls that were meant to protect the terminal from terrorist attacks, shouting at the crowds. They were just as helpless as the rest of us. After a while the crowd became impatient and moved towards the main entrance to the terminal, which was shut. They pushed and pushed but the glass door was strong. Finally, however, the hinges of the door gave in and the big glass door fell flat onto the ceramic floor, shattering into pieces. The crowd rushed forward. We also tried but could not get in. After a while the soldiers managed to block the entrance. They fired into the air to deter further attempts at invasion. That worked.

By this time I was thirsty and becoming dizzy from the heat. I looked at Fariba to check how she was doing but I'd forgotten about Khalil, a kidney patient who needed to drink water all the time. In a situation like this, we think mainly about our children and ourselves. I asked Khalil how he was and he told me that he was not suffering, which I thought was a lie and I urged him to look for water. He said the only way he would find water would be to get out of the crowd and find a shop selling water. But how was he going to find us when he came back? We moved just as much as we could to find a landmark visible from an electricity pole. However, these poles all look the same. Nevertheless, Khalil took a chance, I think because he was suffering. I had been about to collapse and, until he returned when it was almost dark, I had no energy to move. I was glad that he brought plenty of water as Fariba and I could not separate our mouths from the necks of the bottles. It was certain that we would spend the night there.

Night came and we all sat on the floor, no one could stand for ever. The darkness did not reduce the noise around us but there were noises in my mind too. Fear of the Taliban circled in my mind. The airport was the only place not occupied by these savages. If they invaded it, many women, children and old people would be killed. The Taliban know no mercy. According to them, they are the only correct Muslims and the rest of the nation is wrong and has to be corrected. For them we were all infidels escaping from an Islamic country ruled by correct Muslims.

Once again I was running from the Taliban, but can everyone run away from them? All 35 million people cannot escape. So what happens to the rest of us? I knew there would be the stoning to death of women, the whipping of men on the streets for not growing beards, the cutting off of hands for stealing a piece of bread, the checking private parts of men to see if they have shaved their pubic hair. Women would be beaten for wearing high-heeled shoes because the sound a woman makes wearing them as she walks on pavements would arouse the Taliban, who also punished women just for wearing white socks. The Taliban destroy our national heritage. Whatever is judged to be not Islamic, like the Buddhas of Bamyan, must be destroyed.

Running away from such darkness for the second time put me in a quandary. I had a moral duty to save my daughter, but what about Khalil who'd put his life in danger accompanying me to this unsafe place? How about my friends and then the whole nation? How could I stop these feelings? If once again I managed to board a plane and land in America, part of me would still remain in Afghanistan. I would be constantly listening to the radio and thinking about my country and its people.

Afghans stunned the world after the fall of the Taliban in 2001 by sending their children, both boys and girls, to school. School attendance was three times higher than UNICEF's estimate. Where schools had been burned or damaged by the Taliban, lessons continued in tents or even under the trees. There was a story published in *The Guardian* newspaper of a poor farmer who walked with two of his children, both girls, for an hour each way in order to take them to school. This meant leaving his work, the source of his family's income, because he believed that the most important nourishment was education. I predicted that it would be impossible for the Taliban to take up arms again because the whole nation was extremely tired of war and the Taliban would not confront the might of NATO. I was both right and wrong. Right that the nation was still extremely tired of wars and wrong because no one could foresee the unlimited madness of the Taliban – a small group comprising fewer than one percent of the nation – who were mad enough to commit suicide, mad enough to destroy their own country and the rest of the world.

All the progress made since the fall of the Taliban in 2001 would be lost. Once again girls would not be allowed to go to school, women not allowed to go to work. Cultural institutions would be shut or replaced by mosques. Libraries would be closed and books burned. So many publications came into existence after 2001. Newspapers, radio stations and television channels mushroomed. Once again all of that would be gone. Television sets found in houses would be hung from trees, windows would be painted over so that no one could look in and see so much as even a corner of a woman's scarf. Women would cease to exist. There would be a complete darkness.

The darkness of the night in the airport terminal could not hide the fear in our hearts and on our faces. During the night, whenever I heard shooting, my heart leapt. We were unsafe, sitting between the foreign soldiers who were protecting us from our countrymen, the brutal Taliban. All I could do was put my arms around Fariba and hold her tight, just like any mother who thinks she can protect her child. Sitting cross-legged, I could not close my eyes even to have a nap but Fariba put her head on my lap at about 10 p.m. and fell asleep, stretched out on the hard floor. For me, sleep was a difficult venture, even in a comfortable bed in my own home. I looked at the sky, amazed by the brightness of the stars over a country with less pollution to affect the visibility. When I was a child sitting on the flat roof in summer-time before sleeping, my mother told me the names of the stars.

"Those are the Seven Sisters," she would say, pointing them out to me. "And that circle belongs to the Forty Sisters. Next to them is *Sohail*, the star that brings luck and in the past used by the caravans to find their direction."

Exhaustion closed my eyes just before sunrise and I only woke up when Khalil shook my arm and shouted: "Get up! The crowd will step on you!"

Immediately, I shook Fariba awake and we both stood up next to Khalil, confused, not understanding why the crowd was pushing towards the terminal's entrance, carrying all three of us with them. Then we found out the reason. The Taliban had started arresting people at the far back of the crowd and some people had been beaten badly when they resisted. Panic was driving the crowd towards the terminal building because we all thought we would be safe there. We did not realise that if the Taliban wanted, they could have killed us all. If the whole of NATO and the Afghan National Army had been defeated by the Taliban, how could it be possible for a small number of soldiers to protect us and guarantee our safety? I remembered the massacre in Srebrenica when the Dutch forces just watched while the Serbian soldiers murdered men, small boys and old men, and then raped the women.

Unable to resist the pushing of the crowd, we had to go with them. We were panicked, just like everyone else. All through the night, many flights had left Kabul, all filled by those who were running away from the nightmare of the Taliban. The terminal, therefore, now had space for more people. The soldiers wanted to let the crowd in, in an orderly fashion, checking papers to make sure that only those with the appropriate documentation could travel. More than half of the crowd did not have the appropriate documents and were prevented from boarding a plane. I felt sorry for them. But now the fear was so strong that people pushed without thinking of their safety or the safety of others. We all wanted to get inside the building. Many Afghan soldiers also appeared to help the British and together they managed to control the crowd, if necessary by hitting people. We were lucky and eventually able to get into the terminal. By then I was almost half alive, breathing with difficulty, my asthma making it difficult for me.

A woman screamed: "My baby is dying of thirst! For the love of God please give me a sip of water."

I looked at Khalil and innocently pointed to the last bottle of water we had. But what would happen if we were stuck there for many days? I knew that we could endure hunger but without water one could easily die, especially with a massive number of people in a space made like a sauna by the summer heat. But a mother can understand the pain of another mother, so we all took a sip from the last bottle and handed it to someone to pass to the woman who asked for water.

I became calmer inside the building, thinking we were safer, but then a huge explosion happened just outside the terminal, shattering the windows.

"They are going to slaughter us," I shouted at Khalil, completely forgetting the impact what I was saying would have on Fariba who had grown up in America. She was not used to such violence. Fortunately, as we were all so tightly packed in the crowd, we were not hurt.

"Nothing can happen to us here," Khalil said, pointing to the building and the soldiers.

I did not believe him but said nothing, fearing the effect on Fariba. The Taliban could send a suicide bomber to force his way into the building but, at the same time, I felt it would be much easier for them to do the same outside the building. The impact would be the same. All they wanted was to kill and it did not matter if it was inside the building or outside. Inside the terminal, people were pushing towards the exit on the other side, trying to reach a massive army plane on the runway tarmac, and we were pushed along too.

But how will they check documents? I thought.

Soldiers with guns stood near the plane checking travel documents very quickly and allowing only western passports or documents showing the person's connection with western countries, like those who worked as interpreters for the western army in Afghanistan, to pass.

In that confined place everyone was pushing against each other, causing irritation, making women swear, children cry and men to become agitated. Just metres away I heard first a child's scream and then a woman, I suppose the mother, started swearing at the person who had made the child scream. Immediately, two men from each side of the family started throwing punches, making their women and children scream with fear. For a moment no one dared stop them, but then some strong young men separated the two.

"Don't damage your beautiful face brother, the immigration officer in the US would not like it," the young man who had separated the fighters joked and that made me smile. Even in the worst situation, Afghans keep their sense of humour and, indeed, it is humour by itself that kept our nation alive through forty years of war, probably the longest in our history.

Thirst makes people desperate and they gathered around the vending machines. But soon they were empty. Those who came later inserted their money but got nothing and became very upset. The vending machines were ransacked. Angry men jumped on airline computers, smashing them to pieces. They did the same to chairs, desks and tables and I thought the idea behind that was to make the foreign forces allow people to board quickly. We all prayed for more planes from the US to come and take us to a safe place, before the airport was invaded. The violence continued – men took the large framed photos, including President Ashraf Ghani's, off the wall and smashed them, shouting "You traitor! You're now in a safe country while the nation is in the hand of terrorists."

Next to me a baby was wailing continuously. Someone pointed to her, saying that the baby wanted milk.

"I know but I don't have any milk," the mother said.

I realised that was because she was dehydrated and now the baby was dehydrated too. It was obvious we were all becoming dehydrated and, if not killed by the Taliban, we would die from thirst. It was nearing the end of the day. Now the terminal was half full. Those near the exit door to the tarmac, or those who were strong, managed to board the planes. But for us I thought there would be another long night. However, the army had managed to block the entrance to the terminal and that act provided us with some space. We also got a ration of water provided by the British soldiers. They saved our lives.

We spent one more night, this time inside the destroyed terminal and I don't know if it was because I felt safe there or because of sheer exhaustion that I slept for two hours. When I opened my eyes, I noticed our gathering had decreased significantly. I cursed myself for falling asleep because we could have boarded the plane too if I was awake. With regard to Khalil, he could sleep in any condition because he lived through wars in most dangerous places, bombarded by different faction groups, and Fariba was the same. Although she had not seen wars but once she closed her eyes only a big shake could make her wake.

Fortunately, at around seven o'clock in the morning, our turn came.

After initial chaos, disorder and violence, the soldiers were now in full control because their numbers had increased. I don't know why they were not there in the first place but realised that they also had been stunned by the fall of Kabul and had no clue where to be and what to defend. Their presence somehow gave me more comfort and the other matter that brought peace to my mind was seeing the reduction in our number because many had boarded the planes and left. Those not accepted because of lack of documents were sent back using a gate far away from terminal, mainly used by the army. I must say our group was very orderly and I didn't know if it was because we were all extremely tired or because those who were travelling for the first time to the US thought they must behave now otherwise they would be reported to the immigration authorities and turned back.

About 100m from the plane, I was about to hug Khalil and say goodbye when a mob, not those among us but those who were kept outside the terminal, invaded the tarmac after breaking fences or climbing over the surrounding walls. I screamed. Now we would never be able to board a plane. The mob filled Pamir Airlines' private plane, which was not scheduled to fly anywhere because our transportation was organised by the US Army. I could see men on the roof and wings of the plane as well and they were those who could not find a place inside the plane. They really thought that they could fly sitting on the roof.

People surrounded the huge US Hercules army plane, which was supposed to take us on board, but the entrance doors to the plane were immediately shut. Nevertheless, young strong men attached themselves to any part of the plane they could. I think to give the army a chance to control the situation and also to make sure that those who attached themselves to the body of the plane would let go, the plane started moving. It had some effect on most of the men, but some still managed to hang on. Now the pilot had no choice but to fly with those on board and come back later when the tarmac was cleared.

I could see a young man still holding on to the body of the plane as the plane taxied on the runway. I almost shouted at the man to get off because it was suicide, and could not believe my eyes when the plane sped up with a man still attached to the outside. The plane took off and reached a considerable altitude. Was it possible that the young man could keep himself attached until it landed again? My question was very quickly answered when first one man and then another fell through the sky. They had attached themselves on either side of the plane. Obviously, their dreams of reaching the US were buried with them. This is how people paid for freedom and escape from the reign of the Taliban.

How desperate we had become to leave the country we all loved before the troubles started. First came the communist regime supported by Russia, and then the Russian invasion. We tolerated the communist regime because we loved our country. At the beginning, our life was not badly impacted. The war only existed in faraway places, in rural areas. Kabul was safe and the communists provided more freedom for women. But then war came to the cities. After their defeat, the Russians left and the Mujahideen became new rulers, and they killed indiscriminately. The rest you all know, when the Taliban took over. I started weeping but tried to hide my tears from Fariba and Khalil. My tears were for those two men who had lost their lives in their search for freedom.

Time passed very slowly and I don't know when the army trucks appeared and drove directly towards the crowd to disperse them. More soldiers appeared and after a long struggle the area around the planes was secured. The crowd also learned that by attaching themselves to the plane they would suffer the same fate as those two men who'd fallen. Probably whatever foreign soldiers left were there to secure the safety of passengers and not there just for the Afghans. Among us were white Europeans and Americans too, and their lives of course also mattered.

The soldiers managed to impose some order and men started to check documents on the tarmac. We were fortunate to be chosen for the next flight. I hugged Khalil for a long time and cried on his shoulder. He was sobbing loudly too. Would I see him again? We were both already old. How had it come to this?

Note to myself

Of all beings, man is not free. Birds fly away to another sky, animals run to another mountain or jungle, but man can't go anywhere. Do you think those refugees escaped wars? Do you think they left their countries? No. They carry their prisons with them, no matter where they go. Their minds are their prisons.

Chapter 2

Great loss

To lose one member of a family is very hard. To lose all of them – my parents and my siblings – eight in total, is unbearable. That is what happened to me one night, all those years ago.

My mother telephoned me in the office around 3 p.m. asking me to come to dinner at my parents' house. She surprised me when she said, "Come alone, and soon because I need you to cook before the guests arrive."

I was in the middle of editing articles due for imminent publication. However, my first responsibility was to my mother so I decided I would start early and leave late the next day in order to finish the work on time. When my parents had invited guests, it was not unusual to help my mother. But to be asked to come alone had never happened before. I usually took my small children with me while my husband Kabir, a doctor at the hospital, would join us after he finished work. I thought that maybe my parents had invited a large number of guests and wanted me to help without being interrupted by the children. Of course, my younger sister Parwin could help to some extent, but she was very young and I was also known for being an excellent cook. I telephoned Kabir at the hospital to tell him that my parents needed my help and that I would be home late that evening. He didn't sound happy knowing that his food would not be ready for him when he got home and besides that he would have to look after our daughter Lida and our son Haseeb.

I left the office half an hour earlier than usual and went to get the Number 6 bus to Taimani. The bus stop was crowded. Trucks full of soldiers, tanks, and other armoured vehicles were passing noisily, but they had become a normal sight on the streets after the novelty of the first few days when we had watched them with our eyes on stalks. When the bus arrived, there was a stampede to board. I was one of the women and old people who were left behind as well as an old man with a cane who had almost been knocked down in the frenzy to get on the bus. Feeling sorry for the man, I approached him and asked where he was going, which was two stops before my destination, and hailed a taxi. Needing to hurry and wanting to do my good deed for the day, I offered to share the ride with him as paying for a taxi was not a problem. Kabir was a successful doctor and I was a journalist for *Bakhter*, our national newspaper based at the Ministry of Information and Culture.

No smell of food came from the kitchen when I entered my parents' house, which was odd because each time my parents invited people the aroma circulated around the house, making me hungry. Only important dishes like kofteh and Kabuli palaw were left for me to prepare. But today, the air inside the house was just as fresh as outside with all windows open towards the garden. In the living room all members of my family were sitting quietly.

"Nothing is happening in the kitchen," I said after exchanging greetings.

"Nothing unfortunately, Deeba jan," my father said.

"Oh, I see. Is it cancelled?"

"Nothing is cancelled because no one was invited," Mother said.

"Is this some kind of joke?"

"If it is, it is a very sad one. We have decided to leave the country and emigrate to Pakistan."

This, I thought, was definitely a bad joke. How could they even think of leaving everything and emigrating to another country when there could be no possibility of return? Taking refuge in another country branded you an enemy of the people. If you ever dared to come back, you would be prosecuted.

"I don't understand, Mother," I said, still not believing what I had heard.

"It is true, Deeba. But I understand it is hard to digest."

"Why, for heaven's sake?"

"Your father made a simple comment about difficulties of life in his office and his superior, who is a Communist Party member, warned him that such remarks will not be tolerated. People cannot keep their mouths shut for ever. The *Parchamis* consider any comment anti-government if it is not in praise of the government. Besides, your brothers will soon become conscript soldiers and almost certainly be killed fighting for the communists – who they do not support – and fighting against their own people, the poor peasants."

After the communists gained power, people began emigrating in large numbers. A proverb circulated, 'Walls have mice and mice have ears', because the Khad Secret Service had countless agents everywhere, any one of whom could be your best friend or even your brother or sister. Fear ruled the country because many men and women ended up in jail or lost their life simply by confiding in those they loved and trusted.

"But Kabir is a party member, he will be able to protect you," I said.

"He might be able to protect your father if your father complained about economic hardship, but he cannot stop the government from conscripting your brothers into army service. And you know that within a year they will be dead."

My family had not trusted Kabir since he had revealed himself to be a senior Communist Party member after we got married. That was the reason they did not want to say goodbye, fearing he would report their departure to the police. It was a time when brother could not trust brother, far less a son-in-law.

"When are you leaving?" I asked with a trembling voice, submitting myself to the will of God.

"Tomorrow," Mother said, and then she burst into tears, which started me off as well.

"To…mo…rrow?"

"Yes," she said.

"What happens to your belongings?" I asked.

"The house is sold and you can do whatever you want with the rest. We cannot take them anyway."

"Oh, Mother! You've been planning this for months and never told me," I wailed.

We have a saying. If someone dies you can tolerate his loss after some time, but if you lose someone who is still alive, it is impossible to bear. In my case I lost eight members of my family overnight.

I was angry with my parents for deciding to leave so quickly and not letting me know in advance. When I calmed down I realised they'd had no other choice. When a bomb had exploded where my father worked, he had been arrested, put in prison and interrogated. We considered ourselves lucky because Kabir had been able to help that time and my father was released after only a few days. For others it was different. Anyone suspected to being anti-government was arrested and put in prison pending investigation. Sometimes it took months before the communists questioned them, often torturing the prisoners until their morale was so low that they would admit to crimes they'd never committed.

After his release, my father talked about sharing a cell only suitable for four with ten other prisoners. There was no bed, just a concrete floor, and the only connection with the outside world was a small, iron-barred window near the ceiling. They were not even allowed the ritual ablutions to say their *namaz*, and to humiliate them even further, a Turkish-style toilet in the corner of the room meant they had to defecate in front of others on a pot that was often blocked because little water was available. One can only imagine the smell in that room. There was no chance of sleeping on the floor since there was no room to stretch out and they could not sleep standing up.

After that terrible experience, my father was not the same, fearing for his safety and the safety of his family. He was no longer interested in the job he had loved and he feared meeting his friends in case they worked for the Khad Secret Service. No one could be trusted, not even a brother, as there were stories of brother reporting brother to the Khad. This sort of empowerment by the communists provided an opportunity to people who had scores to settle with those they hated, usually brothers and cousins, caused by disputes over inheritance. Now with the communists' willingness to imprison or eliminate people, the animosity increased and forgotten quarrels were refreshed.

One day my brother Hanif disappeared and the shock sent my mother mad. Where was he? There were many reasons for the disappearance of a young man. Either someone killed him, an action not uncommon in our country, or, like my father, he had been caught and put into a prison. The communists were ruthless towards young people while they thought an aged man like my father was not a real threat.

My father and my two other brothers, Salim and Azim, started looking for Hanif, asking friends and relatives about his whereabouts. But we all knew that searching in those places was fruitless. He'd no history of spending the night in any friend or relative's house without informing us. My father went to the police, but the police were not interested because it was common that communists caught a man and put him in prison where he would wait to be eliminated. When a week passed we were worried that we might lose my mother too, because she refused to eat and could not sleep, reading the *Quran* the whole night, praying.

On the ninth day of Hanif's disappearance my mother came home after going to a ziarat to pray for Hanif's return. She was shocked to see a soldier sitting in her living room, probably thinking he was there to arrest someone. I was there.

"Don't panic, Mother, he has brought some news about Hanif," I said and took a piece of paper from my handbag. "This is a note from Hanif."

"From Hanif? asked my mother. "Why a note? Where is he?"

"He is serving the army in Panjshir," I told her.

"What are you talking about?"

The soldier shuffled to the edge of the couch and explained that when Hanif was on his way to the university, at the checkpoint he was interrupted by soldiers who checked young men's identities to establish if they were eligible for army service. Hanif produced his university card, but they did not believe him. After tearing up his ID card, he was loaded onto the truck with other young men and sent directly to Panjshir, where the fighting was intense between the government and the Mujahideen. Of course, they knew he was a student and could continue studying until graduation, but the government was not interested in seeing young men studying. The communists wanted these young men to defend their country against the Mujahideen. Or, in other words, defend them, the communists.

We were surprised to listen to this brave soldier, but soldiers were condemned to death by defending the communists in Panjshir. Not many soldiers came back alive.

"Hanif and I are in the same place," said the soldier. "We even sleep in the same barrack."

"How did you manage to leave your post?" asked my mother.

"Every six months we get a week's break. I came directly here because I knew how much you would be worried."

"God bless you, my son," said my mother, and she asked me to read the note:

> *Salaam all. I have been conscripted as a soldier and I am serving the army in Panjshir. Please don't worry. I am fine. Unfortunately, I cannot write much because it is hard to find a piece of paper here. All be well, Hanif.*

After I read the note out loud, the soldier stood up to leave, but my mother insisted he should eat with us. The soldier could not accept because he lived far away and wanted to see his own family. My mother pushed a 100 Afghani note in his pocket, thanked him many times for bringing news of Hanif, and thanked God that her son was alive. But for how long?

Hanif's disappearance happened after the incident with my father and by now we were all worried that none of them was safe. Apart from me, because I was the wife of Kabir.

When my father came home after hearing about Hanif on the phone, my mother was both delighted and sad. Delighted that Hanif was alive and sad because she knew that Panjshir was known as the graveyard of soldiers.

"You must do something about it." She looked at my father with eyes of a mother seeing her child in danger.

"What can I do?" My father waved his hands in dismay. "They will not listen to me."

"But you can prove that Hanif is still a student," said my mother.

"Of course, I can get a letter from his university," said my father. "But will the army listen to me?"

"With proof they should," I said.

"Not with that proof but your approval, Deeba," Father snapped.

"I don't understand, Baba."

"I could not get out of prison without the help of your husband. Surely he can do the same for his brother-in-law."

I knew this was not an easy task. Kabir would not happily jeopardise his position for the sake of helping his brother-in-law. For the communists, their ideology came before family ties, before husband and wife relationships. But I had no choice. I loved Hanif and I had to try to help him.

Instead of my father going, it was I who went to the university. I introduced myself to the dean, a new man from the Communist Party, and to my delight he knew Kabir very well. In no time he provided me with a confirmation letter and in the evening, when Kabir came home, I asked for his help. Dealing with him was much more difficult than dealing with the dean, but in the end, unwillingly, he gave me a small note. In the morning I phoned my office and declared that I was sick and asked Father to accompany me to Panjshir.

After his release, Hanif had no interest in going to Kabul Faculty of Engineering. My father paid a guide to walk with him all the way from Kabul to Pakistan, which took about five days. They could not go by the normal road, taking a bus, for fear of being caught at the checkpoints. Fearing that Kabir would be angry, we kept Hanif's disappearance a secret. That was not too difficult because Kabir did not like to visit my family very often and my family had the same feeling towards Kabir. But why was I married to such man?

My mother decided on my marriage during my third year of working as a journalist. Before Kabir's proposal, I tried to keep advances from other men away simply because I considered myself to be the same as a man and I wanted to help shoulder responsibilities with my father in bringing an income home. I wanted my father to be able to retire early. He'd been working too hard in a country known for corruption, and life could not get better for poor and low-income people.

Despite high unemployment in the country, I was sure I would be able to get a good job working for radio or television because I was doing very well and my professors were willing to give me letters of recommendation. After graduation, however, *Bakhter News* offered me the position of editor. When I talked to Professor Hakim, who knew me very well and had always been a good adviser, he suggested that *Bakhter* was a much better place than radio or television, because it had the best reputation and was filled with top journalists who produced daily news about Afghanistan and the rest of the world.

Enjoying my work, having great support from my colleagues, and admired by the editor-in-chief, I was a long way from thinking about marriage and unaware that I'd been noticed. Kabir himself admitted that he spotted me one day at the bus stop and said to himself, "If this girl steps on the bus with her left foot, she will be my wife." Apparently, I stepped on with my left foot and it took several days for him to find out where I lived.

The regular appearance of Adai, who I later found out was Kabir's mother, in her sixties with grey hair and a wrinkled face, annoyed me.

I disliked her slow walk as she left our house, pushing her heavy body. On the day my mother finally decided to have a chat with me, I saw Adai sitting in exactly the same spot she sat in each time she came to our house. It made me think that she probably never left. Aware of her purpose, I went straight to my room after greeting her coldly and started editing the *Bakhter News*. I enjoyed my work to such an extent that I often continued working after reaching home. Deep in my work and listening to music, I did not hear the knocking on my door and seeing my mother inside my room surprised me.

"You didn't hear me knocking?" she asked with annoyance.

I put my pen on the table and stopped writing. "Sorry, maybe the music is loud," I said

"No," said my mother. "It is not that loud, but your mind is not here, as usual."

"Maybe you are right," I said smiling to make the impression softer. "Is there something you want to talk to me about?"

"Yes, and a very important matter too," she said sitting down. That suggested she was going to talk to me for a long time, despite it being her usual period to be in the kitchen preparing supper.

"Tell me, Mother. What is it that you want to talk about." I asked.

"I cannot get rid of Adai," she said.

"But why not, Mother? You did not have trouble with any of the other suitors."

"She is an old lady with charming sad eyes and, besides, her son is a good doctor. You know I do not care to have a rich man as my son-in-law, but I respect a man with a good education.

"Mother..." I warned.

"No, please. This one is different," she said. "She brought a photo of her son for you to look at it. Please be careful before you decide to reject him."

"Mother, don't you want me to live here with you?" I pleaded.

"My dearest, it is not that. I admire your support but I don't want you to sacrifice your life for us. We are not poor. I was 15 when I got married and you are now 26 years old. You know once you reach 30 no one will want you. That is the truth about our culture."

I kept talking with my mother and said that if I never married I wouldn't mind, and mentioned obstacles such as different ethnicity. We were Tajiks and they were Pashtun. Ethnicity played a major role in marriages, but my mother had made up her mind.

"I will just leave this photo here. Please look at it and think carefully," she said and left my room. I ignored the photo and went back to my editing. We had a happy dinner and I was glad that my marriage issue was not discussed further. But when I went back to my room, I looked at the photo of a young man who had hypnotising black eyes, naturally trimmed eyebrows, long eyelashes and a chiselled brown face.

He was very handsome.

Kabir kept his true identity secret from me before the marriage and I did not know he was a communist. My parents did not like communists for religious reasons, thinking they were atheists. But like many other young and educated Afghans, I was extremely unsatisfied with our corrupt government and supported the leftist groups who wanted change, like the communists, without becoming a member. When the communists came to power, first I was delighted and could not understand why my father was not happy about it. The communists claimed to be defenders of the poor and would help those people have a share of the wealth that was currently in the hands of the super rich, who acquired their wealth through corruption or cheating. The majority of our people were peasants and I thought now it was their opportunity to take land from the rich landowners.

At the beginning that happened with the government introducing land reform. However, when the same peasants were told that they no longer had the right to prevent their daughters and wives from doing what they wanted to, they turned against the government. Not only was this excessive liberty a big challenge to their lifestyle, also the communists were anti-Islam. They'd heard about Islamic countries like Tajikistan, Uzbekistan and Turkmenistan, where the mosques were destroyed and nightclubs were opened at the same spots encouraging young men and girls to drink. Although the communists did not destroy the mosques, the girls openly started to drink Russian vodka in the bars and chose their own boyfriends. This was not the economic progress I was hoping for and seeing this and what happened to my own family, my view gradually changed. That caused friction between me and Kabir. Initially proud of my husband, I now saw him as a man who put the party first. For him, the people, the country and the family came second, just like the other communists.

Note to myself

I found my position unbearable. First, my mother arranged my marriage when I was unprepared. Now, I had to keep secrets from my own husband. And that would have terrible consequences. Kabir was not the type of a man to easily forget and forgive.

We are a nation of secret-keepers. First my husband hid his identity to make sure I married him. Now it is my turn to keep the departure of my family a secret. But for how long?

Chapter 3

Too little, too much

My mother was busy at her sewing machine, frantically making new clothes for my brothers and sister in preparation for *Eid*, our biggest Islamic celebration, which was fast approaching. Mother was a star in all aspects of house management. She was an excellent cook, a great gardener, growing her own vegetables as well as colourful and soft-scented flowers. Her industry saved my father considerable amounts of money that would otherwise have been spent on a cook, a servant and a gardener. Also, her thirst for learning was unquenchable. She learned to read and write at the age of 36, taught by us, her children who she had sent to school. Hanif and I were happy to become her teachers and admired her love of learning, her attitude making us work harder and perform well in school and university. How she managed to juggle so many activities in her life was incomprehensible to us. She was a superwoman!

"Salaam madar jan," I said to announce my arrival.

"Oh, you are here." She glanced at me through her reading glasses and then, taking them off, said: "You come so quietly."

"Not so quietly, madar jan," I said smiling, reaching her, planting a peck on her cheek. "I rang the bell and Parwin opened the door."

"Really?"

"I'm glad you are enjoying your meditation, madar jan," I said.

"What else have I to do, my dear? I am not lucky like you, about to be taken out."

"What do you mean?" I asked.

"Kabir, your fiancé, phoned to say that he is coming to take you out for the evening," she said.

"Oh no! I have work to do. Besides I only saw him two days ago for lunch."

My mother reached for the teapot and carefully poured green tea into her cup. "Deeba, Kabir loves you. He wants to spend time with you."

"And if I don't finish my work?" I asked, "Which is the more urgent?"

"I don't understand you. You earn the same as the others yet you still bring work home. Don't you know there are other people working in offices who count the minutes until they are free to go home? Spending time with your future husband is also important. You must get to know each other before marriage. When you are married you will face responsibilities – children and God knows what else."

My mother had a point. She was very young when she married Father. She hadn't sought to win his approval by working like a slave but rather by learning how to keep him happy, keeping the romance between them alive, and in so doing had had a happy marriage. While she loved her children, she also made time for her husband by creating opportunities for them both to visit historical places, of which there is no shortage in Afghanistan. They both loved such places and sometimes went to areas like Badakhshan just for the exceptional natural beauty.

I did not argue but went to my room, thinking of my work but worrying that it would not be a good start to my relationship with Kabir as he might think I was using the work as an excuse not to go out with him. So, about half an hour later, I was sitting in Kabir's Toyota that, as usual, he was driving fast, scaring other drivers, pedestrians and me. I tried to keep quiet but eventually I had to say something.

"You are in a hurry, Kabir," I said.

"Yes, a little," he replied.

I had to ask. "But why?"

"I want to show you the sunset in Qargha and I am afraid I might miss it."

I was surprised. "We are going to Qargha?"

"I know, I know, but Qargha is not the end of the world and it wasn't easy to leave the hospital early to be with you. But you're not in a hurry, are you? I was thinking of making it a special evening for us. I love the Spozmay Restaurant, I love sitting in the garden watching the sunset."

"Thank you," I replied, genuinely pleased. "But you know I am very busy and sometimes I bring work home to make sure I have done a good job."

"You will be fine," he said encouragingly, adding, "don't worry."

We had been engaged for almost three months. While I always asked Kabir about his work in the hospital with much genuine interest, he seemed to have no curiosity regarding my work. He was a scientist and no doubt his daily activities were different from mine, but my father was an engineer and still he wanted to know about politics, history and even art, subjects that he always liked to discuss with my mother.

Status was very important to my mother. She had often told me: "We are capable of managing our hearts. Only fools are prisoners of their feelings. Love will come after marriage, not before. That is everlasting love, if we try it. Otherwise it is just infatuation and when challenges come we forget love, and run away from marriage."

Unusually, most of the tables in the garden of the Spozmay Restaurant were empty apart from just a few. At one table there were four French-speaking people – one woman and three men – drinking wine, talking loudly. Three other tables were occupied by Afghan men and women in elegant suits and dresses. The restaurant was my father's favourite and sometimes he brought the whole family for a treat. Also, he occasionally visited with his friends, especially Mr Osman, to have a non-alcoholic drink and to look at the lake. But only when he had some money. High profile officials and rich people frequented the place and I was told that even King Zahir Shah had enjoyed the garden in the evening.

The Spozmay Restaurant was where Kabul's elite showed the depth of their pockets. The restaurant's garden was a large artistically contrived landscape containing exotic trees imported from neighbouring countries like India and Iran, varieties of magnificent fragrant, colourful flowers, and with a mountain on one side and a big lake in front. Kabir took his time choosing a table, ignoring the white-uniformed waiter trying to seat us. Finally he selected a table he liked just 2m from the lake, with full views of the mountain and surrounding area. A gentle breeze wafted the scent of *Raat-ke Rani*, the Queen of the Night, flowers in the garden that had been imported from India. The heavenly scent and the beauty of nature diverted my thoughts from work and helped me see that I was sitting next to a very handsome man who always tried to please me. I was admiring the garden, the mountain, the lake and focusing on the last breath of the day, the magnificent sunset that we had come for when I noticed that Kabir was busy looking at the men. Was the sunset only for me to look at or were we there to share the beauty of life?

"Where are they?" Kabir was irritated, looking left and right to catch a waiter's attention, which I found unnecessary. In my experience, after giving menus to the guests, the waiters left the guests enough time to choose with care, rather than rushing them.

I smiled trying to put him at ease. "They always take a bit of time."

"But I want my wine now. The sunset with wine is more beautiful."

"You want wine?" I asked, still smiling.

"Don't you?"

"No, Kabir, I never drink alcohol." Was Kabir genuinely wanting me to drink with him? Even in the most liberated and educated families, alcohol for children, even when they reached adulthood, was not permitted. My father, being a traditional man, never drank alcohol and never permitted his children to do so.

My father said to me: "Once you are married you will be responsible for your own home and its rules, but while you are living with me, you follow my rules."

Was Kabir testing me? He didn't seem to me to be very liberal. He got upset when men looked at me in the street, which was common in Kabul. He seemed jealous or even possessive. Was his behaviour a sign of love?

I could see the irritation on Kabir's face growing when none of the waiters noticed him. He started waving his hands but only attracted the attention of other guests. In desperation he called to the waiter who was closest and when that failed, shouted at the one who finally responded to him. "Where the hell have you been?" he demanded.

The waiter kept apologising and I felt sorry for him.

"Go quickly and bring me a bottle of Chardonnay immediately!" he commanded.

"Yes, sir." The waiter almost ran to the bar.

When the waiter returned with the wine and two glasses, Kabir again asked me to drink but I refused. Kabir started drinking, and drinking fast. I am not sure if he even noticed the sunset. He ordered *chopan kebab*, *mantue*, *ashak* and many small dishes – a dinner for at least four people. The drinking and seeing so much food made me lose my appetite. Kabir's conversation became mere prattle. On the way home, I thought about my mother saying that love would come after marriage. Would it?

Two days later the editor-in-chief asked for me to come to his office. He was a man of 50 but looked much older with uncombed bushy white hair, a shirt that was always untucked with its pocket full of different coloured pens, including my enemy, the red one. He was a chain-smoker who made his office grey with smoke. I often wondered how he could breathe and I wanted to leave his office as soon as I entered it. Noticing my reaction, he opened the window immediately. He was a nice man, but a self-killer.

"Well, well, well, Deeba," he said, two grey columns of smoke streaming from his nostrils like chimneys.

"Well what, Akram?" I asked uneasily. I had spent two days editing this piece and did not want him telling me that it was rejected or that I must do more substantial work on it.

"This is not what I asked you to do," he began, holding up the sheets of paper almost apologetically.

"I think Ustad Sarahang deserves better than a piece of hack journalism," I responded. "He was the court singer called the Mountain of Music. In India beautiful women bowed to him and spread their hair on the ground for Ustad to walk on. I know the government has changed, but President Daud is the cousin of the former king who had invited Ustad to his court. At least the Shah likes listening to his music but now Ustad is completely ignored and living in poverty in Kharabat, a place without a road, without water."

"I like your piece," Akram answered apologetically, "but you must not suggest that Ustad's situation is the fault of the current government. You are clever enough to tell Ustad's story without putting my head under the guillotine. I love life." He burst into fits of laughter that ended in a fit of coughing.

I waited until he could breathe normally again. "If you love life you ought to give up those stupid cigarettes."

"Thank you, Mother," he replied drily.

"Or at least smoke a better brand!" I added.

"With my salary?" He started laughing again. I was delighted that it did not end in coughing. "Rewrite this quickly, be a little less critical of the government, and then get ready to go to Aqcha first thing in the morning with Mohsen the photographer."

"Aqcha? What for?" I was very surprised.

"The Father of the Nation wants it," he said waving his hand at the big portrait of President Daud on the wall behind him.

"What do you mean?"

"The Father of the Nation has built a new canal there. He wants the story to be covered by us and the television. Make sure you write in such a way that your material can be used by Afghan television too."

"So quick?" I asked him.

"You have done rush jobs before," he replied.

I left Akram's office thinking it was true that I had undertaken such tasks before, but that was before I had become engaged. Deep in my heart I was very happy to go to Aqcha, a place famous for its natural beauty. But Kabir would also certainly have views about the task and I had to know what his reaction would be. While I looked forward to being among the Uzbeks of my country, a very hospitable people known especially for their *Uzbek Palaw* dish, I felt that as a journalist it was my duty to know the nature of the people and their culture. I decided that the best way for me to tell Kabir about having to go to Aqcha was to invite him to dinner that evening. I made a lot of effort to cook Kabir's favourite dishes and did nothing on my work or to prepare myself for my trip. Fortunately, when Kabir came, he was in a very good mood, complimenting me on the food as we ate with the family. I said nothing about my trip until we were both in my room.

We talked about issues related to his work and I was a good listener. When he was relaxed enough I said, "My editor-in-chief wants me to go to Aqcha to report on the construction of a new irrigation canal."

"What did you say?" he asked, apparently not believing what he'd heard.

I sat next to him, holding his left hand. "I am going to Aqcha tomorrow."

"But so suddenly? Why didn't you tell me in advance?"

"I only just got the assignment today. It is very important because the government wants great coverage – it is a publicity issue you know."

"But so suddenly?" he said again.

"It is because the Minister of Rural Development has decided that tomorrow would be the best day for him to open the project officially. You know reporting is a matter of instant response."

"I really wish you would concentrate on working only in the capital," he insisted.

"My dear, I have no choice," I replied. "Covering something in which such a high-ranking officer is involved will be good for my career."

"Personally, I think being a teacher in a primary school in Kabul would be better for you."

"But I have the qualifications to work as a journalist," I argued.

"And what happens when we have children?" he asked and turned away towards the window.

"My dear, I am hoping that by the time we have our children, I shall be the chief editor and able to send someone else on such a mission."

"Do as you like!" he said.

Mohsen arrived with the driver at around 6:30 a.m. the next morning. Mohsen had worked for *Bakhtar* for more than ten years and had been in the region many times before. Although Mohsen was worried we would be late, I insisted that I could not go to Aqcha without first giving him and the driver tea. It is our tradition to be hospitable.

This was my first assignment away from home and I was excited about it, despite Kabir's reaction. I hoped that Kabir would change as time passed and come to respect my work. I sat in the back seat while Mohsen and the driver chatted in the front. Mohsen played the role of tourist guide as we drove, telling me about the places we passed descending from the Kahirkhana hills into more open country and then plunging into a long green tunnel under the arching roof made by the *chinar* trees. I opened the side window and let the fresh air into my lungs. Not many cars had air-conditioning in those days and our Volkswagen was no exception.

"This is Istalif, Deeba," Mohsen said excitedly. On both sides of the road were rows of shops selling colourful handmade cooking pots, plates, bowls and tea cups. Their beauty was unique.

"We'll have a break here," Mohsen said.

"What? We have hardly been on the road an hour," I protested. "And you wanted me to leave home as soon as you arrived, remember?"

"I know, Deeba jan, but anyone who passes this way and does not try the *doogh* is a fool."

"I am only worried that we may be late," I said.

"My dear, the distance to Aqcha is about 700km and no one has made it in one day. Besides, we must make sure Murad is not too tired. The road from Mazar-e Sharif to Aqcha is treacherous so I propose we spend the night in Mazar."

Mohsen asked for three glasses of *doogh* and we sat ourselves on a charpai. The first sip of this drink, made with sour milk, made my mouth and throat feel fresh and by the time I had drunk half of the glass I felt rejuvenated. What a treat!

I watched sophisticated women wearing western clothes travelling with their families who, just like us, sat on a simple charpai drinking *doogh*, cracking jokes, laughing. A bus full of long-haired hippies also stopped and its passengers rushed to buy *doogh*.

"They pay double price," Mohsen said laughing.

"Oh, only experts like you know the real price," I teased.

"No, only foreign fools don't know the actual price," he said, standing up. "Let's go."

"No, you told me that we are spending the night in Mazar," I replied. "I want another glass. Besides we want the soul of Murad to be refreshed."

"That is my lady. That is my Deeba jan. I'll pay for such an expensive drink," he replied.

"Don't cheat," I said. "It is a very cheap drink and by paying for this you are guaranteeing that I pay for an elaborate dinner."

We continued our journey, again passing through that magnificent green tunnel all the way to Charikar. Once again Mohsen described the beautiful hills surrounding Charikar and he mentioned Arghawan Mila, where jacaranda trees with purple blossom cover the hills, and families from Kabul came to celebrate the arrival of spring after a harsh winter. I'd been there many times with my family, eating the special cheese mixed with raisins and walnuts, but I let Mohsen describe the place using his own poetic imagination. This was my first independent journey. I tried to forget Kabir's bad mood, thinking I would be able to change him.

We reached Salang at two o'clock in the afternoon. Mohsen asked Murad to stop the car at a restaurant on the bank of the Salang River. I thought it was a perfect place. The fresh air and the journey had made me very hungry. We were led to a balcony from where we could see the noisy wild river splashing against the rocks that protected the restaurant garden. Lines of poplar trees on both sides of the river stretched as far as we could see. On the hills I saw houses made from stone and wood blending into the landscape, with goats running about freely without anyone guarding them. In rural areas there was complete trust and very little burglary, unlike the big cities. Smoke rose from the chimneys of houses and I smelled fresh *chapatis* baking in *tandoors*. I could see the white mountain tops covered with snow where the snow leopards lived – and it was the hottest month. What a magnificent sight! But my critical mind began working. I thought of the residents of all those houses who had no electricity or proper heating in the harsh winters. No wonder our school textbooks told us that winter was the killer of the poor people. What appeared so beautiful to a person like me was a harsh life for those living there. Mohsen, the photographer, went off with his camera and did not return until our delicious food, *chopan kabab*, was on the table – I licked the delicious meat from my fingers.

It was dark when we reached Mazar-e Sharif and I was glad that Mohsen had arranged for us to stay in Mazar for the night. Country roads snaking through mountain passes are narrow and dangerous. Many accidents happen at night, mostly thanks to trucks driving just by moonlight without their lights on.

From our hotel I could see the shrine of Ali, the cousin of the Prophet Mohammad and the 4th Khalif. The turquoise domes reflected the moonlight and I could see the beautifully calligraphed verses from the *Quran* carved into walls decorated with blue, green and yellow mosaic tiles exposed by the electric lighting. The huge courtyard, where men performed *namaz*, was paved in marble and I remembered the coldness of that stone against my bare feet in the summer years before, when my father took us there for a pilgrimage. But now I knew that Ali was not really there. The legend describes how, when Ali was wounded, he told his followers and his family that if he died they should put his body on a camel and let it wander without a guide until it stopped – that place would then be the place where his body should be put to rest.

As a child I believed that incredible story. Now I know that the distance between Saudi Arabia, where Ali was killed, and Mazar is such that it would take months for a camel to walk, during which time the body would decompose, plus the fact that a lone camel cannot walk non-stop without water and food. Yet my people believed in this story because of their strong faith and the way that the uneducated mullahs influenced ordinary people. Government corruption and the misuse of religion were the two main reasons for poverty in my country, a vast and beautiful land with abundant rivers. But writing about the impact of the government and mullahs was dangerous. The only way I could write about these issues was in coded ways that could only be understood by the elites. What I wanted was to make the majority of our people aware.

The road between Mazar and Aqcha was not tarmacked. It was narrow and it wound through the mountains. On the right the bare mountainside reared up above me and on the left the land fell over a precipice into the gorge of a fast-flowing river. Drivers had to negotiate passing each other very carefully, slowing down or stopping while the other tried to pass. Our car moved slowly, bumping over potholes and passing oncoming vehicles carefully. But I enjoyed the scenery and became used to hitting my head on the roof whenever the car encountered an especially big pothole and Murad misjudged the speed. I hoped that such punishment would not give me a headache and render me unable to write.

We reached Aqcha in the afternoon where the Rural Development Minister who would inaugurate the canal project the following morning was already at the government guesthouse where we were also supposed to stay. I really wanted to stay in a hotel, but I was told that there was no hotel in Aqcha – a shocking realisation that a district in Afghanistan did not have a hotel. The car park of the guesthouse was filled with cars belonging to those I assumed had accompanied the minister. It was very common for the completion of a small government project to be given maximum publicity. The advantage of staying in the guesthouse meant

I would have an opportunity to interview the minister over dinner. That was the only advantage.

During the dinner I counted twelve men in suits accompanying the minister, sitting at different tables. Their western suits were at odds with the rural area, as was mine, and I realised how different the people from Kabul must appear to the people living in rural areas. The manager of the guesthouse, also wearing second-hand western clothes, was a charming man, smiling all the time, asking his guests if they wanted anything. He was between 25 and 30 years of age with brown skin, shiny black hair, charcoal eyes and big hands, supervising his staff as they served the guests. He could have been a Bollywood film star.

Notebook in hand, I approached the minister after dinner knowing already what he was going to say because I had read the same sort of statements in the other newspapers. It would be something like: *Our government is dedicated to improving the life of its ordinary citizens, especially those living in rural areas…* That was a complete lie because rural areas did not exist for these people and I was sure that none of their children had ever seen what was happening in those parts of the country. But I had an obligation to interview this minister as part of my work. Afterwards I remained with Mohsen, writing notes, mainly about my journey, wishing I could share this with Kabir because, in general, men in my country had little interest in work done by women. Yet in both the cities and the provinces women shouldered the burden of work with their husbands. In rural areas, especially in a place like Aqcha where farming was the main activity, women participated in all aspects of agriculture. I had seen women carrying small children wrapped in cloth bags on their backs as they bent over the earth planting seeds, tending crops, rushing home to fetch food and water for their husbands also working in the fields, or working at home weaving carpets by hand from dawn to dusk. In the cities women worked as teachers, doctors, engineers, factory workers and compositors for the newspapers. Women also entertained the nation by singing on radio and television.

Before leaving the dining room, without telling Mohsen I gave a handsome tip to the manager of the guesthouse. Although he tried, I would not accept his refusal. "Just share it with your colleagues," I said in case he thought it was only for him.

In the morning I went to the courtyard for a stroll. Murad was there smoking a cigarette. He greeted me, saying: "Too early for a lady from Kabul."

"Not all ladies from Kabul wake up at nine," I said, enjoying the fresh country air. Then, seeing a hand-dug well at the centre of the courtyard I asked: "Will you kindly draw some water out because I want to splash it on my face."

"Deeba jan, you could use the bathroom," said Murad. "They have water there."

"I know," I said approaching the well. "But the water in the well is so cooling. Of course, no rush, only when you have finished smoking."

After a wash I asked Murad if he was willing to drive me around. I wanted to discover Aqcha for myself, not in the way it was described by the government. It was six in the morning and the inauguration was organised for nine, but it would be late. These ministers always appeared late, making everyone wait for them.

"I thought you'd never ask," he said.

Driving away from the government guesthouse, I was delighted to see large fields of brown wheat with men and women working in them. These were the people who produced food for the nation.

"These lands are irrigated by the new canal," Murad told me.

It was a fine day under a cloud-free sky. As we drove further, I saw a vast area between the mountains that was just barren desert, not even suitable for the camel of the cousin of the Prophet. "I think our great government has built that canal just for the benefit of our feudal landlords," I said.

"The poor are always ignored, Deeba jan," Murad said, driving carefully to avoid the potholes. "The land where you saw men and women working belongs to the big landowners who were behind the building of the canal."

"But there is a big river!" I argued. "I am sure the rest of this place could be irrigated if they built more canals."

"Do you want all the farmers to become independent?" he asked.

"What do you mean?" I said.

"The feudal landlords don't want the government to build more canals because they don't want to lose their workforce. Here, they are like small kings. They decide who gets married to whom and who is entitled to live and who must die."

"A challenge to central authority?" I asked.

"No. Contrary to what you might think, these powerful people control the rural areas and, in a way, are agents of the government.

It was very close to ten in the morning when I accompanied the minister and his colleagues to the place of inauguration, where the ordinary people had been waiting for two hours. The affair was just as I had seen on television a hundred times. The minister cuts the ribbon, the water flows, and the idiots and innocents together with the corrupt officials all clap. I was glad when it was over and angry with the system that required a journalist like me to be present just to rubber-stamp the official purpose, nothing else. I was looking forward to leaving Aqcha at the earliest opportunity.

I was reading *Dr Zhivago*, which I had borrowed from Kabir, in my room at the guesthouse when there was a knocking on my door. I opened it to find Jamshid, the guesthouse manager,

"Madam, I would like to invite you to dinner at my house this evening," he said.

"Oh no, you don't have to do that," I said putting my book down.

"No, I'd really like to do that."

"But who is going to look after the minister this evening?" I asked.

"I have an assistant who is just as good as me. After all, it is just dinner."

The house where Jamshid lived was about half an hour's drive away and a car couldn't go all the way to the house. We had to leave the car and walk the rest of the way because there was no road. We walked through an alleyway bordered by the walls of the villagers' orchards. On the way I saw a herd of sheep being shepherded to where they were kept at night. The strong acrid smell of their wool filled the air and overwhelmed the aroma of *chapatis* baking in *tandoors*. The doors to each orchard were made of solid wood but loose or crooked, none had a lock. The simplicity of life in such a place was refreshing and contrasted strongly to the way of life in Kabul. City life was not so simple.

The three of us, Mohsen, Murad and I, were guided by Jamshid to our guestroom where cotton-filled mattresses and cushions were set against the walls. The walls were plastered with mud and its earthy smell filled the room. We all sat cross-legged on those mattresses, resting our backs against the cushions. The room had a big window and through it I could see trees under the moonlight. In the light of the hurricane lamp I saw a single shelf holding books covered in expensive cloth, which I knew were copies of the *Quran* or other religious texts. There was only one framed portrait hanging on the wall and, when I got close to it, I recognised the face of Jamshid, holding a whip between his teeth, wearing the clothes of a *chapandaz*, riding a beautiful shiny brown horse. This modest man was a *chapandaz*, one of the best riders of our country and probably an excellent one among the best. This is what I should write, about a man who competes in front of foreign dignitaries and is a pride of our nation but lives in such modest conditions, serving government officials who don't have a minute to learn about him, and who is treated no better than a servant. That is the life of people in rural areas where there is no electricity and no roads.

Jamshid's wife Halima and their two children joined us when the food was served. Halima had an oval face, arched untrimmed eyebrows, long eyelashes, soft looking *myna* eyes, plaited long brown hair. She wore a scarf around her neck and never tried to cover her hair. She was a good example of a beautiful woman from the rural areas. Her fair skin in contrast showed that she did not work in the fields, unlike her husband who played *buzkashi* under the sun and acquired a brown skin. One little girl was 9 years old and the other 7, and they proudly told me that they both went to school, which I imagined was a long walk there and back. Husband and wife helped each other put an extravagant variety of food on the *dastarkhan* cloths – *Uzbek palaw*, *sabzy*, *kofteh*, *mantu*, *ashak*.

"Oh, Jamshid so much food! It's enough for twenty people," I said.

"We don't get many guests like you, Deeba jan."

"You didn't tell me you were a *chapandaz*," I scolded him.

"Oh, it is just a passion, nothing significant, he replied."

Their modesty surprised me and I wished I was allowed to write about Jamshid, his passion for horses and his family, instead of having to write about a minister who grew up in France and only came back to his country to become a minister, knowing hardly anything about the rural affairs of the country.

Note to myself

Jamshid has two daughters, one 9 years old and the other 7. They have brown hair and fair skin. So far, their skin has not changed while walking under the hot sun going to school – a distance of one hour. He is a famous *chapandaz* and has competed in front of foreign dignitaries in Kabul, winning trophies for his team. He works as a manager in a government guesthouse in Aqcha earning a salary that barely allows his family to survive, while he serves the officials who come from Kabul.

Still he is considered a very lucky person. Aqcha, like many other distant districts, has no electricity and most of the peasants are paid to farm the huge estates belonging to feudal landlords because they do not have any land of their own. The recent government project of constructing a canal only serves the feudal landlords. There is a vast area of desert and a river full of water, but more canals are required to turn that unlimited desert into farming land. If such projects did happen, Afghanistan would become self-sufficient in agriculture and be able to export its produce to other countries.

Aqcha, situated on the old Silk Road that once connected Europe to Asia, has been ignored and has nothing but a civilised history, because there is only one secondary school and one small clinic with an unqualified doctor. If someone gets seriously sick, they must travel to Kabul – if he is lucky enough to become sick in the summer. In the winter the road to Kabul is blocked with snow, and anyone with a serious condition has little chance of surviving.

Chapter 4

The Truth about the Saur Revolution

I had been married to Kabir for more than a year. He was the second eldest son with two brothers and two sisters and had grown up in a conservative rural area in Laghman Province until his family moved to Kabul twenty years earlier. It was the custom of rural people that the men shared the same house with wives and children while unmarried women left only after their weddings. His sisters were already married and they lived in their own houses. Kabir expected us to share his family's house with his mother Adai and his two married brothers. Cooking and cleaning for such a big family would be a great deal of work, much of which I suspected would fall on me. But I only wanted to be responsible for just the two of us.

With some difficulty and persuasion, I convinced Kabir that we needed our own place, for privacy. "How about your friends when they come to visit us?" I said, pointing out that it would be more relaxing if he had his friends over for a drink in a place where no one else could watch us. Like my own parents, Adai was a religious woman and I was certain that she would not appreciate her sons or daughters drinking alcohol. She was certainly not aware of Kabir's drinking.

We found a very nice two-bedroomed apartment in Kart-e 4 that had been built in the 1970s, so it was new. We had two bedrooms connected by a corridor on the first floor, and the ground floor consisted of a bathroom, living room and a kitchen. I loved the basement because I could store as many household and food items as I wanted. I learned that from my own parents. To ensure we were given the best prices for food and ingredients, Father bought in bulk and we stored it all in our basement. A hundred kilogrammes of rice, 50l of cooking oil, and many other things were not unusual and they disappeared very quickly. I didn't have to buy that much but still felt comfortable if we had stored enough food for at least three months. Kart-e 4 was well connected to other parts of the city, including my office. I preferred to take the bus to work because Kabir's working time as a surgeon in the hospital was irregular. Sometimes he left home at 6 a.m. and sometimes as late as 10 a.m.

After my engagement and marriage, I went on many assignments out of Kabul and Kabir accepted that it was part of my work. Through the travelling associated with assignments I discovered my country for myself. Marriage was also a journey of discovery through which I was learning about my husband. I found that his library was full of Russian books, novels by Tolstoy, Gorky, Pasternack, poetry by Mayakovski and Akhmatova, and philosophical works by Kant, Engels and Marx revealed that Kabir was a communist, a member of a leftist group called *Parcham*. Once a week Kabir met with his friends, Comrade Nabi and Comrade Jafar, sometimes at one of their homes, sometimes at ours. When they came to our house, I could hear their heated conversations while I was preparing tea for them or working on my editing. One discussion I remember was about an operation in the rural areas to awaken the peasants, preparing them for revolution. In my heart I admired their commitment and sincerity but prayed that they would not go into the rural areas. I feared separation from Kabir if he went alone or, if he wanted me to go with him, of losing the job that I loved and being away from my family.

He told me that the reason he did not reveal his political passion was his fear that he might lose me before the marriage because he was aware how religious my parents were and how much they disliked communism, the source of atheism. That revelation made me a little happier to believe my husband had really wanted me. After we were married everyone in my family knew about his political views, but while Kabir allowed me to continue working as a journalist he kept me away from politics. He wanted his wife to have freedom, yet to not be involved with public affairs or have political responsibilities.

While President Daud disallowed public protests, political parties held meetings in small groups in private houses and planned for the future of Afghanistan, believing one day there would be an end to Daud dictatorship. But during the reign of Shah, Daud's cousin, mass gatherings were common to the extent that the flow of traffic at the centre of Kabul City was blocked for days and sometimes even weeks. To stop the protest the government had no choice but to close Kabul University and schools for months. Although the king's government was corrupt, the king was a peaceful man who avoided arresting political party leaders. Many political groups existed but among them all only four were dominant:

- The Parcham and Khalq political parties were directly supported by the Soviet Union and people guessed that their leaders received financial support from the USSR.
- Shola-e Jawid, Immortal Flame followed Mao's philosophy and as China had denounced a Kremlinesque communism, Shola also detested Parcham and Khalq.
- Saudi Arabi and Kuwait financed the fourth party, Ikhwan al Muslimin or the Muslim Brotherhood, later known as the Mujahideen. But in those days they had very little public support and were regarded as backward.

Daud managed to suppress these political groups but they were even more active during the reign of Zahir Shah going forward, influencing the army, which was supposed to avoid politics.

While political publications were unlawful, parties distributed shabnama or night letters secretly at night to houses, condemning the government.

On 27 April 1978, I was in my office when I heard military planes. To hear the occasional plane was not unusual but the difference this time was the continuous roar of them flying overhead. It was a beautiful spring day after a very long and harsh winter that had brought much suffering to our people. The extreme cold took many lives while the heavy weight of so much snow caused some roofs to collapse. But it was spring and the suffering of winter was behind us, yet the frequency of these planes passing overhead made me uneasy. I tried to focus on my work, avoiding looking out of the window. Then, early in the afternoon, I heard the sound of rockets exploding nearby.

"They are attacking the presidential palace, Deeba," Akram shouted, rushing into my office and dragging me to the window.

"What? Who?" I asked. The noise of the planes was deafening, appearing even louder after Akram mentioned an attack. "Impossible," I protested. "No one can attack the presidential palace. It must be elsewhere."

"I tell you it is the palace!" Akram said. "I've just been told by a man who was in the vicinity."

On the street below us, several army tanks were moving fast towards the presidential palace, their tracks screeching on the tarmac road.

I was shocked. "Oh my God, you are right. What should we do?"

"We'll close the office and go home," he said. "It is better and safer to be with our families at times like this."

As soon as I reached home I switched on the radio to hear music and patriotic songs endlessly repeating. I could find nothing being broadcast to explain the circumstances of what Akram had told me.

Late in the afternoon of 27 April, the continuous music and singing on the radio was interrupted by a man speaking in heavily accented Farsi, who introduced himself as Major Aslam Watanjar and announced that the country was under the control of revolutionary forces. What a shock! This Aslam was a junior army officer, a Pashto speaking in Farsi. What was happening? President Daud, we thought, had the full support of the army. He picked and promoted each senior army officer himself. How could it be that a junior officer was in charge?

Just one day before, a leader of the Parcham leftist group was assassinated and at his funeral other leaders of the group denounced the murder as the work of the Afghan police. These leaders were arrested and put in jail and, as a precaution, the presidential palace had been guarded by the tanks. I discovered later that the man in charge of these tanks, Major Watanjar, turned his tank against the palace and that was the beginning of the change of power – a simple *coup d'état*.

I became anxious about Kabir and when he came home he seemed worried. "Our comrades are behind this," he said.

"Really?" I asked, still unable to believe what I had heard on the radio or what Kabir was telling me. I was thinking that such an action against our president was impossible.

"Yes," Kabir confirmed. "But they have only taken the radio station so far."

"So why is this major saying that they are in control of the whole country?" I asked.

"Fierce fighting is going on in the capital and in the provinces. It's just to convince the rest of the military that they should stop fighting us. God spare us if it fails."

What he told me was enough to give me a sleepless night. We went to bed still listening to the radio but it was playing nothing but patriotic music until the radio station closed down as usual at 11 p.m. We both tossed and turned the whole night listening to each other's breathing yet not daring to utter a single word. Certainly, this would be my husband's last night if this *coup d'état* failed. Nothing like this had ever happened in our history. If the king changed, it was because his brother rose against him, not a common man. Now we had a president, but in our eyes he was just like a king because he was the cousin of the previous king and he was ruling exactly like a king himself. Thousands of people would lose their lives and I would be a widow after just one year of marriage. Now I could see that it was wonderful to play with the idea of change and revolution until your own life and the lives of those that you love are in danger.

I don't know what time of the night it was that I decided to go to the bathroom. The cold water on my face gave me a new feeling and I recited verses from the *Quran* while tears flowed from my eyes.

Standing in front of Allah in our living room I read *nafl namaz*, which is not a five times a day prayer. Only very religious people do it during the night, spending the entire night in prayer. The verses from the holy *Quran* softened my heart and I felt the presence of God in that room. Tears continued flowing, making the *sojada* wet when I touched the floor with my forehead each time I did *sajda*. After *namaz* I continued in *sajda* pose, praying in whispers, asking for Allah's mercy, begging for his protection.

Sheer exhaustion made me fall asleep there just before dawn. My heart jumped when I felt someone shaking my shoulder. Was I about to be arrested?

But it was Kabir. "Wake up, Deeba, listen to the radio!"

"What? What happened?" I asked him.

"We succeeded. We succeeded. We did it."

The speaker on the radio was Colonel Qadir, head of the Afghan Air Force, announcing that President Daud had been eliminated and the country was totally in the hands of a new government, of which he was the acting president.

I still could not believe what I was hearing. It had all happened when terror appeared in the sky the previous day. That was the first sign of a change that has shaken our country continuously for the past forty years and which no one can foretell when it will end. But at that moment I thanked Allah for sparing the life of my husband.

Kabir was first to leave the house. Half an hour later I left to face a new Afghanistan. The city had woken to find itself in the hands of new rulers and could not comprehend it. Was it true? There seemed to be no difference until I saw an army tank near the Ministry of Information and Culture where my office at *Bakhter Press* was located. A soldier wearing a helmet stood on the roof and two others with Kalashnikovs on their shoulders in front. They were surrounded by onlookers.

So, it is true, I thought.

The office was quiet as there was no agenda for publication, nor was there any sign of the minister, his deputy, or any other high-ranking people. I sat down and listened to the click, click, click of the clock hanging on my office wall.

Two more days passed before the radio announced that Noor Mohammad Taraki, the new president of the Republic of Afghanistan, would be addressing the nation. In his broadcast, Taraki informed us that the former president had been killed and the country was in the firm hands of the Khalq and Parcham communist parties, supported by the Soviet Union. He also introduced his cabinet, one of whom was the new Minister of Information and Culture – for whom I would soon be working. It was obvious that the previous ministers and senior officials would be put in prison and new communist officials would be introduced. The radio told us how the communists had toppled the old regime and named the army heroes, political leaders and those who fought the president to the end.

The new president also informed the nation that the former presidential palace where the tyrant and his family had lived was being opened to the public so that everyone could see for themselves the difference between those who had lived in the Arg and ordinary people. I had always wanted to see the Arg and so on that day I rushed to go there. Nothing was happening in our office anyway.

In the square fronting the Arg I noticed destroyed tanks, soldiers carrying Kalashnikovs, and soldiers in helmets posing for photos. There were undamaged tanks too that people were allowed to climb over, opening the hatches, getting inside, climbing out. It was not obvious to whom the tanks belonged. Were they the tanks of the soldiers who defended the president or did they belong to the communists? I got closer to an undestroyed tank that had tulips thrown onto it. A soldier sitting on it smiled at me. Instead of smiling back, I rushed towards the entrance to the Arg. Once inside, I saw that the walls were riddled with bullets, windows were shattered. With difficulty I managed to push through the crowd to enter one of the halls, which had broken furniture, torn paintings still hanging on the walls, walls stained with blood, shattered chandeliers, and a big carpet cut into pieces. A loud voice distracted me and I could not believe my eyes when I saw Omid, one of my former university classmates. He stood on a windowsill shouting at the spectators, telling them that finally the end had come to tyranny, that right now the masses were in control of their destiny and the new army belonged to the people. People clapped and Omid continued with his speech, his voice hoarse from so much shouting. He was not aware of my presence as the hall was packed and for me to push through the crowd to reach him was not easy, especially to the windowsill where Omid stood because everyone wanted to hear what he was saying.

When finally I reached him, my head was level with his knees. I looked up into the face of a man who had become very thin but whose eyes were gleaming. For a long time he did not notice me, even though I shouted his name many times. At last I grabbed his leg and he saw me, jumping off the windowsill, hugging me like a brother who has been united with his sister. Tears appeared in our eyes but we both fought them back.

Omid suggested that we should talk outside the noisy hall filled with people. He was my classmate and had been my best friend at university, until he disappeared during our second year.

"What happened to you, Omid?" I asked as soon as we could talk.

"Disappeared," he replied.

"I know you disappeared," I told him briskly. "But why?"

"They made me disappear."

"What are you talking about?" I asked him.

"Do you remember the poetry of Nasrin Azizi published in our newspapers and magazines?" he said.

"Of course, we discussed her poetry. But she disappeared as well," I replied.

"We both disappeared together."

"I don't understand."

"I am Azizi. I thought that by disguising my identity I would be safe and the police would not find out."

"So, you were in prison?" I said.

"Yes. But I'm happy to be alive," he replied.

We talked for a long time and he told me about the prison conditions, about his poor treatment, his desperation for having books to read but could not get, and his poetry writing in secret. "There are volumes, thanks to prison," he said with a sad smile on his face.

"But you can publish them now without fear," I told him.

We said goodbye and I felt sad for his loss of years, his loss of university education.

On the fourth day of the *coup d'état*, which Kabir referred to as a revolution, both Akram and I were summoned to the office of the new minister, Comrade Asil, a young man aged between 30 and 35 who sported a pitch-black walrus moustache. He wore a grey suit and a red tie that did not match and I don't know if his hair was shiny or oily.

He introduced himself and then told us, "The government has decided to change the name of this publication to *The Truth of the Saur Revolution*." And he talked at length about our commitment in this new era, and that the country is ruled by the people for the people.

Saur is the second month in our calendar, which coincides with April, when the revolution happened. So I too started to call it a revolution. What difference does it make what one calls it? I thought. I wanted the end of corrupt governments and was hoping to see our nation lifted out of poverty. The minister also informed us that there would be an official coming from Moscow to advise us on what materials we should publish. I did not like this part at all.

I told Kabir about these changes and he fully supported Comrade Asil, and then he said, "I have news for you too."

"What is it?" I asked excitedly.

"Nabi has been promoted to the position of a general in the army and Jafar has become Deputy Minister for Foreign Affairs."

"Unbelievable," I said, almost jumping up from my seat.

"Wait, there is more."

"What else?" I asked.

"I have been appointed as the head of the People's Hospital," he declared.

"Oh God!" I said. "That is the biggest hospital in our country."

"Wait, I have not finished."

"You can't be serious?"

"Oh I am," he said with laughter and shining eyes. "I invited both of them with their wives to come here to dinner next Friday evening. For the first time we will celebrate and not talk about politics.

I was glad that Kabir had invited his friends on the Friday, which was a public holiday and would allow me plenty of time to cook, because on other days we were busy working until late into the evening on Minister Asil's historical first issue of *The Truth of the Saur Revolution*. A photo of President Taraki filled the whole front page of the paper followed by pages of photos of his cabinet members. After announcements about the change of power and the future of the country, there was the news that former President Daud had been killed along with his brother, his sons and daughters and his grandchildren. In total, seventy-two members of his family and friends. I did not like this part of the revolution. I compared it to the 1917 Russian revolution when the last czar, Nicholas II, was killed with all his family, including the children. At least they were given some time and a trial, even if it was all pretend. But in our country the president and his family were killed without delay.

Kabir went shopping early in the morning and I started preparing special dishes, the sort usually done by professional cooks for big celebrations and weddings – *Kabuli Palaw*, *Sajji Kabab*, *Borani Banjan*, *Kofteh*, *Mantu* and *Ashak*. I cooked some of the dishes in the evenings during the week after I came home from work. Yes, I wanted to celebrate that our country would be lifted out of poverty, but also because we had survived. It could have been the other way around with Kabir being arrested and shot or hanged. I would have become a widow, unable to ever find a job again.

At about five that Friday evening, General Nabi and his wife Rahima were the first to arrive in his chauffeur-driven official car. Deputy

Minister Jafar and his wife Simeen came not long after, again in an official chauffeur-driven car. I was delighted to meet their wives for the first time. They had come especially early to have a drink before dinner, and Kabir had asked me to prepare some finger food and salad to go with the drink, which was normally vodka.

Our guests had brought two bottles of Stolichnaya vodka, the most commonly available in our country. Both Nabi and Jafar had studied in Moscow and had learned the way that the Russians drank. It was there that both men had been indoctrinated with communist ideas and the wish to transform their country into a facsimile of the Soviet Union.

Rahima and Simeen were born and brought up in Kabul. Simeen had met Jafar in Moscow, where she was also studying, and they fell in love with each other and the Soviet Union. I also discovered that, like her husband, she was a good vodka drinker while Rahima took only slow small sips, probably not too keen and just keeping company. For myself, I would never drink alcohol in that party or ever. I could not forget my upbringing in a religious but modern-thinking family that did not approve of the drinking of alcohol by any member.

Both ladies were wearing western clothes. However, while Rahima's appearance was modest with a little make up, Simeen had a deep red lipstick and her face was heavily powdered. Simeen also talked only with the men and kept drinking while Rahima and I made smalltalk. But when I went to the kitchen to prepare the food, neither of them offered to help. By the time they all left they had finished the two bottles of vodka and almost all the food that I had cooked. I was exhausted, almost falling asleep.

Changes became visible quickly. The new government spent a considerable amount of money on publicity, including the hanging of massive red flags on all government buildings, both as a symbol of the party and because it had become the flag of our country, just as red as the flag of the Soviet Union. Radio and television broadcast mainly the political speeches of President Taraki, and our newspaper then printed the same speeches, releasing me from the task of having to produce anything original. At first I liked this because it gave me an easier job. But it soon became repetitive and boring.

There were also other changes, such as the creation of an Afghan Komsomol patterned after the youth clubs in Russia. The goal of these organisations was to educate young people in politics, but in the different cultural context of Afghanistan it opened the door for young men and girls to meet and have affairs, which made the more traditional elements of our society uncomfortable. Girls and boys could be seen in bars drinking vodka, now cheap and easily available, which again worried many parents. For myself, what I really liked was the introduction of the reforms that redistributed land from the big landowners to help poor people become farmers of their own land.

Problems began, however, when the government announced a new decree that girls would have freedom to select their own husbands and would be able to do whatever they wanted, without family interference after the age of 18. That merely surprised people in the cities but it shocked those who lived in the rural areas who feared that their daughters would openly drink vodka and have affairs like the girls in Kabul. Resistance against the new government began with the peasants in the rural areas and soon it spread to the provinces. Kabul, however, remained safe and peaceful. The government appeared to have turned against the very people it said it wanted to protect.

Once a week, as usual, I went to have dinner with my family while Kabir either worked late or met his friends to have a drink and enjoy life, as they had reached their goal. My parents were indifferent to the revolution but my brother Hanif was sympathetic, like me thinking that the new government would help our country out of poverty. I always enjoyed talking with him about serious matters including the politics of the past and the same type of conversations had continued after my marriage.

We were in the living room when Hanif put his university textbook down and looked at me with serious eyes.

"I heard they are killing the peasants now," he said.

I tried to explain, "You know Hanif, there is bound to be some discontent among those who lost position and power. I know there is some resistance but to say they are killing the peasants is an exaggeration."

"An exaggeration?" he said. "How do you know that?"

My reply was quick. "Kabir told me."

My mother, leaving the task of peeling potatoes she had brought into the living room to be with us, joined our conversation. "Will Kabir tell you that his party is killing the very peasants they wanted to help get out of poverty?"

"I don't know, Mother," I replied. "But I will try to find out."

"I hope so dear," she said. "Especially because of the nature of your work."

Note to myself

I don't know about the majority of our people or their opinions regarding the new government, but I am surprised to find out my own family is not happy with the way our government is handling the country, which I believe is temporary and that the government would have the support of everyone soon. Hadn't we all cried for change? What is unnecessary is the fear and mistrust among the people. I feel bad that my own family is unsure that our government is dedicated to help our nation. I also notice my friends are reserved with me. My editor-in-chief, Akram, does not share his views about politics and life in general anymore. They all behave in such a manner because I am the wife of a Parcham political party person. But they don't know that I am not a party member and even if I tell them, they are not convinced.

There is a rumour about an uprising in some parts of the country, but I think it is unpopular and the people behind it are reactionaries – those who lost their power and wealth. How can a peasant act against his own benefit and take up arms against a government that fights for the right of peasants and poor people?

Chapter 5

War was the only project

Pavel, our adviser, was a Russian who spoke perfect Farsi. I did not like him. He was arrogant and treated Akram like an idiot – choosing all the major topics, leaving the small and unimportant matters to Akram and myself. My task was to type President Taraki's long speeches and send them for printing. Those speeches were broadcast on television and on radio and then printed in *The Truth of the Saur Revolution*. Pavel insisted that it was very important to inform the masses about what our leaders thought regarding our present and future. No one dared question him. There was no variety. How many times must the same story be told?

One day, after about four months, Akram came to my office. "Well Deeba, it is goodbye," he said.

"Where are you going?" I asked, seeing that his usual cigarette was shaking as he held it.

"Nowhere," he replied, slumping into the chair by my desk and pulling the ashtray I kept specially for him closer to hand. "I am not going anywhere but home."

"I don't understand," I protested.

"It was bloody Friday that did it for me," he said.

"Akram, please explain!"

"I couldn't go to the volunteering day on Friday. They thought that meant I was acting against the government," he explained.

"No! You can't be serious?"

"I am," he replied. "I am being dismissed for failing to participate in a voluntary activity."

Although Friday was a public holiday in our country, the government had proclaimed that all men who worked in factories, offices and similar places must participate in voluntary work on Fridays building houses for poor people. While that seemed like a great idea, people who worked hard the rest of the week wanted to spend Fridays with their families. I believed it was fine if they could give up the time. After all, it was supposed to be voluntary work. But what I had not known was that anyone who failed to participate was judged to be anti-government. Akram had become one of them. He was the father of five children and one of them was disabled. He needed his Fridays to be with his family.

I discussed Akram's dismissal with Kabir, begging him to do something for the poor man, but his reply was brutal. "The government does not dismiss people unjustly. If I tried to help one, then I'd have to help others too."

The following day I was called to Pavel's office. The first thing I noticed was a bottle of vodka and three glasses on a coffee table and then a young man of about 30 years of age sitting on the couch next to Pavel.

"Come, Deeba, we are celebrating the appointment of our new editor-in-chief." He indicated the young man who looked at me and smiled. "This is Comrade Sharif. He studied in Moscow and I am sure he can handle the job much better." I lingered by the door, looking at the two men and the vodka. "Oh! Come, join us," Pavel insisted.

"Sorry, but I don't drink vodka," I said.

"The wife of a comrade who does not drink?" queried Pavel, pouring drinks for himself and Sharif.

"Is that all, sir?" I asked, thinking how ridiculous it was to make me participate in a drinking session. This Russian man had no clue about Afghan culture. Maybe he spent many years in Tajikistan and it was there perhaps that he learned Farsi with a Tajiki accent. Obviously, the Tajik women influenced by the presence of Russians, watching Russian women drinking, picked up the habit. But in Afghanistan, women rarely drank and those who did were either educated in the west or their husbands had liberal views.

"Yes," he replied. "I just wanted to make your task easier by choosing Comrade Sharif."

Easier? I am just a typist these days, I thought. *How much easier can it be?* I soon found out that Comrade Sharif had indeed studied in Moscow – but not journalism. He had replaced a highly respected journalist, a decent man too, who had simply wanted to spend a day with his disabled child.

After work that day, instead of taking the bus, I decided to walk home, thinking it would clear my head. It was a beautiful summer day with clear skies, people going about their business, and traffic flowing normally. I loved watching the fruit sellers piling the different fruits – fresh mulberries, grapes, our melon, the famous *kharboza*, which was Babur's favourite fruit. Babur was the first Moghul king. He told his friends that Kabul had become his home and that he'd forgotten all about Fergana (now part of Uzbekistan), where he had been born and for which, at first, he had fought many times trying to regain it. He became happy to have found Kabul and wrote, when he was in India conquering it, 'I must go back to Kabul because I miss that city and especially its *kharboza*.'

This story has always stayed in my mind because it shows how much love a king has for his country that he leaves his campaign and returns even though very close to victory.

When I got closer to the man with *kharboza* piled on his cart, he said cheekily, "Come on madam. It is a test of knife." Which means that he would first cut a slice from any melon I chose and ask me to try it. If I liked it, then I would pay for it. Otherwise, I would ask him to cut another slice from a different melon. I liked his cheekiness because usually it is only men who are asked to try.

Taking a shortcut through Zarnegar Park, I saw a huge crowd standing around a small man-made hill on the top of which was a stage where, when I got closer, I saw our famous vocalist Hamahang singing *The beautiful lady walked in the garden of desire*. I had seen his concerts before when people, if they were lucky enough to get a ticket, paid substantial amounts of money to watch him sing. But there he was singing for the people for free. I was even more surprised when he was followed by Parasto, who I had never seen at a live concert because she rarely performed in public. She was rich, beautiful and beyond approach, but still the communist government demanded she perform for the masses free in the park.

She sang *He came one evening when it was raining and filled my room with the scent of his body.* The audience laughed and clapped. I was delighted but this sort of event camouflaged the misery of the people. People in Kabul were not happy even though the city was still safe, guarded by government soldiers. But beyond the city in the provinces a serious war was going on. Now even I, the wife of a senior member of the Parcham Party, was doubtful that the government had taken the right path – and I was not the only one who felt that way. Some real communists had become disillusioned. I chose to take a neutral stance while watching for both the positive and the negative impacts of the new government.

Our country had become a one-party-state in which all other parties were illegal and any group that stood in opposition would be prosecuted. Discontent was growing, dividing families. Two brothers I knew, one a communist and the other critical of the government, stopped talking to each other. In some cases, family members betrayed each other and many ended up in prison, or worse.

The censorship and restrictions on freedom of speech made me worry for the safety of my brother Hanif, who was regarded as one of the best young poets of our country. His poems had been published in literary magazines and broadcast on radio. His most recent poem was a long one containing the lines:

> I heard that the mouth of the earth moved and said
> When the gardens are emptied of beautiful flowers
> The black bat is the only flower left.

That poem drew on the actions of the current government that either killed or imprisoned intellectuals who were not members of the Parcham or Khalq communist parties, only allowing their members and supporters to flourish. Since the 'black bat' drinks blood, Hanif was accusing the communist government of sucking the blood out of the people. I had told him that he must destroy that poem if he wanted to go on living.

Hanif came to see me at my office to invite me to a café for tea. That was not unusual as I loved being with him, listening to him reading his latest poem. We went to the Khyber Restaurant and sat outside the main building, just by the fountain. The wind blew some of the water towards us, giving us a fresh feeling, yet I noticed signs of worry in Hanif's face.

He began the conversation obliquely. "How is your pregnancy going?"

"You haven't come here to talk about my pregnancy, Hanif," I replied.

He shrugged. "Not exactly."

"Anything wrong?" I asked.

"No, not really."

My response was to provoke him. "Ah, then it must be love!"

He smiled, gazing into his black tea. I knew everything about Hanif – his studies, his poetry and the girls he loved. Like his poetry, which always sought to discover new dimensions, his loves also changed. Initially he had loved only beautiful girls, but more recently he wanted someone with an ordinary face but a poetic mind like his own.

He took his eyes off the tea cup and looked at me squarely. "Love is not something I think of these days."

"What is it then?" I asked.

He hesitated before saying: "You know Samad has left?"

"Left? Where's he gone?"

"He left the country," he replied.

I was shocked. "But why? And where to?"

"Anywhere, Deeba. People are just leaving."

I knew people had started leaving the country but I thought they were mainly from rural areas where fighting between the government and the Mujahideen was the most fierce. This Islamic group had existed even during the time of President Daud but had assumed the leadership of the peasants who were fighting the government, turning their struggle into a momentous fight between Islam and the infidels. Samad was Hanif's best friend, so the thought of someone like him leaving the country seemed unrealistic. Like Hanif, he loved his country and, besides that, he was engaged to his cousin whom he loved very much. How could he leave without her?

"I am thinking of leaving too," he admitted.

I was shocked and angry. "Are you mad?"

"No. I am being careful," was his calm reply.

"Listen," I said. "For years you've told me that you wanted change and now that the government has changed and is committed to eradicating poverty, you are leaving. Besides that, Samad is the son of a rich man. He has relatives in California who might help him to get there. What are you going to do? You'll be stuck in a refugee camp like so many others in Pakistan. You must wait to give this government a chance."

It was with difficulty that I managed to convince Hanif not to emigrate. At the same time, I was also praying in my heart that the troubles in the rural areas would soon be ended and the people be enabled to return to normal life. There was no way to go back to the past and imagining a backward group calling themselves the Mujahideen coming to power was inconceivable. I knew how they treated women and I knew that they would close schools and make them madrasas. If, however, I could not convince even my own brother that the future was going to be better, how could it be possible to convince our people? Not only was there a serious war in the rural areas, but Kabir had begun hinting at a struggle between Khalq and Parcham, the two communist parties, both supported by the Soviet Union and both sharing the government of our country. Kabir and his friends belonged to the Parcham Party.

"You know what?" Kabir seemed happy and relaxed when he came home that evening.

"What?"

"Moscow is calling to me," he said.

"I don't understand," I replied.

"The government has decided that I should go to Moscow to study medical developments there," he explained.

"That is nice," I said, hoping I would be included. "For how long?" I asked, but fearing he would be going alone.

"One month."

"That is a long time."

He laughed. "Oh! Don't tell me that you will miss me."

"Of course I shall!" I protested, adding: "And don't forget I am six months pregnant."

"Nothing will happen in a month, Deeba," he responded dismissively.

After my marriage I had become used to having Kabir around and the prospect of not having him hit me very hard. My mother had told me that 'love begins after marriage' and that proved to be true. I missed him from the moment he said goodbye at the airport and I cried all the way home. Every day after work, to compensate for my sadness, I met with my family, who were extra kind to me. My in-laws, unfortunately, blamed me for making Kabir live apart from them with the result that there was little opportunity to be close to them during this time or, for that matter, any other time.

One day my sister Parwin suggested we should go to the Park Cinema to see the film *El Cid*, which I accepted with delight as I loved both Sophia Loren and Charlton Heston, the main actors. After such a long time, seeing a great movie made me very happy and I thanked Parwin many times.

Before I was married I often used to go to cinema with friends and siblings, but after my marriage to Kabir, it never happened because he did not go to movies with me, only with his own friends. Then, a day later while I was eating my dinner alone in our living room, Adai burst in and without greeting me as is normal in our society, raised her voice, saying, "Madam, you have been spotted in a cinema!"

"Yes," I admitted. "I went to watch a film with my sister."

"Shame on you!" shouted my mother-in-law. "How can you go to the movies and sit next to strangers?"

She fulminated for a long time, saying many other things while I was hoping that she would leave. But she didn't. I kept apologising. I said that such a thing would never happen again. She, however, threatened to inform Kabir, to tell him that I had behaved like a loose woman. She terrified me. I could not sleep at night thinking that Kabir would really believe that I was a loose woman. What seemed to be an ordinary event in my family was, I discovered, considered shameful in my in-laws' eyes. I resolved to be careful and make sure Adai would not find another excuse, deciding not to go to my parents' house again.

A few days later I was shocked to find Kabir sitting in our living room. It was only eighteen days since he had left. I knew the number of days because I had counted every single one since his departure. A sad smile appeared on his face when he saw me.

"Why are you back so early?" I asked, sitting next to him, looking at his eyes and face.

"They sent me back," he replied.

"Back? What for?"

"There has always been a power struggle between Parcham, our party, and Khalq. President Taraki belongs to the Khalq group and he decided to sack all the Parchamis in high positions. They also decided to cut my visit to Moscow short."

"You've lost your job?" I said.

"I don't think so, but I'm sure Jafar could lose his."

I tried to comfort him but I knew it was not going to be much use. I was worried too because I had read about the rivalry between Stalin and Trotsky and then what happened to Trotsky. What was taking place in our country was similar to what had happened in the Soviet Union, like killing the previous rulers, their friends and their entire families.

The following day, Kabir went to work as usual. Kabir's post was not a political one so I doubted he would lose it. I did not dare, however, ask him further about Jafar or Nabi. Four days passed until, on the fifth day after his return from Moscow, he didn't come home. At 8 p.m. that night I phoned his office at the hospital. No one answered. I could not go to the hospital because of the curfew. The government's nightly 6 p.m. curfew in Kabul city had been in operation for more than a week with the aim of making the city safe, as the fight in the rural areas spread further and fiercer. Sometimes Kabir slept in the hospital, in case he was needed. But he always called home first. I thought perhaps he had forgotten to phone me and hoped there was nothing to worry about. Nevertheless, I could not sleep all night. In the morning, instead of going to my office I took a taxi and went to the People's Hospital, only to find out that Kabir had been arrested.

My life turned upside down at that moment and I don't know how I managed to reach my parents' home.

"Mother, he is in prison!" I burst into tears as soon as my mother opened the door. She was alone.

"What?" she said. "Who is in prison?"

"Oh God, how am I going to live?"

"Don't kill me, tell me what happened."

I choked and could not talk, only wail. "They have taken Kabir."

My mother was both surprised and worried. She brought me a glass of water. It took a long time for me to calm down enough to tell her what had happened and why. She insisted I should stay with her until I felt better, which would have been the wiser option. But I told her that I had to deliver this bad news to my in-laws and I went to Adai's house.

"Your child brought bad luck to our house," Adai said, referring to my pregnancy of seven months. These words came from the woman who had come almost every day to my parents' house to secure my marriage to her son.

She had become poisonous. It took me some time as her daughter-in-law to discover that there were other reasons for Adai not liking me. She had wanted her son to marry one of his cousins, the daughter of Adai's sister. Even more than that, because as I had initiated separate living arrangements for us, Kabir had stopped contributing to the family expenses – to which he had previously contributed more than his two brothers put together. It appeared that I could expect no support or even sympathy from my in-laws. How was I going to cope with my pregnancy during this time? And where had Kabir been taken? I knew that political prisoners were moved to Pol-e Charkhi Prison, but only after some days of interrogation by the secret police in Khad. So, was he in Khad or Pol-e Charkhi?

I phoned Rahima. "They are all in Pol-e Charkhi," she said wailing.

I did not go to my office for the next few days and when I finally did, I found out that I had been sacked. I did not dare to ask the reason why and went straight back home. How was I going to survive without Kabir and my salary?

My in-laws ignored me but my own family did not. Every day at least one of them came to see me and Parwin physically moved into my apartment to look after me during my late pregnancy and, once again, my father took responsibility for looking after me financially. My mother started knitting socks and cardigans for the baby and Rahima also came frequently. She had become a close friend and we were both overjoyed when, finally, we found out our husbands were alive and imprisoned in Pol-e Charkhi. We were not allowed a visit and no matter how we begged, the authorities would not allow us to take food to them. But we could take them clean clothes. All we knew was that the three friends, Jafar, Nabi and Kabir, were in that prison. We did not know if they were in the same cell or kept separated.

As I was folding a jacket to take to Kabir, a number of photographs fell onto the floor out of an inside pocket. When I picked them up, I saw

Kabir next to a woman, who I assumed was Russian, in many different places, one in front of Kremlin, holding hands, smiling, looking into each other's eyes. My heart started racing, my hands and lips trembled. I just sat frozen. Fortunately, Parwin was not at home. After some time I managed to get up. I folded the jacket but did not know what to do with the photos. I couldn't ask Kabir about those photographs or what they represented. Like a fool I wanted a reasonable explanation for an obvious situation. I felt lonelier than ever before, more even than since Kabir's disappearance. Why were these things happening to me, one after another? How was I going to give birth to this baby who had brought bad luck to Adai? How cruel life is sometimes.

Seeing how terrible I looked, Parwin suggested that we go shopping for new clothes for her. She had passed the entrance examination for university. To celebrate her success, my father had given her money to buy new clothes and also to prepare herself to go to university in three months. After purchasing what Parwin wanted, we went to a restaurant to eat *pekawra*, our favourite. After leaving the restaurant, I saw a fortune-teller sitting cross-legged in front of the Shah-e Do Shamshira shrine.

"Come Parwin, I want to ask this man to read my future," I said pulling her by the arm.

"You can't be serious!" she said, unsure whether I was joking.

"I am."

"You never believed in this rubbish before," she argued.

"I am not sure what to believe any longer," I replied.

I squatted in front of the fortune-teller. He rolled his dice, counted the numbers on the dice, consulted his book that looked centuries old, and told me exactly what I wanted to hear. My future would be perfect.

Then, just a few days later, the prison warden would not accept the clean clothes I had brought for Kabir. That meant he had been eliminated. And that was the end of my life too. Or at least that was how it seemed to me.

Note to myself

Now I want to turn the clock back and I wish this so-called Saur revolution had never happened. The revolution not only hurt the majority of the people in the rural areas but now I feel its impact in the capital and, moreover, in my family. My brother is planning to leave the country and my father is worried for his own safety. My own husband, who worked for the revolution to happen, has disappeared because of it.

How is it possible that both Jafar and Nabi are still alive and a doctor is not? Surely those two had much more important posts than Kabir.

Chapter 6

Life and death

On 21 October 1978, I gave birth to our son Haseeb. That is the name my husband chose when he discovered that I was pregnant. "We'll call him Haseeb if he is a boy," Kabir had said and I had agreed. I would have preferred to call him Iraj after the seventh king mentioned in the *Epic of Kings* by our great Persian poet Ferdowsi. Haseeb is an Arabic word and I would rather that my son had a name inspired by Persian poetry. But I have come to love this name and it becomes poetic because my son bears it.

The pain of his birth was almost intolerable and I tried my best not to scream. Parwin had suggested informing Adai, but she was the last person I wanted to be near me during that time. Instead I asked Parwin to call our mother to come immediately. I did not want to go into hospital. In those days people had the option to give birth in a hospital or at home. I opted for home, not because of religion or tradition, but because it was simply my preference. My mother was an expert, having given birth to five children and assisted at many other women's confinements. In a way she was more qualified than a midwife and, to be honest, I trusted her more than I would a doctor.

My pain moved in two different directions, hurting my soul and my body. My child would be born fatherless, the worst scenario for any child, and that pain was much worse than any bodily pain. Fortunately, Haseeb chose to arrive during the day as the night curfew would have made it impossible for my mother to be with me. He was a healthy baby, weighing 3kg when he was born, certainly not small but mothers accept the pain of bigger babies with love, no matter how hard the birth is. Immediately he was my king, communicating with his eyes, his hands punching my face, his feet kicking. He was a very healthy child – but was he able to fill the vacuum in my life?

No.

War dominated our lives. It was spreading from the rural areas into the cities. Kabul was still safe, but only because the government made that a priority with soldiers patrolling the streets and imposing a curfew. The government was attempting to show that it was in control of the country while more and more areas fell to the Mujahideen. Many young soldiers forced to serve in the army as conscripts lost their lives and the growing number of casualties was yet more proof that the government was lying and its entertainment in parks, bringing in musicians to perform for free, was just window dressing. I did not care whether the government would survive despite fearing the Mujahideen. At least they had not killed my husband.

The government continued imprisoning and executing members of the Parcham Party, to which Kabir belonged. They did not stop there because the rivalry between Khalq party members continued as they struggled to gain better positions, although one member kept his position throughout. Prime Minister Amin was so faithful to President Taraki that he earned the nickname 'Taraki's loyal dog', reputedly willing to lick the soles of Taraki's shoes. Amin called Taraki the 'Great Teacher', 'Great Leader' and even 'Genius of the East' until, one day, the radio announced suddenly that President Taraki had died. That was hard to believe as just the day before 'Taraki the rubbish talker' had been seen by the nation in perfect health and good humour appearing on television lecturing for hours and even laughing at his own jokes.

After Taraki's death, Amin became the sole ruler of the country and soon proved himself to be the cruellest and most ruthless of all the rulers our country has ever had, killing or imprisoning thousands because of their connection to other parties or for supporting the Mujahideen. It was obvious that he had gained absolute power by killing the 'Great Teacher', 'Great Leader' and the 'Genius of the East'.

He also unleashed his mad dogs on ordinary people – one of them being Arif Alamyar, the guardian of Kabul University.

I found out about Arif Alamyar from Parwin, who was studying pharmacy at the university. There had been some student protests and he had been sent there to make sure that no such action should ever take place again. She told me it was impossible to avoid Arif Alamyar because his chauffeur-driven Soviet Zil, one of the best Russian cars of the 1980s, was constantly circling the university compound. He sat in the passenger seat, windows open, smoking. A thick walrus moustache, popular among communists, covered his upper lip, his hawk nose sniffing out anyone with anti-government tendencies, his big eyes watching every step, capable of seeing inside the minds of ordinary people at the university.

Parwin's classmate Sanam paid a heavy price simply for being beautiful. Arif Alamyar spotted her one day going to her faculty and decided that, no matter what it took, he would marry her. The fact that she was engaged and soon to be married did not deter him. He sent someone to Sanam's parents' house asking for their permission to have Sanam as his wife. When they informed him that she already had a fiancé, Arif Alamyar had the fiancé put in prison and sent a message to Sanam's family that if they wanted to continue living, they must accept his proposal for marriage. Sanam's family had no choice because even if they sacrificed their life for the sake of their daughter, he would have kidnapped Sanam and married her by force, which would have been even more dishonourable.

One night, Haseeb was peaceful and letting me sleep when a loud banging on the door of our apartment woke me up. For a moment I thought it might have been in my dream. Then I heard a harsh voice: "Police, open the door!"

Immediately I put on some clothes and went downstairs, not sure whether to open the door because it seemed very late at night. How could I be sure it really was the police? Then I realised that, because of the curfew, only the police and the army could move at night. I opened the door and three men in police uniform burst in, pushing past me into our living room. Haseeb was awake and wailing.

"What is the matter, officer?" I asked the one who was bending down searching under the couches.

"We have an order to search your home."

"Search? But why?"

"Don't ask. Just go and make that child quiet and let us do our job."

Frightened, I did as I was told, picking up Haseeb and sitting on the edge of the bed. Another policeman entered and started going through all our cupboards and belongings, making piles on the floor of all the clothes, bedsheets and towels that I kept in our bedroom. Was I a suspect now? Did the government think that just because I was the wife of a Parcham Party member that I must be against them? That fear prevented me from saying anything as they went through every room, including the kitchen and the bathroom. It was a long time before they left.

After they had gone, the first thing I did was to go to the living room where we kept our books. They had searched every page of every book, then thrown them on the floor, including my prayer book with verses from the *Quran*. No one respecting our religion would have thrown such a book on the floor. Books were the only possessions I was worried about because, apart from the books written by Russian writers belonging to Kabir, I had books written by western writers and I knew that our government now only allowed works of Russian writers to be translated and published while the work of western writers was banned from being published. Was it now a sin even to have such books at home? I didn't know and prayed that they would not be back to take me to prison for possessing books by western authors.

By December 1979, Haseeb was a little more than a year old. The government could no longer hide the fact that its forces were unable to defeat the Mujahideen and the Soviet Union was invited officially to send forces to defend the Afghan government against the Mujahideen. On 24 December 1979, the Soviet Union invaded Afghanistan. Their arrival marked more than a year since the disappearance of my husband.

One of the Soviet Union's first acts was to install a new president. His name was Babrak Karmal and he was from the Parcham faction of the Communist Party. The first thing he did was release political prisoners. I thought that did not matter to me as my husband was dead.

Then, one afternoon, a man with long hair and a beard, wearing torn clothes knocked on the door. I thought he was a beggar, failing to recognise my own husband Kabir who was alive although he had a foul smell. Without any control I jumped on him, hugging him tight, kissing his neck first where my lips reached, pulling him down, lowering his head, kissing his dirty greasy hair, reaching his dirt-coated hands, rubbing my face on them. I was in a state of madness, frenzy, crying loud. Stepping back looking at him to make sure it was Kabir, then jumping at him again. A dead husband had come from his grave, just for my sake. I was certain that like thousands killed by the government regardless of their innocence, his body was under metres of soil in a mass grave now excavated.

"Please talk to make sure I am not dreaming," I wailed. "Is that really you or I have become mad imagining it is you?"

"It is me, it is me, calm down," he said.

"I thought you left your son fatherless."

"Son?"

"Yes you have a son. He looks exactly like you," I told him.

I rushed to Haseeb, regardless of him being asleep, took him out of his cot and brought him to Kabir, who was now standing in our living room.

"I have a son, I have a son," Kabir repeated, grabbing Haseeb from my hands, sitting on the couch kissing Haseeb's cheeks, while Haseeb wailed with anger, protesting the interruption to his sleep. But at that moment, such a small discomfort of my child's was not a big issue.

Apparently, another person by the name of Kabir had been executed in the prison and a prison officer had mixed up the identity of the two Kabirs.

I was extremely happy to see that my husband was free but sad as well that our country was no longer truly independent. Considering we were now occupied by the Soviet Union and how Kabir had suffered in prison, I hoped he would leave politics now so that we might live a normal life. Although I no longer supported the government, whether ruled by Khalq or Parcham parties, I went back to my old job, which now involved writing about the Soviet Union's achievements. A new editor-in-chief from the Parcham faction replaced Sharif, who was from the Khalq Party. Torab Ainy had studied literature in Moscow and possessed a good knowledge of old and modern European literature and our own classics, but nevertheless made sure that we published works of Russian authors, especially Mayakovski and Gorky. I liked Torab more than Sharif but the presence of Pavel, who continued in his previous role, made me uncomfortable as he had become bossy and rude since the Soviet invasion. I believe that he thought Afghanistan had become part of the Soviet Union, like countries such as Tajikistan, Uzbekistan and Turkmenistan. He managed my assignments in Kabul and asked me to come to the office one day, which he shared with Torab.

"Deeba, my dear. You've heard of our victory in Kalakan?" he asked.

I said yes, trying to hide my annoyance that he had used the word 'dear'. Either he was ignorant of our culture – only family and close associates use this familiarity – or he did it deliberately to intimidate and disrespect me. I thought the latter as he also treated Torab like his personal servant.

"Well in that case I want you to go to Kalakan and write a good report about it. Take your photographer with you."

The rebellious nature of the people of Kalakan is renowned in our history. First, in 1929, Habibullah Kalakani, a Tajik, fought against a powerful Pashtun, King Amanullah Khan, who had gained Afghan independence by fighting and defeating the British empire's army that had invaded Afghanistan from India. At the beginning, people of Afghanistan loved Amanullah, but when he started his education reforms, including opening schools for the girls and even sending some of them to Turkey for higher education, first the mullahs and then the nation rose against him at the same time the country was going through a difficult economic situation due to civil war and government corruption. Some historians argue that Kalakani rebelled because of the high price of commodities. Others say he fought against the king because he felt that by allowing the girls to go to school, the country was not following the path of Islam, which says the place of women is at home.

Kalakani, the son of a water bearer, gained a small number of followers from the Kalakan district and surrounding areas who were determined to fight against a very much larger army and, in only a year, managed to overthrow a powerful king, and Kalakani himself became a king for nine months. What he achieved in that short period was astonishing, because never in the history of modern Afghanistan had a Tajik ruled this country whose rulers were otherwise only Pashtun.

Following the arrival of the Soviet Army in Afghanistan, the people of Kalakan confronted the biggest army in the world, arming themselves with *jezail*, old-fashioned home-made muzzle-loading guns fired with gunpowder. But the people of Kalakan had the same courage as their forebears. One night they launched a surprise attack on an Afghan post near their district and, after defeating the defenders, got all the modern Soviet-made weapons they needed. After this success, the people of Kalakan attacked some other small posts, giving the signal to the nation that it was possible to fight against the government that was supported by the Soviet Union. In retaliation, the Soviet forces, equipped with modern artillery and tanks and supported by air power, captured the whole of Kalakan in just two days. We heard about this story from ordinary people because the government refused to admit that there was an uprising in Kalakan, just 40km from Kabul. Because the uprising was common knowledge, the authorities decided to acknowledge the uprising in order to show the might of the Soviet Army to the people and provide a lesson to anyone who might think fighting against the Soviet Union was possible.

When I mentioned to Kabir that I was going to Kalakan to write a report about the war, he seemed happy. "Go and write in detail covering the atrocities committed by these *ashrar*," he said. *Ashrar*, bad guys, was the word the government used to describe those fighting the government and the Soviet forces. While they attacked military targets, the government and the Soviet Union retaliated by killing both the fighters and innocent civilians, claiming that the civilians were giving assistance to the bad guys. What kind of bad guys we did not know. By now, regardless of my marriage to Kabir, who fully supported the invasion of our country, I had turned against the Soviet Union and thought their presence in my country was harmful because their army indiscriminately killed people in rural areas. I was very happy that my husband was alive and free but at the same time very sad that many other innocent people were losing their lives daily.

When Mohsen came to pick me up, he was not the same enthusiastic person he had been when we had travelled to Aqcha. As to the reason, I only could read his mind because he would not dare to say anything negative against our government if he wanted to live. After all, I was the wife of a senior Parcham party member and if I were to report him, he would disappear, never to be seen again. As on our previous journey, I occupied the rear seat while he sat next to Murad at the front. Unlike that earlier journey, there was silence in the car as both Murad and Mohsen kept quiet, not even talking between themselves.

After the Khairkhana Pass, I expected to see my favourite green tunnel through the chinar trees. But what I saw was just the circular tops of the stumps of all the trees that had been cut just a little above the ground. The felled trees were nowhere to be seen on either side of the road. There was only an expanse of flat land covered by vineyards and agricultural crops. I felt as if someone had fastened a black rope around my heart and was pulling the noose tight. Were my eyes playing tricks on me? I had no other choice but to break the silence and ask Mohsen, "What happened to the trees?"

"The trees?" Mohsen seemed surprised by my question.

"Yes, the trees."

"You seriously don't know?" he asked.

"Know what?"

"The trees were used by *ashrar* snipers firing at a convoy of Soviet and government forces."

"But how?" I asked.

"They hid behind the trees and fired at the convoys. So the government ordered all the trees to be cut down."

"Oh no! Innocent trees. The green tunnel…"

"All gone, Deeba jan."

There were no shops open when we reached Istalif where last time there had been glazed clay pots for sale and we had refreshed ourselves with *doogh*. All of the shop doors were bolted and the *doogh* sellers had disappeared. No sophisticated Kabuli tourists, no foreigners – just an empty place. Before the Saur revolution, tourists from all around the world, and especially Europe and America, had come to visit our country for its magnificent natural beauty and historical sites such as the Buddha of Bamyan, which would later be destroyed by the Taliban after they had gained power. There were many hotels in Kabul and other cities that had accommodated these travellers while others loved the freedom of camping in our fresh air unaffected by pollution from cars and factories. People even talked about these tourists skinny-dipping in Band-e Amir. Afghanistan became a platform for artists and writers to start their career, like the famous Irish writer Dervla Murphy, a young female who cycled from the border with Iran the whole length of Afghanistan to Pakistan. She slept in the open air alone and without fear as the country was hospitable and safe. Her first book, *Full Tilt*, about her journey through Afghanistan, became an instant bestseller in 1965.

The famous actor Omar Sharif was in a film called *The Horsemen*, which was filmed in Afghanistan. Sharif and his crew of film makers and female actors were all safe and happy to be in such a beautiful country. My brother Hanif, then just a teenager, went to the Kabul Intercontinental Hotel to see Omar Sharif as he came out of the hotel, perhaps even to get an autograph, but he told me that young and beautiful ladies circling around Sharif made it impossible for him to get close. I saw the film when it came out and for years thought Omar Sharif to be an excellent horseman, not realising that it was our Tora, the greatest *chapandaz* of all time, who had doubled for him.

But now only the main roads were safe, and then only during the day. Where we were going had also been secured by the Afghan and Soviet armies, so we would be safe there as well as on the main road – but none of us would dare to venture off-course. Despite Istalif's emptiness, Murad asked if we might have a short break while he smoked a cigarette. I agreed because I wanted to remember how this place had looked when I was on my way to Aqcha. After parking, Murad found a half-damaged *charpai* and sat on the edge of it, searching his inner jacket pocket for his cigarette pack. I watched his face through the smoke and realised how sad he looked. He must have been thinking of many other losses since the Saur revolution and not just the loss of trees or the shops in Istalif. Little did I know that this would be his last trip with me. Weeks later he disappeared and I was told by another driver that he had emigrated to Pakistan. I sat next to him on the *charpai*, carefully making sure that it did not collapse as one of its legs was broken. He was gazing towards the mountain. When he noticed that I was looking at him, he smiled and said, "It is not the same, is it?"

"No it's not," I replied.

He became quiet again and I realised what he said was the height of protest from him to the wife of a Communist Party member. "It is not the same, is it?" I repeated his words in my mind silently, realising that nothing was the same any more. The poverty in our country had worsened and on top of that the country was at war and no longer safe. Trust between people had broken. Neither Murad nor Mohsen dared to say anything against the government for fear I would report them and they would simply lose their lives.

The village of Kalakan was at the centre of the district and not far from the main road to the north. As soon as we turned right from the main road we saw army tanks about every 100m, changing my memories of a peaceful village I had visited before. Afghan soldiers with Kalashnikovs on their shoulders patrolled up and down. I did not see any Soviet soldiers, guessing that once they had secured the area after a heavy fight, the task of guarding the district had been given to the Afghan Army. The soldiers stopped our car at a checkpoint and one of them pointed his Kalashnikov at Murad, demanding: "Show me your ID and open the boot of the car."

"We are from *Bakhtar Press*." I raised my voice from the passenger seat but still he kept looking at Murad's ID. A second soldier, without pointing his gun at us, examined the inside of the car, carefully scrutinising its contents.

"Show me your ID," the soldier with a gun asked me this time. I obliged. After carefully scrutinising my photo and face, he said "No need to check the boot," to the second soldier, and then, turning to Murad, said: "You can go, but drive slowly. Many tanks are parked on this narrow road."

When we reached the village of Kalakan I noticed that at least half of the houses were damaged or totally destroyed and, like Istalif, the shops were closed. I saw only one old man using a long piece of wood as a walking stick, otherwise the village was deserted. I asked Murad to stop the car and went to the old man.

"Salaam, uncle, can I talk with you for a while?"

The old man looked at me as if noticing me for the first time. He also saw the car. "Salaam, welcome."

Greeting and welcoming has always been an important part of rural culture. When men and women passed each other in the village, they said *khoosh amadi*, welcome. I thought such a greeting was ironic in a village destroyed by war. "What happened here, uncle?" I asked.

"Why are you asking?"

"I am a reporter from *Bakhtar Press*."

"You mean you work for the government?" he said.

"Yes."

"Oh, my child. *Ashrar* had taken this place but thanks to our army, the village is liberated and our army has provided us security."

I wrote what the man told me in my notebook, and would report it, but I did not believe him. Clearly, he was too afraid to say anything negative about the government and the soldiers who had destroyed Kalakan.

In the rural areas people did not lock or close the doors to their houses but, as we walked and peered into the courtyards, we did not see anyone until, in one of the courtyards, I noticed an old woman sitting under a walnut tree, resting her back against it, her chin touching her chest, probably asleep. I told Mohsen and Murad to wait outside and stepped in. When I got closer, the woman heard the sound of my steps and raised her head.

"Salaam, maadar jan," I said.

"Salaam," she replied.

"How are you?" I asked.

"Why? Why do you ask?"

I was taken aback. There was no greeting, no welcoming. I squatted in front of her and looked at her tired eyes.

"I am a reporter and want to find out what happened in this village."

"What happened? You can see what happened. Men are dead or ran away. Women are widows now and children without fathers. Write that I ask God's justice in judgement day. My son just 46 years old and my grandson only 17 escaped to take refuge in the *Kariz* when soldiers took men out of the houses and shot them in front of their families. My son and grandson did not fight anyone. They were simple farmers. The Russian soldiers heard about men taking refuge in the *Kariz*. They went there and set fire to the *Kariz*, burning both of them alive together with many other men, children and women. Go and see it for yourself.

Tell your government what they did to us. Tell them. May Allah burn all of you in hell. Go away. You are not welcome here."

Her words and looks frightened me. Immediately I got up and almost ran towards the door. Mohsen and Murad were chatting with each other some distance away, but when they saw me hastening towards them, they rushed to meet me.

"What is the matter?" Mohsen asked.

"It is terrible."

"What is terrible?" Murad asked.

"I need to drink some water," I said.

"There is a spring at the centre of the village," Mohsen said, pointing.

They did not ask any further questions while I drank water from the spring, sitting next to it watching the water flow, wondering how I was going to lie? How was I going to write a false report?

"We must find where the *Kariz* is," I told them and got up.

"What for?" Mohsen asked.

"You will see. Find someone to ask for directions."

We waited at the village square until a boy about 10 years old appeared. Murad went to him and asked for directions to the *Kariz*.

A *Kariz* is a system for transporting water from a water well to the surface, through an underground aqueduct. This is an ancient system of water supply that allows water to be transported over long distances in hot dry climates without much loss from evaporation. The system has the advantage of being resistant to natural disasters such as earthquakes and floods, and to deliberate destruction in war. Furthermore, it is almost insensitive to the levels of precipitation, with only gradual variations in flow between wet and dry years. *Kariz* are constructed as a series of well-like vertical shafts, connected by a gently sloping tunnel. This taps into underground water and delivers it to the surface by gravity, without need for pumping. The vertical shafts along the underground channel are purely for maintenance purposes, and water is typically used only once it emerges from the end point.

On the way to the *Kariz* we saw Russian soldiers and their tanks. We were walking and were stopped by the soldiers who asked us what we were doing. With some difficulty, as none of us could speak Russian and they did not speak our language, I managed to tell them that I was a government press reporter there with my colleagues. Near the *Kariz* we saw old men, women and children standing, shouting, crying, trying to draw the attention of the soldiers. It appeared that the Russians had blocked the entrance to the *Kariz* with big boulders. The crowd were shouting and crying all together, making it difficult to understand what they wanted. I saw a teenage girl stamping her feet in frenzy, shaking her body violently, pointing to the soldiers and screaming. Her state frightened me but I thought I must ask her what she wanted.

"They don't allow us to take our dead family members out of the *Kariz*. God curse these Russians. They burned them alive and now they don't allow us to take their bodies – if anything is left of them."

Mohsen took up the task of enquiring himself. He found out that when the Russians surrounded the village they immediately started killing men and boys. Some men with their families, including wives and children, managed to escape and thought that no one would find them in the *Kariz*. The Russians searched all the houses and surrounding areas until they found out that many people were hiding in the *Kariz*. The Russians poured a large quantity of petrol down the vertical shafts of the *Kariz* and set it alight. But not before they had blocked all of the entrances so that no one could escape. All the people who had taken refuge there were burned alive.

We had no choice but to leave those desperate people in their misery, knowing Kalakan would not be the only place where the Russians had committed such atrocities. They wanted to show anyone who dared to resist them how savagely cruel the Russian Army could be. I knew then that we were going to become another Tajikistan, Uzbekistan or Turkmenistan.

Note to myself

I have to lie but I am not good at it. Unfortunately to survive now one must lie. I have to write that since the army of the Soviet Union came to defend our country against the western intrusion – countries such as the UK and the US – our country is safe and *ashrar* are in retreat. After securing our country from the invasion of the western powers and *ashrar*, our country would progress to become self-sufficient and prosperous, using the USSR models adopted in Central Asian countries, now part of the Soviet Union. But the truth is I don't see western invaders, I don't see any *ashrar* but ordinary Afghan people who do not want the Soviet Union interfering with their freedom. They don't want Afghanistan to become like Tajikistan.

At the beginning of my journey when I saw trees cut and shops closed, I felt sad for such loss. But my loss is nothing in comparison with the loss of people in Kalakan now without houses, without their men and women, and not allowed to bury their dead.

Chapter 7

Russians on the streets

In the summer after Kabir's release we planned to celebrate with Nabi and Jafar at the Qargha reservoir, famous for its cool weather and natural beauty. Of course, we'd celebrated their release many times, throwing parties in our own houses with friends who were mainly party members. But to go to Qargha was very special. Our deposed king had owned land and properties there to which he had invited foreign dignitaries. Ahmad Zahir, our very own Elvis Presley, had been a frequent visitor, drinking wine and playing music with his friends and girlfriends. We set off in three separate cars, Kabir and I in his own car while the other two used their official cars as there were no rules restricting use for private purposes. As soon as we arrived, the men chose a quiet spot under a eucalyptus tree near a fast-flowing stream and opened a bottle of vodka.

"Hey, wait!" Rahima protested. "Let us spread the *kilim* first and we'll prepare some salad to go with the drink."

"We are thirsty," Simeen laughed, joining the men in their drinking.

Simeen's smile revealed sparkling teeth and I wondered how she could keep those teeth so white despite smoking and drinking with the men. It seemed to me that she did not behave like an Afghan woman at all. Was that the result of her spending time in Moscow? I was glad that Rahima behaved like me as we helped each other spread the *kilim*, and we prepared some salad. Our men always ate salad as they drank their vodka while Russians knocked back their drinks in one go, saying *Davai!*

The men were drinking heavily and Simeen seemed to be keeping up with them. I don't know how much vodka she consumed. She never offered to help Rahima and me to prepare and serve the food. They all became loud with laughter and there was no talk about politics or helping the masses out of poverty. The result of the excess alcohol was not a pretty sight. I thought it was becoming obvious that the communists had forgotten what they had promised the people. The only change in our country was the people who ruled it. I was starting to think that the whole idea of bringing revolution to our country was simply to gain power to enjoy privilege, forgetting all the promises that had been made.

The Mujahideen were gaining ground in their fight against the government, conflict spread from the rural areas into the cities and was intensifying. By describing themselves as freedom fighters and defenders of Islam, they began to influence the army, with the result that some major units with all their weapons defected to the Mujahideen. With more men and almost the same weapons as the government, the Mujahideen were now winning with alarming speed. In response, the government increased the service period of conscript soldiers from one year to three years and reduced the age of eligibility to join the army from 21 to 19 years old, only deferring service for those boys studying in school and university. As soon as they finished their studies, they were forced to join.

Hanif, my brother, was then a student at Kabul University. Despite being a *bona fide* student, he had been stopped at a checkpoint, transported to an army compound with other young men picked up on the street, and sent to Panjshir. With Kabir's help we managed to prove that he was a student but, although we had been successful in bringing him back to Kabul, he had stopped going to university and very rarely went out of the house, fearing he would be caught again. So, when he came to my office on a hot Thursday I was pleased to see him.

"I think on a hot day like this you deserve to take a break and have a cold drink with me," he said with his big familiar smile.

I was pretending to look busy because I no longer had much interest in the sort of news coverage the government, and especially Pavel, required me to write. I was looking forward to Friday, the day when all office workers were freed from their work.

"Oh that would be great! I am not busy," I told him truthfully.

We went to *Khyber*, our favourite café, where we enjoyed each other's company. He ordered a Coca Cola and I a fresh lemonade. We sat outside by the fountain in front of the café, watching passers-by on the street, and trying to ignore the soldiers, tanks and trucks that made Kabul appear to be a city under siege.

"I've finally decided," Hanif said, but then sipped his drink and only elaborated when I encouraged him by nodding expectantly. Almost reluctantly he continued. "I'm going to leave the country. I must do it before I am caught again and sent somewhere to serve in the army. I am very serious. I've already planned my way out. Father is helping me."

"Oh, God!" I said. "How will we manage without you?" I understood the reason for his decision, but even so could not imagine losing him again.

"If you want me to have a chance to live, you should encourage me to leave."

"But getting to Pakistan won't be easy. And how can you survive there without a job?"

"Father will give me enough money to tide me over. When I'm there he'll send money secretly. There is a system. *Sarafs* – people involved in money exchange – can do it using codes. Father will deposit money with one of them here in Kabul and I'll get that money in Pakistan."

"Oh! So you've worked out all the details," I said, wiping tears from my eyes.

"Yes, sister. I've even found a guide to take me to the border."

I lost interest in my job. I did not bring work home any more. Instead, I cooked dinner, ate it with Kabir, and then went to read a book in the living room. The government encouraged people to read only

Russian authors and books by western writers were becoming less easily available. I avoided Russian authors and even our own writers who had to praise the Saur revolution or the Soviet Union if they wanted to be published.

One evening, as I was reading *The Old Man and the Sea* for the third time, Kabir looked up from his book, which I assumed was written by a Russian, and announced: "I have been invited to go to Moscow."

"You are going again?" I asked politely, not wishing to reveal that I was annoyed by him interrupting my reading.

"Yes. There is a conference about new medical developments and the Ministry of Health thought it would be good for me to be there."

"For how long?" Remembering the photograph of Kabir with the woman, I knew that he would not be going to Moscow just for a conference and visits to health institutions. Or perhaps he would be meeting some other woman. But I did not have the courage to confront him with my suspicions.

"About two weeks," he replied confidently. "One for the conference and another to see health institutions in the rural areas."

I was not in a position to doubt or argue with him. The government was sending people from many different backgrounds to the USSR in order to show them how developed that country was and how happy and satisfied were its people. It was not only people in Kabir's position. Ordinary people like school teachers, students and factory workers were also given a chance to visit the Soviet Union. Included among these visitors were mullahs and other religious leaders, who the Russians were trying to convince that the atheistic USSR was not destroying mosques but actually building new ones. What these religious leaders in fact discovered was that the mosques they were being shown were devoid of worshippers and the people of Tajikistan could no longer speak Farsi – demonstrating that both the religion and the language of the people were disappearing. The Russians, thinking that these religious people were from a poor country, provided them with good food and accommodation in excellent hotels, no doubt believing that such treats were so extraordinarily generous that they could win the support of mullahs and religious leaders with such obvious bribery. I wondered what would happen if the government decided to send me to the USSR. Would Kabir allow me to go there to meet Russian men and drink vodka with them? In fact, the government did not send many women, apart from seriously committed communists belonging to the Khalq or Parcham factions. Resigned, I doubted that this would be Kabir's last trip to Moscow.

Since the Saur revolution, Afghan radio and television could not be relied upon to provide honest government news so like many others, I became a serious listener of the BBC. Each evening a little before 7 p.m., I switched the radio station to the BBC and waited until it said 'This is the BBC'. It was through the BBC that I learned there had been a major uprising in Herat, Afghanistan's second largest city, just eleven months after the Saur revolution.

I discovered that ordinary people had gathered in very large numbers and began to demonstrate, eventually attacking the Afghan Army post in the city. After a bloody fight the citizens, among them some army officers and soldiers who had defected to them with their weapons, took control of the army post in Herat. The remaining government forces were driven out and virtually the whole city was in the hands of ordinary people. I found it hard to believe that a city had fallen into the hands of people who lacked any form of military or political leadership. But the Mujahideen did not claim that it was they who had taken the city. As the situation in Herat continued, I yearned for a successful uprising by ordinary people all over the country. My hopes were for a genuine popular uprising – ending the communist government but without simply replacing them with the Mujahideen. Was that possible? Nevertheless, I began to hope that the people of Kabul would soon do the same and rise up. But I was totally wrong.

To recapture Herat, it was Soviet forces that responded instead of the Afghan Army. The dreadful Russian helicopter gunships levelled the rebel-held army compound and then went on to destroy most of the city's residential areas. Soviet forces recaptured the city for the Afghan government and, by the time fighting ended, about 30,000 civilians had lost their lives.

The Saur revolution had divided both the people and the nation. I was not the only one who thought communists were wrong, despite my own husband being a party member. My mother was from Nijrab – a beautiful district about 60km north of Kabul, where her brother had three sons: Khalil, Amin and Wasi. The eldest, Khalil, remained uninterested in politics while Amin was a member of the Parcham Communist Party. Wasi disappeared after the Soviet invasion of Afghanistan. It only came to light much later that he had joined the Mujahideen and was moving arms from Pakistan to Afghanistan and fighting against the government.

Ordinary people paid the ultimate price after the Saur revolution, either by being imprisoned or killed. They were regarded as the enemy of both the communist government and the Mujahideen. News also came that Golbudin Hikmatyar, the most radical leader supported by Saudi Arabia, was hinting that those Afghans who had worked for the government in the past and then emigrated to Pakistan were subject to his radical 'justice', no matter where they were. His groups killed innocent people who had run away from the communists to take refuge in Pakistan. The news worried me so much that, initially, I could not sleep well, thinking about Hanif and the rest of the family who had gone to Pakistan. Not many months after Hanif had gone, my parents and the rest of the family also left. Were these stories really true or just government propaganda that gave the Mujahideen a bad name? Later, when the Mujahideen took over, they proved my fear of them by committing despicable atrocities against the people.

Since my very first visit to the Arg, the presidential palace, in the aftermath of April's Saur revolution, the damaged building had been restored and I had become a regular visitor to the formulaic press conferences I was required to report on. About a year after the Russian invasion, I went to the conference room at Arg where foreign and local journalists waited impatiently for the new president to arrive. Most of the faces in that room were familiar to me and I knew which organisations they worked for. After a long wait, President Babrak Karmal appeared wearing military uniform. The approach was similar to that of Fidel Castro, showing the revolutionary face of a successful revolutionary leader, tough and ready to fight to the end.

The press conference began with the usual questions by the Eastern European pack, which always consisted of more praise than questions. The intention was for the new president to showcase Afghanistan's achievements since the revolution and to protest against the world's unjust accusation that the fraternal assistance offered by the USSR was not the 'invasion' President Reagan of the US repeatedly insisted it was. Much of the world became united in condemnation of the actions of the Soviet Union. Allies of the Soviets had no choice but to agree with the USSR and we noticed the arrival of many soldiers from Eastern Europe and Cuba. The Soviet Union had humiliated the US during its war in Vietnam so, in retaliation, Reagan sent weapons to the Mujahideen. Not because he really cared about our country but because Afghanistan was becoming the Soviet Union's Vietnam and the Mujahideen the US's proxy Cold War warriors.

After praise from the Eastern European countries, the BBC journalist managed to grab the microphone and ask a serious question. "Mr President!" he exclaimed. "Can you please tell us why the Soviet Union forces are here?"

After the journalist's question had been translated, Karmal stared at the journalist for some while until we thought maybe he had not heard the translation. Then, with real anger in his eyes, he replied, "The small contingent of the Soviet Union's forces is here to defend our country from the aggression of the US and UK, which are staging an unjust war against us, threatening our freedom."

The BBC journalist continued. "But Mr President, we have not seen any US or UK soldiers fighting in your country. The Mujahideen are from Afghanistan not the US."

"Stop!" the president roared. "You are a spy pretending to be a journalist from a country that we have defeated three times and, I tell you, your country will be defeated again despite your cunning plans."

The BBC journalist tried again. "But Mr President... Mr..."

A security officer grabbed the microphone and, although the brave journalist tried to shout, he was forced to leave the room. I felt sorry for the reporter and yet admired his courage, wishing that I and the Eastern Bloc journalists were as brave. Then I realised that the BBC journalist had the backing of his government. If I did the same, I would have been punished severely, losing my job and even risking being put in prison. My action would have also affected Kabir. Any one of us who said something to annoy Karmal or the Kremlin would pay with our lives.

The language Karmal used was the language of force the government had used since the Saur revolution, which I referred to as the 'Sour revolution'. These people forced their way into power and the Mujahideen were even worse. If they came to power, Kabir would not be left alive. Oh God, in my mind I sounded so pessimistic and anti-government now, yet could not express my feelings to anyone, not to Kabir nor to my own relatives.

After the BBC journalist had been removed, business returned to normal with the president confidently explaining the achievements of the Saur revolution, demonstrable examples of which, apart from the devastating war, I found very hard to believe. Afterwards, I did not feel like going back to the office. The interview would be shown on televisions around the world to people who, it was hoped, would agree with our president that he was directing our country towards a better future. Rather than return directly to my office in the Ministry of Culture, I took a detour to look at the flowers in Zarnegar Park. I had fond memories of my father taking me and Hanif – the other children were not born – to the park where the three of us walked slowly holding hands, Hanif on one side and I on the other. We listened to our father as he talked, sometimes reciting a poem of Hafiz or Saadi, his favourite Persian poets, and then explaining their meaning. His influence on us made me become a journalist and my brother a poet.

While walking through the park I heard the sound of *Allahu Akbar!* in the distance. I sat on one of the park benches and waited to see what was happening. Shouts of *Allahu Akbar!* became clearer and louder as the minutes passed, until I saw a huge number of demonstrators coming from Jada, marching towards the Arg. I didn't believe what I was seeing. Did I have sunstroke? But it was real. We have a proverb, 'The knife has reached the bone', and it occurred to me that our people had reached the height of suffering and were now prepared to lay down their lives for freedom. To them, living in such circumstances was like a slow death anyway.

Because I am a journalist, curiosity is in my nature, and I walked towards the demonstrators. From their age and appearance, I guessed that they represented people from many different backgrounds – students from the university and schools as well as factory workers, and even workers from government offices. I hadn't seen such a big crowd before. There were so many that I imagined the crowd stretched all the way to Kabul Zoo. The sheer number of them must have made them feel safe to express their feelings, shouting that they wanted Soviet forces to get out of Afghanistan. They probably thought that the government could not put every member of that huge crowd in prison. I walked with them.

Near the Ministry of Education, their progress was halted by a line of big army trucks blocking the road. Soldiers carrying Kalashnikovs stood on army trucks and officers shouted orders at them. Seeing the determined faces of the soldiers and their officers, the crowd stopped. As time passed, however, they found the courage to go a little further forward, demanding that the road be opened for them. At that point the officers ordered their soldiers to fire into the air. The sound of gunfire created panic. Some of us ran away, but then returned. I decided to get to the edge of the mob to avoid being pushed forward or hit by a bullet if the officers ordered the soldiers to shoot into the crowd.

One young man, who I assumed to be a university student, climbed onto the roof of a traffic warden's cubicle and shouted louder than the others: "Death to the communist government, death to the Soviet Union, death—" And then his shouting stopped. I saw him reach for his chest with both hands and then fall into the crowd below. One of the soldiers had shot him. I ran into a shoe shop. The owner kindly allowed me to stay, but immediately shut the iron door in case others tried to get in. Outside the noise gave the impression that it was mayhem. The sound of bullets being fired, the sound of bullets hitting something, and beside all these noises the shouting prayer of the old shop owner praying for his safety and the safety of the nation.

"Oh, Allah have a mercy up on us," he screamed non-stop, and his behaviour made me even more nervous. When I heard the sound of screeching of the army tanks on the pavement I thought a massacre was going on outside. Obviously, the government wanted to make sure that such a demonstration would never take place again, and the style used was the same as the Soviet-installed governments in Eastern Europe. They ruthlessly killed to teach the people a lesson.

I don't know how long it took before it became quiet again, but still I had no courage to leave the shop until the shopkeeper decided to open the door to get out. I urged him not to open the door, but when I looked at my watch I noticed it was late and I'd been there for a long time.

The first thing I saw when I got out was wreckage and bodies everywhere. The soldiers were pulling bodies from the street, loading them onto trucks, among them the injured as well. But no one paid attention. I could see blood everywhere under the streetlights.

I walked home on shaking legs, not having the strength to go back to the office. The next day I found out that the soldiers had killed and wounded many demonstrators. They had also filled their trucks with captured demonstrators – these would be interrogated, tortured, and then put in prison.

Among the many, many deaths I was especially shocked by the loss of my colleague Timor. He worked for *Anis*, the next most important newspaper after *The Truth about the Saur Revolution*, for whom I worked. He had been on his way to the Bamyan Province to see his parents when his bus was stopped by the Mujahideen along the way. After they searched him and found out that he was a journalist working for *Anis*, they killed him along with others who also worked for the government. They did this in front of the other passengers to teach them a lesson and to spread the word that anyone who worked for the government was an enemy of the Mujahideen and would be killed without investigation.

The war against the Mujahideen intensified. Of all the places, Panjshir district, surrounded by high mountains, remained impossible to capture, no matter how hard the government and the Soviet forces tried. The leader of the Mujahideen, a young man with an engineering degree, had become very famous for his resilience and ability to defend Panjshir, the graveyard of Soviet Union and government forces. Western journalists walked all the way from Peshawar, the border city in Pakistan, to Panjshir to meet this man called Ahmad Shah Masoud who, they said, had brought the Soviet Union to its knees. In fact the Soviet Union had been brought to its knees because of the collapse of its economy, having spent incredible amounts of money on its war in Afghanistan and losing many soldiers and army officers.

Babrak Karmal was failing to bring peace by winning the war against the Mujahideen. In fact, the Mujahideen were taking more and more land from the government, even successfully taking cities and holding them for a while until, after intense fighting including bombing the cities, they retreated to the districts again. It appeared that the Soviet Union was losing its grip on Afghan affairs, no longer convinced that Karmal was the right person to be president and the leader of his country. It seemed that the Soviet Union thought Karmal was too lenient, too weak and that it would require a strong and a cruel man to deal with the Afghans, someone able to punish them and bring them to submission. In desperation, after six years of carnage, the Soviet Union replaced Karmal with Dr Najib.

Dr Najib, or Najib the Bull as he was known among those who hated the Parcham Party, initially appeared at demonstrations prior to the communists taking power, holding a wooden stick as big as a cricket bat, always ready to attack the police when they tried to stop the demonstrators. He was a bodybuilder but also a medical student who became a doctor before the Saur revolution. The new communist government first appointed him as the head of Khad, the national secret service, and soon he earned the name of butcher as he sent his victims to specially built horror chambers, to be tortured before being sent to prison to wait for their execution – a bullet in the head.

It was evident that there had been no loyalty among communist leaders since they came to power. Every individual wanted to be the ultimate leader, every individual wanted to rule the nation. After years of turmoil we had a country in which everyone who thought they had some power wanted to be king. No one cared for the nation and the only thing anyone seemed interested in was toppling the previous government. I lost interest in my work. I started reading the world's literature in the office, novels that I photocopied from the books so that it looked as though I were reading work documents. The work had become so simple and repetitive since all I had to do was rewrite speeches of political leaders, my task had become the work of a secretary – a-cut-and-paste job. No creativity.

I was in the middle of reading *To Kill a Mockingbird* and drinking green tea when our office building shook and the windows shattered, some of the shards landing on my desk but, fortunately, not hitting me. For a moment I was stunned and couldn't move. As I was about to run out of the office into the corridor, I met our watchman, who burst in asking me if I was all right. Without answering, I rushed past him into the corridor and further away from the front of the building. On the way I heard another explosion, but this time the sound was weaker, which made me believe it was somewhere further away from our building. The centre of the building was our assembly point. We were all frightened, especially the women. The watchman told us that a rocket had hit the street in front of our building. He was lucky to have survived because the explosion was just metres away from him. But he was saved by the wooden cubicle in front of the building where he sat all day.

Later that day, with trembling feet I left the office, praying that another rocket would not land in the vicinity. The following day I saw the damage to our building and to other buildings nearby. The watchman told me that four people had been killed and many injured. There was no news about this incident on radio, television or in the newspapers. Those two rockets marked the beginning of the Mujahideen offensive against Kabul, a nightmare in which all we could do was hope that a rocket would not hit us, shamefully forgetting it would take the lives of other people. That is what war does to human beings. Kabul was not safe any more. The war had come to our home.

The war may have been a catalyst for the disintegration of the Soviet Union, but it also resulted in the killing of about 1.5 million Afghans, ninety percent of them innocent civilians, and it created the biggest refugee numbers in the world, a total of 5 million people living in harsh conditions in both Iran and Pakistan. Refugees suffered from hunger and had no medical assistance if they got sick. Women were vulnerable to rape in both countries although Afghans would never report it, as rape brings great shame and dishonour on a woman.

By this time I'd had my second child, a beautiful girl with deer-like eyes, named Lida, a Russian name that means 'loved by the people' – chosen by Kabir. I later found out it was the name of a city in Belarus. Was it also the name of his girlfriend who lived in Moscow?

That autumn I was knitting sweaters for Kabir, Haseeb and Lida. I was considered the fastest knitter among my friends and I had chosen our bedroom that evening in which to continue my task while Kabir was in our living room. Haseeb was with him and Lida in the bedroom with me. Sometimes I heard *Allahu Akbar!* but tried to shut my mind to the sounds and, by doing so, block out my worries.

Suddenly Kabir burst into the bedroom shouting, "What is this?" He was waving some sheets of paper in his hand.

"What is what, Kabir?" I answered, surprised by the way he had addressed me.

"This, this!" He raised his voice with anger.

Seeing that he was not going to explain, I left my knitting next to Lida, who was watching us with wide eyes, and went to look at those sheets of paper Kabir was holding. I glanced at them and said, "It is my writing."

"Writing all this rubbish against the government?" he shouted.

"It is not against the government," I said trying to calm him down. "It is merely an observation."

"Notes to yourself? This shit can't just be observations." He grabbed my arms with his strong hands and shook me while still holding the papers in his right hand. "Stupid idiots like you provide fuel for the Mujahideen," he shouted.

I was frozen. Lida started crying, which helped stop Kabir shaking me. But before leaving, he tore my work into pieces. After that, he thought I was a traitor and not a loyal wife. That incident marked the beginning of his abuse.

Note to myself

This time I record the note to myself in my mind, not on the paper. Everything is revealed now. The communists are not what they claim. They are people with ambitions to rule the country but are even worse than the previous rulers. At least the previous government did not try to hide its identity and did not have to lie again and again. They knew that they were corrupt and we knew too. But the new government is corrupt and cruel. Anyone who stands against the government is either put into prison or killed.

I also know my own husband Kabir now. He is not what he portrays himself to be – neither in public, nor in private.

Chapter 8

How to forget these days?

28 March 1985

The spring breeze was strong when I reached the shaky footbridge called Pol-e Larzanak. I was on my way to meet Fatima, a friend who was a teacher at the Aisha-e Durani girls' secondary school. For as long as I had I known Fatima, she had been interested in the political teachings of Mao Zedong, the founder of the Republic of China, who had once been close to the Soviet Union but later became an arch-rival. Like the supporters of the Soviet Union's brand of communism in Afghanistan, Mao also had his supporters in our country. Similar to the two countries, these two groups of supporters were opposed to each other. Fatima was also interested in literature and lent me a book of twentieth-century Chinese poetry and I was surprised how good it was. In our country, we knew nothing about them but heard about Russian poets and read their works. That day I was returning her book.

While Fatima was political, I stayed neutral but curious, hoping for change to end the poverty in our country. Even after my marriage to Kabir, a senior Communist Party member, I stayed aloof but worried that Fatima would stop being my friend, fearing that I would spy on her because of Kabir. However, I was delighted that she trusted me to keep her politics secret. Our country's brand of Soviet communists believed no one was more dangerous than the Maoists. Her trust was sacred because if the government found out she was a Maoist, she would have been put in prison, if not executed.

I was crossing that shaky suspension bridge very cautiously to avoid falling through the holes caused by missing planks and at the same time wondering what kind of jokes Fatima would be cracking. It was about a week after our government had celebrated the anniversary of its coming to power with military parades, displays of the most modern Soviet weapons, military planes overhead, and patriotic songs blasted on national radio or performed live in the parks by famous Afghan vocalists. Streets were decorated with huge new red Afghan flags, similar to the Soviet flag, hanging in their thousands from the windows of government buildings. I knew she would say, "What was that about? Celebrating a disaster?"

At the middle of the bridge, holding the huge metal cable from which the bridge was suspended, I looked at the clay-coloured Kabul River, filled by melting snow and the springtime rains, running wild and scary under the bridge. On the far bank was the King of Two Swords mosque, which looked more like a museum in a German town than a mosque. It had been designed by a German architect on the orders of the late King Amanullah Khan, who I loved because of his ideas to bring progress in our country. But his reign was shortened by mullahs and fundamentalists who thought his modern ideas were not Islamic. The mullahs told the king that, for example, opening schools for girls was un-Islamic. The right place for women was at home, cooking, cleaning and bearing children. Looking at the mosque and the girls' school not far from it, a question came to my mind: "Why do our mullahs always treat the mosque and the school as places of opposing ideas? They are both centres of learning." However, if learning is misused, it is not only harmful to the nation but the individual also. I remembered a poem by Rumi:

If knowledge touches your heart, it moves you and others
But it becomes like a snake if the brain misuses it.

I remained standing in the middle of the bridge watching the world around me, ignoring the passers-by. How the city changed from season to season. In just a few months, when summer was here, this river would be breathing its last breath and by the middle of summer, there would be nothing but a dry bed. What a contrast with winter when everything lay beneath a blanket of deep white snow.

Two girls were coming across the bridge towards me. They were wearing school uniform but with their headscarves on their shoulders. At school they would wear them as required but, like most girls, once out of school they let the scarf drop around their shoulders to be free. They were beautiful and so young. A man ran from behind me towards them. I saw a bottle in his hand. When he got close he sprayed something into the faces of two girls. They both screamed, rubbing their hands on their faces in a frenzy, stamping the ground. Staring in panic I saw the man reach the end of the bridge and disappear.

The following day the newspaper reported that the faces of two school girls had been disfigured by someone throwing acid at them. That man had probably belonged to the Golbudin Hikmatyar Mujahideen group – the most radical of all – who were completely against girls going to school.

July 1986

Two days after the Herat uprising and just after evening prayers, I heard *Allahu Akbar* carried like a whisper on the wind, a faint sound but voiced by many. I looked at Lida, who was on my lap, as if she might be able to tell me what it meant. Haseeb, unaware of anything but his game, was playing with his toy car on the windowsill, making it fly like an aeroplane, imitating the sound of a car engine: Vroooooooom!

"Haseeb, quiet please for a second," I said, looking towards the window where the sound came from.

"But why?" he snapped.

"Can't you hear the sound of *Allahu Akbar*?" He looked at me probably thinking that I was asking a ridiculous question.

"Yes, I hear it. So what?"

"Never mind, Haseeb." The child thought it was normal to hear *Allahu Akbar* in a Muslim country. What he did not know was that it was not the right time to hear it. The call for prayers had already been made about half an hour previously. All five occasions of the daily *namaz* were called at fixed times. The Faithful had either been to the mosque or already prayed in their homes. I took Lida off my lap and went to the window.

The sound of *Allahu Akbar* was spreading and had reached our neighbourhood. I could see men and women on the flat roofs of some of the houses shouting loud, and I realised what it was for. They were protesting against the massacre in the historic city of Herat where about 30,000 citizens had been killed by Soviet forces fighting to take control of the city out of the hands of ordinary people who wanted the Soviet Union to leave our country. Scared that they would be shot by the army if they were to pour onto the streets and march together, the people of Kabul had come up with a different way to protest. It didn't sound like the voice of angry people, rather the voice of those who now referred to Allah as their protector, asking for his hand to take the nation out of this terrible situation. At least that is how I interpreted it. Then I joined in. First like a whisper but rising until my voice filled the room and I noticed my children looking at me in amazement.

"Come on! Let's all of us shout that God is great. Shout my beautiful children! Shout *Allahu Akbar* and ask for His mercy and forgiveness."

"But why, Mother? It sounds frightening," said Haseeb.

"Nothing to be frightened of. It is just affirming God is great and that would help all of us to live in peace."

They both joined me with innocent smiles on their face. Tears came to my eyes, but I held them back.

By the time Kabir came home just before midnight, the children were fast asleep and I was glad because I did not want them to tell their father what we had done. These days he returned home very late and I did not know if it was because of work or because of drinking parties with his old and new friends from the Soviet Union. I could smell alcohol on his breath as he lay down next to me. Only senior communists could roam around in the evening and if they were lucky they might find themselves in the company of Interior Minister Golab Zoy, who brought female musicians from Radio Kabul to sing for his guests and other females from unknown places to dance and provide sex. I wasn't sure if the communists were aware that the citizens of Kabul knew all about these things – were they arrogant or simply ignorant?

I prepared my usual lavish Friday breakfast to my own recipe – eggs, potatoes, onions, tomatoes, cheese, some *Bolani* (a dough stuffed with *gandana* or potatoes and then fried on a *taba*, the big flat frying pan popular in Afghan households) and accompanied by homemade jam that I bought from a neighbour whose relative made it in Kariz-e Mir on the outskirts of Kabul. I let the children sleep longer because Kabir got up late. He said Fridays, the public holidays, were the only days when he could catch up on his sleep because normally he worked very late, although I suspected not all lateness was due to work.

Haseeb, who had not seen his father the previous day, was happy that we were all together and announced excitedly: "We said *Allahu Akbar* with Mother and the rest of people, Baba."

"What?" Kabir exclaimed, his food hovering between plate and mouth.

"Yes, yes. *Allahu Akbar*. Mother told us to say it."

Kabir scanned the whole family and then he looked at me. I'd also stopped eating. "Is that true?" He asked me.

"It is nothing, dear. Just an affirmation that God is great."

"But you know it has another meaning in Kabul."

I tried to give reasons, telling him I was not supporting those who wanted the demise of the government and Soviet withdrawal from our country but he was boiling with rage. Eventually he asked me to come to another room. I followed. There he slapped my face hard and said, "I don't want my wife to support the Mujahideen." My face burned and I ducked to avoid another blow, rubbing my left cheek where he'd hit me.

28 October 1987

I went to the Ministry of Justice through a Kabul painted in autumn colours. The garden of the ministry, managed by the best gardeners of our country, was the perfect canvas to display these colours in a nation entranced with nature but ravaged by war. The lawn was green and trimmed. Gardeners were busy attending to the flowers, raking the paths. I sat on a bench just to look, to forget my troubles, to inhale peace. I was in no hurry.

The Ministry of Justice oversaw a system of justice delivered by judges applying a combination of Sharia and modern law. After the communists had come to power, even they did not dare to ignore Islam and so worked to find a way to make modern law compatible with Islamic justice. An appointment had been made for me to interview one of the new judges, Professor Niazi, who dealt with the rights of abused wives seeking divorce. Almost all cases of divorce were initiated by the husband, and men didn't even have to go to court for that. If a man told his wife *talaq* (divorce) three times, then the wife was divorced. From my research I knew that prior to becoming a judge, Professor Niazi had been teaching in the Faculty of Religious Studies and, therefore, understood Islam far better than many Islamic scholars. What surprised me was that he was also a communist. How could he reconcile his religious belief with his communist philosophy?

Professor Niazi's offices befitted a powerful man. A secretary presided over a large room full of people waiting to have an audience with the judge. There were many more women in that room than men. I introduced myself to the secretary, who showed me into the professor's office. In comparison to the outer office, this room was small and modest. The large framed photograph of the leader of the country, the usual feature in other important offices was absent. Instead, there was a painting of Bala Hisar, the historic fort destroyed by the defeated British during the second Anglo-Afghan war. After the initial civilities I went straight to the point of my interview: "What makes you the best person to decide a woman's right to divorce?"

He smiled, shuffling papers on his desk, taking time to construct his thoughts. "Not all women," he replied, "but only those who, after studying their situation in depth, I feel deserve to be divorced. What gives me confidence in my task is my own knowledge of Islamic law from having studied and taught Sharia in the Faculty of Religious Studies coupled with a post-graduate degree from the Faculty of Law. So I am aware of modern law and the rules of Islam."

I liked to talk to this man and the interview went on for a long time. I felt he was sincere in helping the tortured and abused women who had no support in society. Not only did women have to endure the abuse but usually even their own family did not help them, especially their fathers who were afraid that they would have to provide for a divorced daughter. A divorced woman had a bad reputation. A good woman was the one who put up with disgrace and torture.

"You know, madam," he said near the end of the interview, "these women cannot even write to ask for justice. Most of them are illiterate. When you go out, you will see letter-writers on the street who fill in the application form for divorce for such women."

I left Professor Niazi, thinking that for the first time I had met a real communist who cared for his people. As I passed out of the gate of the ministry, his parting comment sparked my curiosity. I went to the place where the letter-writers lined up.

"Deeba Jan, don't tell me you have come here for me to fill a divorce application for you?" a man with a silver beard said to me. "I am sure you can do that better than I."

I looked at this underweight man sitting cross-legged behind a small, low desk, not knowing who he was or understanding how he knew my name.

"Don't you remember me?" he asked gently.

I looked again, more closely this time. Recognition dawned – was I imagining this? "Is that you, Akram?"

"Who else, madam?" He puffed on his cigarette and coughed. "I am a man with many talents."

Seeing Akram sitting on the bare ground behind that desk and in such poverty broke my heart. The place of a scribe was normally for someone with little education. Akram had been more than just a journalist. He had a vast knowledge of the country and its people. Once, in a meeting of experts of Rumi poetry, he described a new dimension that had not been mentioned before. He was regarded an expert in this field and had almost finished writing a book on Rumi when the communists took over. Not only did he lose the chance of publishing his book, but he was also made redundant. Was this the result of the promise the communists made to alleviate poverty from our country? Could I tell my husband: look what you have done to this man who was probably unique in the whole country?

Once Akram had said to me, "You know Deeba, I don't think men are remembered by their children but by those who read their books."

This was the man to whom I owed my knowledge of journalism. He taught me everything, much more than I ever learned at university. To me he was my teacher, my elder brother, my father. But could I challenge my own husband and tell him that the communists in Afghanistan had got it wrong? Of course not. I ought to go back to Professor Niazi and tell him that it is not only uneducated women who don't have the right to challenge their husband for their right to share their opinions. Even educated woman are denied equal rights. Regardless of what it says in the *Quran* about men and women being equal, in this country we are not equal. Here, men like Akram, highly educated, also have no right because they are not members of the Communist Party.

"Oh no, Akram, I never imagined you in this situation," I said, squatting in front of him. "And I never imagined that the Russians would invade our country."

Regardless of time, I sat there to talk with Akram. People passed by and customers came to ask him to write a letter for them. I listened to the questions Akram asked and the information he was provided by his clients. How meticulous he was in this job, working with complete honesty, advising his clients how to proceed with their applications.

Writing up my interview with Niazi was urgent and I ought to have gone straight back to the office, but Akram's magnetic energy held me until, just after midday, he collected his belongings and turned homeward. There were no clients in the afternoons because offices only accepted submissions up to midday. I gave him a hug, kissing the small part of his cheek not covered by his beard and did not care that people around me were watching. I fought back my tears.

The next day, I told the office I had a doctor's appointment but went instead straight to the bank and withdrew 2,000 Afghani from our joint account before heading to Akram's house, knowing he would not be there at that time of day. I'd been to his house many times when he generously invited his colleagues, including me, to come for lunch on Fridays. He lived in Saraji, an old part of Kabul with houses built with dry mud bricks and seemingly in danger of collapsing.

His wife Jamila was a beautiful woman with grey hair like her husband. Yet she was young. Does poverty make people go grey faster? It was almost unbearable to see Farid, their teenage son, in a torn *piran wa tonbaan*. What Jamila wore was not much better. I could see embarrassment in their eyes. I also was embarrassed for having come without telling them in advance. She was surprised to see me yet, like her husband, so generous that she would not allow me to leave unless I had tea with her. Sitting cross-legged on a cushion, I noticed their many hand-made carpets had been replaced by rough *kilim* of a cheaper quality. The walls were bare and there was no sign of the framed calligraphy produced by Ustad Hoseini, the very best *khatat*, which Akram had inherited and proudly displayed on his walls, telling guests that of all his possessions, these were the items he was most attached to. They were not of huge value in Afghanistan, but if taken to Iran it would have been a different matter. In a poor country like Afghanistan, feeding stomachs was more important than feeding eyes with art. Akram must have sold his carpets and his calligraphy. I remember one of them was a line taken from my favourite poet Hafiz who, our religious people argued, had been very religious. I believed that Hafiz had loved wine and women as only a man who had experienced the love of both could describe them so beautifully.

Good news my heart, someone with Jesus breath would come
Through his breath the scent of beloved could be smelled
Don't cry and complain about separation because
I have predicted that someone would come to silence your painful cry with joy.

After tea I gave Jamila the envelope containing the money and told her not to open it until I had gone. I knew she would be embarrassed, but I justified that by telling myself it was better for them to be embarrassed than hungry.

Chapter 9

Shaky days

Determined to continue with my job as well as be a mother, I interviewed two sisters, one by the name of Soghra, whose name meant modest, and the other called Kubra, the magnificent. They both had worked in the houses of a French mission in Kabul but since the communists took over, the French mission had reduced considerably and these two unfortunate Hazara sisters were losing their jobs. I liked the modest one better and I offered her the job and, frankly, she proved to be a wonderful person. Sometimes out of kindness she cooked knowing I would be late home in the evening, tired and not much interested in cooking. But that was not part of her job. She was there to look after the children, clean the house and do some ironing.

The other reason I did not ask her to cook was because I loved cooking and Kabir preferred my cooking. The only inconvenience was that I liked to cook a variety of vegetables and reduce cooking meat to twice a week but Kabir was a big meat eater and wanted meat on the *dastarkhan* every day. One day I had been busy editing a speech by our president, Dr Najib, which was due to be published. Each time I thought I finished the task and gave it to the editor-in-chief, he called me back after reading it and told me to add or cut something. So when I left the office, I was exhausted and prayed in my heart that Soghra had cooked.

Dr Najib had changed so much since he became president. There was no mention of Marx, Engels or Lenin in his speeches, he did not threaten anyone who did not agree with his views and, in contrast to his predecessors, he talked about reconciliation, peace, brotherhood, love for tradition and country, respect for Islam. He astonished people with his knowledge of the *Quran*, quoting the holy book often, mentioning that we were all created by one God and that our purpose was to live in peace and harmony. He did not talk about the rights of women to marry who they loved but left it to the parents to decide, as it had always been. No land reforms would be undertaken and, in fact, he abolished all seven decrees introduced by the first communist president, Taraki, hoping to win support from the nation. I thought it was too late because the nation already knew that he was responsible for murdering many innocent people.

He was the fourth president since the communists took over and his first role working for the communist government was in charge of the dreadful Khad Secret Service. He definitely deserved to be head of it because he was just as good as any KGB agent with a vast knowledge, speaking many different languages, and capable of fitting into any role. Khad was an organisation for capturing anyone thought to be anti-government. These people were first interrogated, then tortured and put in Pol-e Charkhi dungeon or executed. Did he think our people were stupid not to know what was going on? I must admit, his knowledge of the *Quran* was excellent.

As I entered the house I did not smell cooked food. I was disappointed but after hugging the children and saying goodbye to Soghra, I started to cook for the family. When Kabir came home that evening he was in a bad mood. Instead of sitting in the living room, as he normally did, he went straight to our bedroom. Sometimes he used our bedroom as a place to be alone, to read or do something in private. When he joined us later for dinner he told me that soon the government would announce the Soviet forces would be withdrawing from our country.

"What did you say," I asked, not believing what I heard.

"The Soviets cannot cope. They are losing thousands of soldiers every month. It is causing their economy to collapse," he replied.

"But what would happen to this country, to us?"

"It's not their problem any more," he said.

"I heard from reliable sources within the government that Gorbachev was going to meet Reagan to discuss Afghanistan to end US sanctions against the Soviet Union," I said. "As you know the west imposed sanctions on the Soviet Union because of Afghanistan."

Obviously, this was going to be the end of us. If the Soviet Union could not stop the Mujahideen's advances, how would it be possible for the Afghan Army alone to stop them taking Kabul? Now it made sense that Dr Najib should be sounding like a mullah. Quoting verses from the *Quran* was intended to show the Mujahideen that he was a good Muslim and that there was no need to fight. He even promised senior government posts to the Mujahideen, saying he was happy to share power with them. He talked about a broad-based government and he preached reconciliation. But the Mujahideen were close to taking major cities, including Kabul, and thought they could run the country by themselves. They did not need assistance from Dr Najib.

"This idiot knew it all along and kept it secret from us," Kabir said. The way he said it surprised me because he always referred to Dr Najib respectfully and admired his intelligence. Dr Najib had been specially chosen by the Soviet Union to lead our country.

"What are we going to do?" I asked.

"There will be blood everywhere. Rivers of blood. The whole city will be painted with blood," he replied.

"Please don't say that, Kabir. You scare me."

He looked into my eyes, realising the impact of his words, and became quiet. I laid the food on the *dastarkhan*, washed the children's hands and only then became aware that they'd heard our conversation. We all sat quietly around the *dastarkhan* but, unlike the children, neither Kabir nor I had much appetite. We just stared at the food. After dinner I sent the children to their bedroom to play before bedtime and returned to living room.

"Let's run away somewhere," I said to Kabir, sitting next to him.

"Run away?" He looked at me questioning the logic of what I said with his gaze.

"You know, we could go to Nijrab or somewhere in the countryside."

"What an intelligent solution, Deeba," he sneered.

"But what is wrong with my idea?" I said, taking hold of his hand.

"You've forgotten that the countryside has been taken by the Mujahideen. And they can easily work out why someone has left Kabul to live in a remote place."

In a panic, thoughts streamed through my mind like a wish list. I wish I had my parents and siblings with me in Kabul – at least to talk with them and receive some kind words. My brother Hanif would have been the perfect person for this. Now those people who were affected by the Soviet invasion and whoever thought my husband had helped the Soviets occupy our country would be delighted to see our downfall. They would point us out to the Mujahideen saying we were responsible for horrible crimes. How could I explain that I was innocent? That my children were innocent? And my husband had believed that the only way to get out of poverty was to change the regime to one with a socialist style, sharing the wealth of the small number of rich people who had everything with the majority who had nothing? I wished we had all gone to Pakistan. I knew that life in Pakistan as a refugee would have been hard but at least we would be alive. Kabir was a doctor and a good one. He could have found a job to feed us. I wished he was not a communist but just an ordinary doctor, rather than a political person with a grand agenda. I wished those communists in power had respected the will of the people and not rushed into making decisions, ignoring what our people wanted. I wished I could live in the secure past and had not seen these changes that were affecting all of us and threatening our lives. How long did we have before this government would collapse and we would be faced with the brutal justice of the Mujahideen? No one would be spared, including my innocent children.

Hiding my tears, I went to the bathroom and tried hard to suppress my wailing. I wanted to be in a lonely desert where I might wail out loud, so loud that heaven would hear me because without the help of Allah, no one could make our life secure. God knows how long I stayed in the bathroom. I returned to the living room for *namaz* – to pray in the corner I always used. Kabir had gone to our bedroom. I remembered the night that our former president, Daud Khan, and his family had fought for their lives against the communists' *coup d'état*. That night I had prayed for our survival too. I am sure all those people who were facing death had also asked for Allah's help. How does Allah decide to save one person rather than someone else? Oh Allah! That is a blasphemy, I thought, and whispered: "You know what is best because you are our creator. Please forgive me."

It was hard to concentrate on *namaz*. Even when I closed my eyes and recited verses from the *Quran*, I saw in my mind Lida and Haseeb's eyes and the barrel of a Kalashnikov pointed at us. Cruelty would be replaced by cruelty just as it had when President Daud, his family and friends were killed.

It was about midnight and instead of going to bed I opened the *Quran* and started reciting in whisper:

> *O Allah, it is Your mercy that I hope for, so do not leave me in charge of my affairs even for a blink of an eye, and rectify for me all of my affairs.*

Those words brought some peace and comfort to my mind and because of that I kept on reciting until my eyes became tired. After placing the holy *Quran* on its place on the shelf, I went to my *jainamaz*, the prayer rug, kissed the rug, and put my head on it like a *sajda*.

When I awoke, daylight filled the living room. Rolling my *jainamaz* and placing it in a corner, I went to see Kabir. But he'd already left and the bed was not made. After tidying our bedroom, I went to our children's bedroom. I watched them in deep sleep. Haseeb's bed was next to the window, which opened onto the courtyard, and Lida's bed was on the opposite side. Between the two beds an empty space was left for them to play. I kissed Haseeb's forehead and then went to Lida, lowering my head, inhaling her breath, the breath of a little child. I kissed her cheek gently trying not to wake her but, still asleep she turned on her other side. Perhaps she was communicating with me even in her sleep, wanting me not to disturb her. "Dear almighty, please keep my children and husband safe," I said it quietly. Was it worry or an early start for work that made Kabir leave before having breakfast? I waited until Soghra came and then I too left home for work. No breakfast.

A week later the radio announced that the withdrawal of Soviet forces from Afghanistan would start on 15 May 1988 and be completed by 15 February 1989. Meanwhile, President Najib spent a huge amount of money inviting Mujahideen leaders to a conference on peace and reconciliation, providing the best food and accommodation. But no senior Mujahideen members participated. And any Mujahideen who did participate took no part in the decision making.

I was in my office busy with some paperwork not related to writing or editing, which had become less and less, when the office orderly came to ask me to go to the editor-in-chief. To my surprise, when I entered Torab's office I found the room full of my colleagues. When I asked what the occasion was about I was informed that the gathering was to say goodbye to Pavel. *Thank God the idiot is going,* I thought to myself. Apart from the minister and his deputy, most of the senior officers were there, hugging Pavel, shedding tears, drinking vodka. But instead of joy, which this drink normally created in those people, their faces showed deep sorrow. I knew their sorrow and tears were not because Pavel was leaving. They were crying for themselves, thinking of what the Mujahideen would do to them.

Because it was Pavel's departure, he thought it would be good idea to address the people in the room.

"Comrades," he began. "The time has come for me to leave this wonderful country and loyal colleagues."

My thoughts ran parallel with his speech:

Me: I have been praying for this moment since you arrived.

Pavel: My departure doesn't mean we have decided to leave you alone. Of course, I am sad but we will be with you in many different ways.

Me: Don't lie that you are sad. You must be very happy to be leaving this hell hole of a war-torn country and you want to go back because otherwise Irina is likely to produce children with whom you would not share your genes. Why should she have been here, for God's sake? She lives in St Petersburg, away from wars. I admire her for not accompanying you, a true woman. And what different ways are you going to be with us? You are running away to save your skin.

Pavel: You must be proud of the changes we all have brought to this country.

Me: What? What pride? Proud that this country is almost completely destroyed by war? That is the true change you have brought to our country.

Pavel: We have been here to help you and now you are in a position of not needing help…

Me: Yes, we are in a perfect situation knowing that we are soon to be facing the cruelty of the Mujahideen and none of us will be left alive.

Pavel: We were here to defend you against imperialism and reactionary forces.

Me: Bullshit! You were here to conquer and hoped to reach India's warm waters as you people always have dreamed about. It is the same Great Game. The only difference is now the US stands against you instead of the UK.

Chapter 10

The most un-Islamic Islamic groups

President Najib immediately tried to escape Afghanistan when the Mujahideen, a most un-Islamic bunch of ten parties of Islamic freedom fighters, entered Kabul, but he was prevented by his own generals. He took refuge in the UN office, leaving the capital for the Mujahideen to plunder. The Mujahideen robbed, raped and killed innocent people and then started fighting each other, forgetting their original enemy, the communists. The war now extended to every inch of Afghanistan and the epicentre of this devastating earthquake was Kabul. Kabir was not only safe but in demand, treating injured Mujahideen at the hospital, but his hours of work had become irregular dealing with emergencies at all hours of the day and night. And there were plenty of emergencies. The People's Hospital in Kabul became overwhelmed with large numbers of casualties needing treatment, filling corridors and even spilling outside. Kabir was mentally and physically exhausted, sometimes saying: "I wish they'd killed me when they took over, not like this torturous way of killing slowly."

The government was in the hands of Jamiat-e Islami, a group comprising mainly Panjshiris, who pretended that it was a broad-based government including other Mujahideen leaders. The president was not from Jamiat and his authority was no more than that of a Panjshiri watchman. There was a joke circulating that, when all important posts had been given to other Panjshiris, one Panjshiri complained to Defence Minister Masoud, a close relative, that not a single important post had been left for him. Masoud said: "You will be the watchman for the president but will have enough power to slap him if you get annoyed with him." And that is how it was in reality. Golbudin Hikmatyar, the man who would be called the Butcher of Kabul, rejected joining the coalition, occupied the heights of the mountains surrounding Kabul and from there launched rockets to hit houses.

The Mujahideen claimed that the correct place of a woman was at home and so women were forced, either directly or indirectly, to remain in their homes. As a result, I lost my job and, besides that, my motivation to see my friends or go shopping, for everything from groceries to major items. And I hated my burka too, a new garment for the Afghan women since the Mujahideen arrived. At home one day I wrote about the burka:

1. In 1919 after defeating the British, Afghanistan was the first occupied country to become independent of British rule. Our Queen Malika Suraya was the first queen in the Islamic world to denounce face-coverings. She toured Europe with her husband King Amanullah, surprising the western world with her elegance. She was also the champion of girls' education and in 1927 she was the woman of the year for *Time Magazine*.

2. When I wear a burka, it feels as if I am hiding my identity. My face is my identity. With this face I show my pleasure, sadness, agreement and disagreement. I don't want to shout that I am happy or sad. My face shows that.

3. I don't know how the burka appeared in our country but I know our people did not invent it. In the past, our women covered their heads in the main cities – but not their faces. Even now the burka has not found its place in rural areas as in the villages women cannot wear a burka while working in the fields with their men.

4. If a woman wants to have an affair, it is possible to hide her identity in a conservative society like Afghanistan by wearing a burka. A woman in western clothes seeking romance or sex can easily be identified when she is with a man who is not a relative, colleague or someone she meets for formal business. A woman under a burka can easily meet a man to go with him to his house or some private place.

Chapter 11

It was yours, now it is mine

War keeps people apart. Even when it was safe to travel on the roads, there might still have been difficulty passing the checkpoints set up to protect the territory of the many different Islamic groups that had occupied and divided the city. So it surprised me when my cousin Khalil unexpectedly showed up at our apartment – it had been such a long time since I had seen him.

Whenever my kind cousin had come to visit us, either at my parents' house or my own apartment, he never came empty-handed, always bringing something from the Nijrab District and telling me, "I brought this from your home to remind you that home is missing you." This time, he had brought homemade cheese and *chokida*, a mixture of dried mulberries and walnuts, made like cake in the shared village *jwaz*, a giant stone mortar. Normally we ate this cake in winter because your body temperature increases immediately after eating it – but I love this delicacy so much that I could eat it in the heat of Africa and, yes, it reminded me of home.

People lived like a big family in Jarpiroz Village in Nijrab, where my mother was born. Like all my siblings I had been born and brought up in Kabul but during school holidays we spent two months in the birthplace of my mother where the natural beauty of the place mixed with the kindness we received from my relatives has left an everlasting impression on me. With my cousins, both male and female, we went to Sharshara, the village waterfall, where we stripped naked to go swimming. At that age, just younger than a teenager or perhaps around the beginning of it, not noticing who was male and who was female – until someone cruelly told us that it was inappropriate for girls to stand naked in front of boys. But the people were generous, sharing almost everything. If someone had a bull, he could not say no to his neighbour if the neighbour needed it for ploughing. Houses and gardens were open and even strangers could enter my uncle's garden to sample his grapes, which he said were the best in Nijrab if not the whole world. But perhaps food, fruit and even water tasted better there because of the kindness and generosity of my relatives.

"How did you come?" I asked Khalil, who was sitting cross-legged with both children on his lap, combing Lida's hair with his fingers.

"With my feet." He laughed at his own joke, which made me laugh too.

"Come on, Khalil," I said looking him straight in the eye. "I was asking you how is it possible that you came all the way here from Nijrab without any trouble?"

"There is no war between Nijrab and Kabul," he replied.

"You're teasing me!"

"It is true," Khalil assured me. "Nijrab is next to Panjshir and, as you know, Commander Masoud, who is from Panjshir, now acts as defence minister and he has kept the road from Kabul to Panjshir completely free of trouble."

I did not believe him. "Here in Kabul every part is controlled by a different Mujahideen group. Each group has its own checkpoints. It is impossible to move around freely."

"But isn't Kabir going to work in the hospital every day?" he said.

"Yes I," I replied. "It is because the Panjshiri group need him to treat their injured. They take him through the routes manned by themselves. Every morning he is taken to the hospital in an armoured vehicle and is brought back the same way. I count every minute in between."

"Oh God!"

Although I was glad to see him, I had to ask. "So why didn't you come earlier if the road was clear, Khalil?"

"It only happened recently."

His explanation reassured me. "I am so glad to see you, Khalil jan."

Queen Soraya of Afghanistan in 1927. She opened girls school, provided education for women and with her support for women right to education, her husband King Amanullah Khan sent many women to Europe to learn modern education.

Afghan-women-in-1927.

King Zahir Shah of Afghanistan in 1963. He introduced many reforms including women's right to vote.

King Mohammad Zahir Shah who supported women liberation and encouraged them to occupy important government posts in his visit to England during 70s.

Biology class, Kabul University, 1950s or early 1960s.

Zaieshgah, infant ward, a hospital in Kabul, 1960

1960s Afghanistan – Laboratory at the Vaccine Research Centre.

Entrance to the Faculty of Medicine in Kabul, c. 1977.

Famous Afghan writer Dr Akram Osman attending a wedding party with his wife, 70s.

Afghan Fashion Designer Safia Tarzi in her studio 1969.

Postage stamp of Afghanistan from 1963, depicting an Afghan woman in folk clothing.

Omar Sharif filming in Afghanistan in 70s.

In 70s women were active in all sports.

Bibi Gul a grandmother who dropped bur in 70s, photographed with her daughter ar grandchildren.

Kabul street scene, 1979.

Teachers and students of Malalai School in 80s.

Teachers and students of Malalai school in 80s.

A typical wedding attended by male and female guest in a hall where both genders mixed, ate, drunk and danced, 80s.

Anahita Ratebzad, standing at right, speaks with a group of activists, likely in the 1970s or 1980s.

Students of Kabul University, 1980.

Socialist-Women-Afghanistan in 1980s.

Young Nader Omar, student of Faculty of Engineering, Kabul, with his family going for a picnic, 80s.

Taliban beating woman in public in 90s.

Female school under the tent in 2002. Afghan girls stunned the world by registering to attend school, three times more than the numbers anticipated by UNICEF.

ghan girl from north addressing the crowd in)9.

Captain Nader Omar in 2019 with his male and female crew.

eaker Nancy Pelosi and Rep. Susan Davis et with Afghan women in Qalat, Afghanistan Mother's Day for a roundtable discussion on llenges women face in Afghanistan.

Hoshang Zekria Afghan Diplomate fleeing Kabul, three days after Taliban occupied Kabul. He spent three nights with his three years old son and wife waiting for an army plane to take them to England.

ecrete girls school in Panjshir after e arrival of Taliban in August 2022.

Defying the Taliban, girls attend school in Panjshir where it is not under Taliban's rule.

Photo for book jacket. Nagina Azizi escaped from Afghanistan during Mujahideen rule and became a refugee in Pakistan. She learned Urdu language at home and after immigration to California, studied at Berkeley University. Now a successful career woman.

Ravi Shankar famous Indian sitar player in Kabul surrounded by both Indian and Afghan musician in 70s.

Tribal Afghan women in traditional attire, 1975.

"Come on Deeba jan, let's go to Nijrab – *wakht-e tootaas*! It is mulberry season."

I wanted Kabir to see Khalil and learn about the beauty of life in Nijrab. That day, waiting for him to return, time passed even slower than usual. They had met probably only three or four times since the Russians had invaded Afghanistan.

When Alexander the Great was on his way to India to conquer the rest of the world Afghanistan was not called Afghanistan and Alexander left some of his generals to build cities in his honour along the way. The treasures of the famous Bactrian Hoard found at Tillā Tapa, Golden Hill, contained thousands of fabulous historical artefacts, the work of artists from east and west, and by west I mean Greece. Afghanistan has people with green eyes and blond hair who we assume must be the descendants of Alexander. Khalil is a good example, perhaps having the blood of a Greek general in him with his amber eyes, auburn hair, chiselled face, flat stomach and muscled body – I had seen him shirtless, sweating under the sun when he had been working on his land in Jarpiroz.

Khalil has the deep voice of a storyteller. Every word that comes out of his mouth has a deeper meaning and, as he speaks, the contours of his face change and you become almost hypnotised. I had listened to his stories sitting on the flat roof of his house in the moonlight with the distant grey mountains and the sounds of animals providing a background to his tales. When Kabir came home, both Khalil and I told him about going to Nijrab.

"Are you crazy!" was Kabir's immediate response.

"Why?" I asked.

"Don't you know there is a war going on?"

"It is because of the war that I want to go with you and the children to Nijrab to have some peace," I said.

Khalil spoke to Kabir, supporting me. "Doctor Sahib, I assure you that everything will be fine. The road to Nijrab is controlled by Commander Masoud's forces. Panjshir is just on the border of Nijrab and since Masoud's forces keep Panjshir safe, they also keep Nijrab the same way."

"But I'm a doctor. What about my work?" Kabir pointed towards the window and in the general direction of the hospital.

"Come on Kabir," I urged. "You love driving and the children are tired of hearing the sound of war. It will be good for all of us."

It took some persuading to get Kabir to tell the hospital authority that he needed to be away for some time. The usual excuse in those days was the loss of some beloved ones because of the war.

It had been a long time since Kabir had driven himself instead of being transported in an armoured vehicle. I could see the satisfaction on his face, even a smile. In the past I would have sat next to him, but since the arrival of the Mujahideen, women were supposed to hide themselves. So I took the back seat with Haseeb and Lida, excitedly pointing out to each of them the hills, mountains, trees and vast agricultural lands we were passing through. War did not exist here, at least at that moment. We were stopped many times at Panjshiri checkpoints but, fortunately, Khali's accent was similar to Panjshiri. He told the men at the checkpoints that he was from Panjshir, travelling with his brother-in-law, his sister and their children.

At Gulbahar the road forks. To the right the road goes towards Panjshir and to the left towards Nijrab. Kabir was so struck by the beauty of the valley with the Panjshir River running through the middle of it, that he himself suggested we should eat there. We had started very early and though it was only eleven in the morning I felt hungry. I think it was due to the excitement of running away from war, even if only temporarily, and the fresh air coming through the open windows of the car.

Whenever we had gone to Nijrab with my parents we had taken the public bus and the driver always stopped in Gulbahar for a lunch break. The *chaykhanas*, traditional tea-houses, in that area comprised a *takht*, a big platform covered with carpets, shaded by tall trees and next to the wild Panjshir River where the bus passengers were treated to a variety of delicious *kabab*, views of the green mountains, and serenaded by the music of the river. Those memories came back to me as we stopped. The only difference this time was that I had to stay concealed under the burka. Women had become faceless. How was I going to eat like that? Fortunately, Kabir had selected a secluded corner where I could keep my burka on my shoulders but my face free. At that moment I did not know what I wanted first: to fly over the mountains or to swim in the river with my imagination, or to eat savagely. I was hungry for freedom.

My mind wandered back into the past at that peaceful moment, remembering the days when, as a child, I travelled with my family to Nijrab for the summer holidays after school exams. Our parents told us they would only take those children with them who had done well in school. We were all good students but going to Nijrab was especially motivating. My sleep would be disturbed for a week before travelling to Nijrab because of the excitement and once I woke my parents in the middle of the night telling them we had to leave the house because it was time to take the bus. The only two buses that left Kabul daily for Nijrab both started just after morning prayers, which was the beginning of the day. The drivers knew my father and he was well respected because of his position as an engineer. For that reason, we were always given good seats just behind the driver with good views through the windscreen and side windows, showing us a panorama of the areas the bus went through.

The journey became much more exciting after the fork at Gulbahar because the way to Nijrab did not merit being called a road. The bus swayed and lurched along a rough rutted track, fording streams where there was no bridge, and scaring those who were on the roof who shouted *shakha samal* – avoid the branch – to warn each other to lie down to avoid the many tree branches that overhung the track.

The steep slope before Solanak made the bus moo like a cow and it was then that the bus driver requested all the men to get off the bus leaving only children, girls and women aboard. Hanif was a child but he could not miss the opportunity to get behind the bus, acting like a grown man, pushing the exhausted bus when it had run out of breath and could not move without assistance. For us, the children, that bus was a living vehicle.

Once the bus arrived at Solanak at the top of the hill it had reached a vast land as flat as the palm of my hand. On the right the Panjshir River raced through its valley and on the left a tall mountain. Solanak was the beginning of Nijrab, just about half an hour from our destination. We often heard someone on the roof singing, his voice travelling though the valleys:

> *Nijrab is full of tulips but no use to me*
> *Its winter is like a spring but no use to me*
> *My nights are spent guarding the army compound*
> *My days spent in learning the art of war*
> *And my beloved in Nijrab is waiting for me.*

Obviously, the singer was a soldier on his way home during his once a year break. That poor man had had to serve for two years. Peaceful soldiering in those days was nothing in comparison to what young men are doing today, killing each other mercilessly.

The more difficult the road became, the greater was Kabir's enjoyment of his skill as an excellent driver. Even a smile appeared on his face and I knew he had missed driving. The road was not as bad as it was in the summer season, but I could imagine how hard it would be during the winter. What appeared to us as an enjoyable journey would, in winter, become a journey of suffering. It was because of the poverty and inequality in our nation that I had wanted change – but not the change that the Soviet Union brought us.

When we reached Sharwani Bazaar, Khalil told Kabir to park the car in the same place as the two buses because it was a protected compound and the car would be safe. As far as I knew there was no theft in Nijrab, but children might want to play with the car and could cause some damage. Kabir loved his car, so that was a perfect idea. I wanted to get out and walk for half an hour to the family home, inhaling the smells of walnut trees, corn fields, wheat fields, buckwheat trees and the tempting aroma of *chapatis* baking in a *tandoor*. I wanted to feed my eyes with the sight of lush green and the brown of fields, the sparkle of the river, the colours of life in a place I regarded as heaven, alive with the sound of song, the songs of birds. We had none of those in Kabul.

I knew the children would be extra excited when we reached the river. Because of the war they had not seen even the muddy Kabul River, which became dry in summer and seemed calm even when full in the spring. Here the river was just as wild as the Panjshir River, singing, fighting and arguing with its surroundings, wanting to expand its bed with its frequent flooding. We crossed the river on a bridge made from two tree trunks, which only the locals had the heart to cross. That is how it had been during my father's time and it remained exactly the same, frozen in time. Nijrab had always been ignored by our government. In the past my mother and my siblings had crossed the river on those logs, carried on the back of my uncle, Noor Mohammad. Now the same thing happened again as Khalil carried me and the children on his back to the other side. Kabir insisted that he could cross without help but Khalil did not want to take a risk – so he held Kabir's hand, making sure that he did not lose his balance.

Close to *qila,* Khalil's house, I stood under the poplar tree I had climbed in my childhood, and raised my hands in prayer. The graveyard in front of the *qila* had expanded considerably towards the corn field, but fortunately none of my immediate family members were sleeping there. My mother had almost died when she was a child. She told me that for some reason she had been unable to pass water for days. Uncle Noor Mohammad carried her all the way to the shrine of *Khaaja Ghaar* on his back because she could not walk. Such was the power of belief in this child that she urinated there and, by doing so, angered the shrinekeeper. I am glad she did, otherwise my mother would have been in this graveyard next to Uncle Noor Mohammad.

Not all the dead were buried in the family graveyard. The bodies of two of my relatives were never found. One cousin was an army officer fighting the Mujahideen. He was in his compound when they attacked and killed him, his body turned to ashes as the place burned. His brother, on the other hand, was killed by the army, the enemy of the Mujahideen, as he ran home to bring the animals to safety before his house was bombed. The bomb hit the house just as he reached the front door. There were also stories of uncles and aunts who died of simple illnesses because there were no doctors or hospitals to treat them. War destroyed life in my mother's district.

The beautiful surroundings and the welcome by Khalil's wife helped me to forget the war. They gave their best room for us to sleep in and as before when I came with my parents, they chose the best settings for having lunch and dinner. These rural people were much closer to nature than us, the city people.

Sitting under the old walnut tree planted by my grandfather, I gazed at the mountains that once had been home to snow leopards. Now there was no trace of snow or leopards. "Does war alter the climate? I asked.

"Cousin, as long as we have our land, we cultivate," Khalil replied as if apologising for what war has done to our country.

"But all your vines are gone," I said.

His reply was simply heroic. "Yes, and we are planting new ones."

"But even if you start again, there is no water," I said pointing towards the mountains. "Look, there is no snow on the mountains, and you have had no rain for a long time."

"There is water," Khalil replied, "but we have to buy it."

"Buy it? Where is it? Who from?"

"From Mia Gul Agha," he said.

"How did he find the water?"

"It is a long story, cousin."

"Tell me!"

"Many years ago Mia's grandfather was walking in the hills," Khalil began with his story-teller's voice. "Then, our country was suffering from another drought. He came to a place where he stamped his feet and shouted at the earth: 'I order you to open up and give me water!' Immediately the earth opened up under his feet and since then enough water flows to run two mills, day and night."

"Oh God! Do you believe in that shit?" I said.

"Listen, cousin. We are all followers of Islam. We believe in miracles."

"Is that so?" I snapped back "Then how come our prophet Mohammad did not perform any miracles? Was he less important than his followers?"

Khalil was not prepared to argue with me and I did not force him. In the evening we sat with my relatives on the flat roof having dinner. The gentle breeze brought the smell of sea-buckthorns from the farm below. We were told never to play near the buckthorn trees because snakes liked their scent and lay beneath them in their shade. I saw a snake only once in the Nijrab District, as I was walking with my cousin Masjidi on a footpath along a stream. There was a line of cypress trees casting shadows onto the path at sunset, concealing the snake, which was big and ready to attack. Masjidi quickly took his shawl from his shoulder and waved it at the snake, scaring it away. In those days, the only dangers were snakes and the sharp sting of a wasp on the neck. We were not bitten by the venomous snake of war; we only heard about it on the radio. War was in the Middle East and Vietnam, countries that we only knew about from our school geography books. When the war came to our country no one was safe, including the snakes and wasps.

Around Kabul I had seen burned vineyards and trees, destroyed houses, demolished schools and hospitals, bridges dangling from their pillars into the rivers, half their structures washed away. I had seen crippled men, armless men, blind men, all wandering around in the streets. In some parts of Kabul not a single building was standing. The best you could find were walls without roofs, and yet the spirit of the people had not been completely destroyed.

"Your Mia has taken the water belonging to the villagers just for himself," I told Khalil during dinner.

"But no one complains," Khalil replied.

"I see," I snapped back, annoyed by his complacency. "So no one complains because this water comes from the land of the messenger of Allah?"

Khalil's right hand stopped in the middle of carrying a piece of bread to his mouth. He looked sharply into my eyes. I could see that he was disturbed by my blasphemy, but instead of saying anything he lowered his eyes and said, "Oh Allah forgive our sins."

I had wanted to bring Kabir to Nijrab because he had been so stressed treating the war wounded, sometimes working until late at night without a break. The mountains, the lush green and open countryside, the sound of water, the music of birds all brought him pleasure and I was relieved to see another unforced smile appear on his face. Perhaps that expression of satisfaction was a mirror of my own. I also felt satisfied. No it was more than satisfaction, it was a total happiness.

When the men went out, I sat with Khalil's wife and his two grown-up daughters, Homira and Amina, talking about many things. They asked me about Kabul and I made enquiries about Nijrab. They were poor peasants but at least they were not affected by war. Khalil's wife was just as good a cook as my aunt, the wife of Uncle Noor Mohammad. She slaughtered a *choocha morgh*, young chicken, every day to feed us. In Nijrab it was shameful to feed guests with an old chicken. They had to be young because they tasted better and yet they took a long time to cook because they were not farm chickens but wild ones, growing outside in the field, feeding themselves with what they found on the ground and that was mainly worms. Then, when the men returned, we ate like kings. Then it was time to gather mulberries.

Khalil's teenage son Mustafa climbed the mulberry tree while all the rest of us held the corners of a big canvas sheet underneath the tree. Mustafa shook the mulberry branches with his feet and it rained mulberries, some of them falling on our heads, making us laugh. We shouted at Mustafa for him to watch where we were holding the canvas sheet and he shouted back that it was up to us to watch him and make sure we held the canvas underneath wherever he was. After the harvesting, of course, came the eating.

Mulberry eating has its own ceremony. Once we'd collected them, we put them in baskets and then walked towards the *kariz*, sometimes known as *qanat*, the underground aqueduct that brings water, often ice-cold melted snow, coming to the surface in the village in a stone-lined channel. Squatting on stone edges of the channel, we dropped the mulberries in, picking them out of the cold water one by one. After five or six dips into the water, our hands were frozen up to our wrists. The joy of eating these mulberries, which reminded me of the times my parents and siblings had done this together during our school holidays, was overshadowed by the horror of what I had seen happen to the villagers in their *kariz* in Kalakan. I did not mention any of that, trying not to spoil such a happy moment of escaping from war.

Haseeb and Lida became like village children, lost in the pleasure of running after cows, laughing when the cows farted or pooed, their clothes dusty and stained with mulberry juice. Lida watched the girls playing *joz-bazi*, imitating them as best she could, but she was too young to join in with them. Haseeb joined the boys in playing a game with walnuts, which basically involved holding one between the fingers and throwing it, trying to hit a target, another walnut lying on the ground a set distance away. I loved to watch him, squatting, eyes focused, his face made serious with concentration as he aimed at the target. When he managed to hit the target he, like the other boys, jumped up and down, screamed with joy and went to claim his prize: the walnut he had hit. When he began playing he lost so often that I felt he might finish the whole stock of walnuts belonging to my cousin that had to last right through the winter. But my worries were groundless. Now it was summertime and Khalil had three full *candoos*, barrels made of clay filled with walnuts, and Haseeb learned the game so well that Khalil's stock was never put in jeopardy.

The *sharara*, or village waterfall, which I used with my relatives in the summers when I was a child, became an open-air shower. Lida and Haseeb went under the waterfall naked, shouting that the water was cold, getting out for a minute and then, screaming with joy, going under it again until their skin turned blue. Then they put on their dirty clothes and lay under the sun in the village square. Fun, fun, fun and no war.

Soraya, my cousin's wife, cooked for all of us, starting to prepare lunch at about ten in the morning, and during my morning walks with Kabir I could smell the aroma of *chapatis* baking in her *tandoor* on the first floor from a long way off. Many relatives came to visit as soon as they heard of our arrival in Jarpiroz, so it was not only for us that Soraya baked – God knows! A hundred chapatis for the large numbers of guests who came for lunch, and often for dinner too. She and her grown-up daughters cooked many different dishes – *salata*, a village-style salad with wild peppermint on top of tomatoes and chopped onions was my favourite. I regarded myself to be a good cook but I could not work out exactly what she put in that *salata*. Was it the weather and the amazing setting where we had our lunch or was it the organic ingredients or was it the happiness of being together and the hospitality and kindness of our hosts? During lunch in the open we could see mountains and green fields and during dinner on the flat roof where the breeze brought the smell of wild flowers, we sat under the bright stars – the Seven Sisters, Forty Girls, or the bright *Soheil*, which guided caravans in days gone by.

When Khalil told me that the village mullah would be coming for dinner I felt a little uncomfortable, although I knew it was the custom of the village for each family to take turns inviting the mullah to eat with them, a great custom because, otherwise, the mullahs would have been alone in the mosque. Nevertheless, I was worried that Kabir would find the company of the mullah unbearable because since the Mujahideen had toppled the communist government, he had turned completely against religion. Even I was worried that the mullah might spoil the evening by quoting passages from the *Quran* to make us fearful of the Day of Judgement.

At around 7 p.m., after evening prayers in the mosque, Mullah Naqib joined us on the rooftop. A nice carpet had been laid with cushions on top to make the sitting comfortable for all of us. Mullah Naqib was given the place of honour as a mark of respect. He surprised me by wearing an elegant and immaculately clean *piraan wa tonbaan*, light-blue waistcoat and artistically fastened white turban. He seemed to be a very handsome man aged between 25 and 30, sporting a trimmed beard not at all like the wild beards worn by the Mujahideen. And his clothes smelled of rosewater.

When he began whispering *bismilah-e rahman-e rahim*, in the name of a kind and compassionate Allah, I thought the man was going to start preaching but he smiled pleasantly, welcoming us to Jarpiroz and asking about our life in Kabul, until the magnificent *shola ghorbandi* was served by Soraya and we all stopped talking as it was the custom to pay attention to eating. After drinking green tea at the end of the dinner, I thought Naqib would be leaving us but then Khalil asked Mustafa to sing. I thought I had not heard him properly. How was it possible to sing in front of a mullah? These people, I thought, like only one sound, the sound of verses from the *Quran*. But I was wrong. The mullah moved his head sideways listening to the melodious voice of Mustafa. Mustafa sounded like a professional country singer with the deep voice he had inherited from his father. He made the lyrics come alive. It was a perfect stage for the young performer. The moonlight, bright stars, the grey mountains, the musical sound of the Nijrab River in the background and the flickering light of the hurricane lamp made the show a great success. Unlike in Kabul, people in the rural areas were not shy and sang and told stories easily. After singing a mix of three sad and romantic songs, Mustafa began the last one:

In the middle of the night
Not being able to sleep, thinking of you
I came to your house with apples
And I threw one hundred of them one by one onto your roof
To awake you and make you come out to see me
But you ignored me.

"You must be the son of a very rich man, Mustafa jan," the mullah said, stroking his beard.

"Why?" Mustafa asked shyly.

"You wasted one hundred apples. Some people don't have even one to eat."

We all laughed and I could see that even Kabir found this mullah interesting.

"Next time, throw a hand-grenade into her courtyard!" said the mullah. "Not to kill anyone but make them all take notice of you. *Then* ask her parents to accept you as their future son-in-law." Once again, we laughed very loud.

"No, No, Mustafa – not a hand-grenade," I said. "Throw a pomegranate through their window to hit your father-in-law on the head. Your beloved will enjoy eating it in the morning and she would know it was you. Continue this every night and then reveal to your future father-in-law that you were the pomegranate-thrower and it was time for him to agree to your marriage as the pomegranate season is over." I didn't get us much laughter as Mullah Naqib.

After Mustafa's performance, Khalil went down and came back with his treasure, one of the oldest books I had ever seen, the *diwan-e Hafiz*, the famous Persian poet's words bound in leather and calligraphed with special perfumed inks, decorated with gold and lapis lazuli.

"See our fortune, Deeba jan," Khalil said, handing me the book that I loved so much and always wanted to read from the moment I came to Nijrab.

"Oh no, Khalil, I can't read after that performance by Mustafa."

"Don't be such a city lady!" Khalil exclaimed, handing the *diwan* to me. "Of course you can."

Hafiz is referred to as the poet of *Lisan-e Ghaib*, the secret language, the language in which you could read your fortune by closing your eyes and saying, with the book in hand: "Hafiz of Shiraz, the master of secret language, reveal my fortune." Since it would not have been polite to decline, I started reading aloud:

> *May your goodness always increase*
> *And your smiling face never cease*
> *In our head the thought of your love*
> *Every day is on the increase.*
> *Every cedar and every spruce*
> *From your height may you hear their pleas*
> *The eye not intrigued by thee*
> *Its tear drops a bloody disease.*
> *Your eye for mesmerising hearts*
> *Is a magician and master-tease.*
> *Wherever a heart is longing for thee*
> *Impatiently shears its own fleece.*
> *The beauty of all the lovers*
> *Beside your swan is ugly geese.*
> *The heart that is out of love's lease*
> *From the circle of union release.*
> *Hafiz's soul, your ruby lips ease*
> *Away from base lips, if you please.*

It was past ten when I looked at my watch. The small children, including Haseeb and Lida, had gone to bed. I was surrounded by the happy faces of my relatives just as I remembered them. I knew they were affected by war, yet did not want to mention it.

Because of the war all commodities were less available and prices were much higher. Schools were either closed or, because of the fear of insecurity, parents did not send their children. Those who braved going to school found they were without teachers because no one wanted to teach without being paid. Formal education for the Mujahideen was not important. Before the war, people in Nijrab had taken their seriously ill relatives to Kabul but now, because Kabul was no longer safe, no one dared to take the risk and, therefore, patients died.

My thoughts moved to Mullah Naqib. Here was a mullah I was sure did not become a mullah out of choice but because of poverty. This incredibly handsome man had probably lost both his parents as a child and had been left at a mosque, first to assist and then to become a mullah himself. I could see that the earth was much more in his mind than the heaven normally preached about by other mullahs, whose preaching was always depressing as they talked about our sins and the punishment waiting for us. This mullah had not mentioned a word about sin and punishment or even quoted from the *Quran*, until Khali, the organiser of performers, suggested, "It is your turn, Mullah sahib."

The mullah became aware of our presence at that moment. Was he thinking about the Hafiz poem or his own loneliness? This man was certainly lonely because whenever my father had invited a mullah, he had gone immediately after dinner. Naqib was searching for company, I thought, and probably for the family he'd never had. I could see on his face the map of an unusual life, his laughter and smiles just a thin layer that could not hide his sadness, no matter how hard he tried.

"Oh no, you don't want me scaring you with tales of the fire of *Jahannam*," he said with a light laugh.

"No no, Mullah sahib, for sake of Allah, no talk of *Jahannam* this evening," Khalil said with a bitter laugh. "The Mujahideen have made our country a real *Jahannam*."

"You know they are not the real *mujahid*," the mullah replied. "*Jihad* means struggle and that refers to the path of man in *nafs tazkia*, the cleansing of the soul. It doesn't mean to take a gun and start shooting your own countrymen who are Muslims."

"Yes, let's leave that sad matter behind us. But I still want you to tell us a story. Mullah sahib is an excellent storyteller you know," Kahlil said looking at me first and then Kabir. Mustafa filled Mullah Naqib's cup with fresh tea.

"Well, I hope I won't bore your guests," said the mullah.

"Oh on the contrary, please," I said.

"I shall tell you a story from the *Quran* in which there is no mention of *Jahannam*. Many, many years ago when the moon was closer to the earth and at night you could see the wings of birds flying, there was a rich man by the name of Aziz living in Egypt. He was called *Aziz-e Meser*, Aziz of Egypt, by the merchants, and foreigners who travelled to Egypt knew that when you mention Egypt you must mention Aziz too. It so happens that the prophet Yusof, the favourite son of his father Yaqoob who had run away from home because his jealous brother attempted to kill him, was working as a servant in the house of Aziz.

"Yusof's dazzling beauty captured the heart of Zulaikha, the wife of Aziz, but she resisted her temptation. However, from time to time, she talked about Yusof to her female friends who were married too. 'He has thin and narrow eyebrows, like a crescent moon. He carries an imperious nose well and his angular cheekbones are accentuated by a flinty jaw. His black eyes are orbs darting constantly, agleam with delight and the vigour of youth. They swim with joy. When he talks you are lost between the musical sound of his words and the sight of those full lips giving you a warm feeling as if he is kissing you. His simple morning greeting is like the soft sound of a flute, and I wait in the evening to hear his voice saying goodnight to us after serving us the whole day. When he puts a cup in front of me, I watch his hand and, you must believe me, his skin is like silk.' But the women did not believe Zulaikha and to prove that she was right, she invited all her friends to visit her one afternoon.

"When the friends came, they were served apples on a plate with sharp knives by another servant. Then Zulaikha asked for Yusof to come to the big room where she had received her friends, pretending she needed him to do something.

"It was when the ladies had started taking the skin off the apples before eating them that Yusof entered the room. His magnificent face and body took the attention of the ladies away from peeling the apples. Their eyes were focused on Yusof and were unable to control their actions. Instead of taking the skin off the apples, they cut their fingers without noticing.

"Among her friends, the one who was very close to Zulaikha suggested that she must fulfil her desire by making herself available to Yusof. She justified that by saying, "He is just like your slave, like those women *kaniz* that Aziz has. Slaves he is entitled to sleep with because they are his, like his other belongings.""

This was more of an erotic story and I knew it was not exactly as the story appeared in the *Quran*, but I loved Naqib's talent as a natural storyteller, transporting his audience to a different world. When I looked at Homira, I saw that she was mesmerised. Looking at Naqib's handsome face I realised he was actually looking directly towards her. Was he telling this story just for her? Was the storyteller Naqib projecting himself as Yusof? I don't know for how long my eyes were focused on him but when I turned my eyes towards Kabir, I noticed he was watching me. Was he jealous? Was I like one of those women in the Naqib's story, cutting my fingers with a knife by watching Naqib? Then I remembered that Homira went regularly to the mosque and had become seriously interested in learning about Islam and the *Quran* from Mullah Naqib. Were they in love? Were they lovers? As for me, I wanted to tell my husband that eyes are like rivers, they flow everywhere but I am a loyal and faithful wife and would never let any desire soil my name.

"For a while," continued the mullah, "Zulaikha thought about what her friend had said but still tried to subdue her desire until, one day, she could no longer resist. She was very beautiful and yet Yusof had never looked upon her face. In part this was because he was a shy and polite servant, but also because he respected his master Aziz. How could he look upon the face of Aziz's *mahram*?

"To make Yusof look at her, Zulaikha had her chamber redecorated with mirrors covering all the walls and ceiling. That way, she thought, Yusof would be unable to avoid looking upon her face and by doing so would become aware of her beauty and therefore desire her as well.

"When Yusof entered the mirrored chamber, he could not avoid seeing the face of his beautiful mistress, even when he averted his eyes to the ceiling. Zulaikha ordered him to sit beside her and when Yusof wanted to leave the chamber, she locked the door.

"Now Yusof was running away from Zulaikha because of the fear of God and his loyalty to Aziz, and Zulaikha was in pursuit. In this struggle, Yusof's long shirt came under the feet of Zulaikha and was torn. Exactly at that moment there was knocking on the door and the voice of Aziz could be heard.

"After Zulaikha opened the door she shouted, 'Look what your servant has done. He locked the door and wanted to take advantage of me.' Yusof denied that. At first Aziz was very angry with Yusof and immediately put him in prison, but some days later, remembering that Yusof had always been honest and loyal, he sought the counsel of a wise man who said, 'Find that shirt Yusof was wearing and see where that shirt is torn. If it is torn at the front then it is obvious that Yusof wanted to force himself upon Zulaikha. But if it is torn behind, then it is Zulaikha's fault.' Aziz quickly found that the shirt was torn behind and therefore knew with whom the blame lay."

I thought about Naqib and Homira and felt their love. Perhaps even Khalil and Soraya knew about it, or maybe it was all in my wild imagination. There had been very little romance prior to my marriage. I was busy with my studies while I was growing into adulthood and afterwards I concentrated on my career. Then before I realised it, my marriage had been arranged. Before marriage I had never explored the possibility of a romantic relationship because of the fear of being discovered. Girls who were found dating men had little chance of marriage because, even if their romance was innocent, their honour would be judged to have been compromised. In a place like Nijrab, there was more freedom for lovers in the countryside as, when the corn grew tall, it was easier for them to keep their secrets hidden.

While I agree with those in society who judge girls who have sex, or even a date, with men before marriage, I do wish the parents did not get involved in choosing wives for their sons or husbands for their daughters. I am sure my father would have left the choosing of spouses to his children, but it was my mother's sense of caring for her children that made her employ an indirect way of finding the right partners for them. She had used that indirect method to persuade me to accept Kabir.

The way that my father met my mother is part of our national history. My great grandfather was a senior army officer serving Amir Abdu Rahman Khan, the so-called Iron Amir who ruled the nation brutally, punishing severely those who broke laws or displeased him. He was a tyrant with many enemies who wanted him dead. One of these enemies was also close to the Amir's *Darbar*, and thought the best way of getting rid of the Amir would be to bribe the cook to poison his food. Abdu Rahman knew that he had many enemies, even among those close to him, and employed a man to taste his food to prevent such an event, by tasting the food at the four corners of each plate first. Then Amir would started eating only when he was sure there had been no effect on the taster. What Amir could not visualise was that the cook could still poison him if he put strong poison in the middle of the plate.

Cruelty was not the only quality of the Amir. He was also known for his massive appetite for food and, as I have seen from photographs of him, he was a very fat man. The poison was strong enough to make the Amir unconscious but did not kill him, thanks to the efforts of his German doctor who pumped out the Amir's stomach. If the task had been left to the local *hakim* with little knowledge of medicine, the Amir would have been dead within a day or two.

The Amir's survival meant that those who had planned his demise now faced his wrath. He had the cook tortured in many different ways to admit what he had done and who had instructed him. A boiled egg was greased and put in his anus until he confessed and then he was skinned alive. The man who had planned the poisoning, a close relative of the Amir, together with his sons, was tied in front of gun barrels and blown to pieces while their wives and daughters were taken as slaves. The Amir did not stop there. Believing many people in his *Darbar* had plotted his demise, whoever he suspected, he tortured first and then killed. My great-grandfather, who had been head of the royal guard and was completely innocent, was punished by the confiscation of all his property and forced into exile. That is how he ended up in Nijrab.

In those days, exile to a rural area such as Nijrab was far worse than being executed. Village people knew each other like a family and although very hospitable to strangers, they would never allow outsiders to settle and create a new life for themselves. While my great-grandfather had lost all his property and belongings, he had managed to keep some *Ashrafi*, gold coins of the emperor Ahmad Shah Durani, which he had earned as his award for his services, first in battles and then in becoming head of the king's guard. With the *Ashrafi*, he tried first to buy a place to live and then some land, but the head of the village, who was aware of his misfortune, told him that he could have a small house without paying rent but could not buy land. When a person wanted to sell his land, it was offered first to the relatives. If no relative wanted to buy it, then it would be offered to a neighbour. But never to a stranger from Nijrab, let alone someone from Kabul.

In the Nijrab environment, my great-grandfather's sons were unemployed and uneducated. He'd had no choice but to live on those *Ashrafis*, but even if he had had a huge quantity of them, without an income they would not last for ever. Fortunately, in the case of my grandfather, the head of the village agreed to give his daughter in marriage to him and my grandfather received a bit of land and a house as a dowry for my grandmother. Seeing the effect of not having land or education or a job encouraged my grandfather to enrol his only son, my father, in a school in Nijrab where the children were taught under the trees, and then he sent him to stay with one of our relatives in Kabul.

In Kabul my father did well. After secondary school he went to university, graduating with a degree in engineering. Knowing he would have a very good future he became a desirable catch for the daughters of our relatives in Kabul. My father's heart, however, was in Nijrab and that was the reason he went there whenever he had the opportunity. It had been while walking in Nijrab during one of his school holidays that he had heard the cries of a girl pleading for help. She had fallen into a *gelkana*, or clay pit, and no part of her body could be seen. In that remote place she was very lucky to be heard by my father. With much difficulty, using his belt, he managed to pull her out.

"What were you doing in here?" my father had asked, wondering why the girl had been in such a lonely place.

"My mother sent me to get some *gelawa* to paint our house with," she replied.

When he saw her crying eyes, he knew those were the eyes he wanted to see first thing in the morning. Those eyes changed colour from brown to amber and then a mix of other colours depending on the angle of the light. She was partly fairy, my father said, referring to this discovery. He quickly found out where the girl lived and feared she might get engaged to someone else. Girls married very young in Nijrab. My father sent my grandmother, who was herself from Nijrab, to ask the parents of the girl to agree to their daughter's marriage to my father. There were the usual issues, like our houses, our lands and our daughters are only for the people from Nijrab. But when my grandmother informed them that my father was going to have a bright future and that she herself was from Nijrab, they agreed, provided that my father could offer a large dowry. That was what my father did not have but, after graduating from university, he would have a good job and that would allow him to borrow money from a bank to make his dream come true. My mother admitted to me that the evening after my father rescued her from the clay pit she had prayed to Allah to make her rescuer her husband.

While my mother proudly told everyone in Kabul that she was from Nijrab, my father never accepted Nijrab as his home because the rural community had not accepted his grandfather, his father or him. Instead, with a perfect Kabuli accent, he told people he was from Kabul, and he was right. He had been born in Nijrab but grew up in Kabul – son of a man who had been born in Kabul and all of whose relatives on his father's side were from Kabul.

There in Nijrab I was able to experience total freedom from war and the requirement to hide my face. Women in the village did not cover their faces because they lived like a family and women had to work in the fields. They could not work in a burka or even wear a scarf. We wanted to stay longer, but Kabir had only been given a two-week break and was told it was not possible to have longer when Mujahideen were dying because of the fighting. Of course, we could disappear in Jarpiroz and the war would not help the government search for a lost doctor. But I could not accept making Khalil pay for our living in Nijrab. Although he was the most generous man in the world, he was a poor peasant and Soraya had already slaughtered all her chickens to feed us. Apart from seeing my kind relatives and the country that I loved so much, I felt happy that Kabir had bonded with Khalil and come to appreciate the good-hearted nature of a peasant family who generously gave whatever they had to make our stay pleasant.

The children started crying when we told them the day of our leaving had come. We found it difficult to get them in the car. From the back seat I watched Kabir driving, now carefully and not like when we had just got engaged. The passenger seat next to him, which I occupied before the arrival of Mujahideen, was empty. In the back seat, Haseeb sat on my right and Lida on my left, their faces glued to the windows, watching every tiny trace of the countryside pass by. I was thinking that I must learn how to make our life as normal as possible even while this devastating war was going on. Living with Khalil and his family had been a good exercise in learning how to create normality in the middle of chaos. Proud that I had been able to give my children a slice of peace, I dreamed of the days when it would become normal again – war cannot go on forever. It is not only that innocent people lose their lives, but those who continue fighting for power must one day realise that the cost of gaining power is too high when paid for in lives.

On the road to Kabul we had to pass several checkpoints. We had rehearsed with Khalil to be confident when telling the men at the checkpoints that we were from Nijrab. That preparation had built my confidence and so, as we approached a checkpoint, I would roll down the window and shout, "We are from Nijrab. We are going to Kabul to attend the funeral of my father-in-law." I had to lie to pass these hurdles. My father-in-law was dead, so there was some degree of truth in it as well. It worked until we came to the last checkpoint outside Kabul in Qila Murad Baig.

Kabir stopped the car and I shouted from under the burka, "We are from Nijrab, brother. We are going to attend my father-in-law's funeral."

The man holding a Kalashnikov and wearing a *pakol* hat had a sparsely bearded face, just like Commander Masoud. He looked at me first and then turned to Kabir. "You don't look like Nijrabi to me," the man said.

"I am from Nijrab," he insisted.

"Oh yes, which part?" asked the man.

"Jarpiroz." I was delighted that Kabir remembered the name of the village.

"Show me your *tazkira*." Tazkira is our ID card in which our ethnicity and place of birth are stated.

"I don't carry it."

"Why not?" the man with the Kalashnikov demanded.

"Because it is safer at home."

"Step out of the car," the man ordered.

"But brother, what for?" asked Kabir.

"Don't waste my time," said the man, pointing his gun at Kabir's temple.

Horrified, I shouted "Do what he says!"

Kabir got out of the car and another man started to search him head to toe, taking whatever he had in his pocket out. "Here it is," the searcher said waving the *tazkira*. "You didn't leave it at home after all." He turned pages and then shouted, "You lying Pashtun!"

My heart was pounding as I took my burka off saying loudly "Brothers, I am from Nijrab I swear." I started describing villages and giving an accurate picture of Nijrab, telling them about my cousin Khalil along with much irrelevant information.

The two men left us, taking Kabir's *tazkira* and the car keys with them, and went into a wooden shed at the side of the road. Some minutes later they emerged with another man also wearing a *pakol* hat, a typical piece of clothing among Panjshiris, especially since Masoud always wore one.

"Show me your *jawaz-e sair*," said the new man who we assumed was their leader.

"Brother, we left that at home."

"Lying again. How can I believe this is your vehicle if you don't have a travel permit for it?"

"Brother, you know it is not safe to leave the *jawz-e sair* in the car. People easily steal it."

"No, no, no," the man shouted. "You already lied that you were from Nijrab and hid your *tazkira*. Now you all get out of the car. The vehicle is impounded."

"Oh no, brother, please believe me it is our car," I implored.

"You woman, it is shameful. Cover your face."

"Brother, we are with children," I begged.

"Law is law. No *jawaz-e sair*, no car."

One of them, who had a Panjshiri scarf on his head, said, "Until today it was yours, now it is ours." Then he searched in his pocket and brought out a snuff box, putting some snuff on the palm of his left hand. "Do you think it is fair that we fought all these years defending our country and liberating it from the Russians to end up having nothing? We lost everything. You have your car and, God knows, a posh house." He put the snuff under his tongue before spitting on the ground.

"Please, this is the only property we have left," Kabir pleaded like a child asking for forgiveness. "We don't have a house, we are renting."

"Go! Don't waste our time and yours," their leader said. "Bring the document."

No matter how much we beseeched those men, they would not listen to us. Having no other choice, we tried to find public transport so that we could go home and Kabir could bring the *jawaz-e sair* to prove it was his car. But there was no public transport and Kabir had to promise a lorry driver a large sum of money to take us to Kabul. The lorry driver's assistant moved to the back of the lorry and the four of us were squeezed into an area of one and a half seats with the children on our laps. I felt the lorry was driving too slowly as we needed to get home quickly so that Kabir could return to the checkpoint and reclaim the car.

It was dark when we reached home and it would have been unwise to leave the house at night. After some discussion we both agreed that it would be better for Kabir to go to the hospital first thing in the morning to get support from the head of the hospital, who was a senior member of the Panjshiri Mujahideen Group. Kabir would ask if someone could accompany him to the checkpoint, but that evening he returned without the car.

"It was your stupid idea to go to that place for a holiday in the middle of a war," Kabir shouted, dropping onto the couch.

"Why? What happened?" I asked.

"They moved the car somewhere else. Or that is what they said."

"Did you get any help from the head of the hospital?" I asked.

"Yes, I went with a man, but it was not a great help."

"What did they say at the checkpoint?"

"They said our car was needed urgently for Panjshir to bring some of the injured to hospitals in Kabul for treatment."

"Really?"

"I don't believe they are using it as an ambulance. They simply want to have the car," he complained.

"You must take the head of the hospital with you tomorrow," I insisted.

The experience at the checkpoint was alarmingly common since the Mujahideen had taken over, but we were not aware of it until that time. Fighters stopped cyclists and motorists on the streets, telling the owners that it was their turn to have the bicycle, motorbike or car. Some Mujahideen had also taken over houses belonging to people who had left the country because of the war. Communists like my husband had done exactly the same as the Mujahideen, just in a different way. The communists put their opponents in prison, or simply eliminated them, and then confiscated whatever belongings they had.

Fortunately, Kabir got on well with the new head of the hospital because this man had no medical background or any knowledge of how to run a hospital. Kabir said one day that the guy probably had not finished secondary school. Nevertheless, this man went with Kabir many times over several weeks to the checkpoint. Each time the head of the hospital asked for the car to be returned, men at the checkpoint argued that during the time of *jihad*, it was far more important to have such a car as an ambulance than for it to be used by its owner for pleasure. When the head of the hospital finally convinced the Mujahideen to return our car to Kabir, we discovered they must have used it for joyriding because the car had many dents and its radio cassette player had been stolen. I had loved that cassette player, listening to the voice of Ahmad Zahir whenever I rode in the car. Kabir did not like the car in that condition and, to avoid a problem similar to what happened, he sold it cheaply, and I thought it was not a bad decision.

Chapter 12

The tunnel

I was woken in the middle of the night by the volcanic sound of hand grenades, rockets, bullets, shouting and screaming in the street outside our house. I was four months pregnant with our third child – my children were living and breathing war. Jumping out of bed I rushed to join Kabir at the window, where he was peering around the curtains into the street. He looked worried.

"Must have been a rocket landing on someone's house," I suggested.

"I am not so sure," he hissed, lowering his voice.

We had got used to the sound of bullets and rockets at all hours of the day and night. One must continue with life no matter how hard and unbearable it becomes, not only for one's own sake but for others – particularly my children. What would happen to them if I became sick or was injured? Staying safe was not just about protecting myself.

The sound of shooting in our street was loud but we didn't know where the shooters were. We soon saw them with their Kalashnikovs, running from one side of the moonlit street to the other, taking positions behind walls as men at the other end of the street were firing at them. Bullets were hitting our walls. Our neighbourhood was now a war zone. We both ducked below the windowsill. The children's room was on the other side of the house and had no windows overlooking the street, but they ran into the hallway, screaming with fright. I rushed towards them, pushing them back into their bedroom, which was safer, and calling Kabir to join us. Together we tried to calm the children, but it was not easy. In a matter of seconds our apartment seemed to have become a target for all those fighters.

Blood pumped in my ears. My heart expanded. My rib cage felt small. My feet tingled, glued to the ground. My head turned on my neck as I watched for fear in every corner, following the sound of where a bullet hit. Uncontrolled body movement. Ducking, diving, loud explosions. I pushed the children to the floor, shouting at them to stay down.

"We must go to the basement," I yelled.

"You can't! It is too dangerous," Kabir shouted back.

He was right. The window at the end of the corridor had been shot to pieces. If we left the children's room, there was more chance we would be hit by the bullets.

"What should we do?" I asked, holding the children tight. "We cannot stay here for ever. The basement is safer."

"I know, I know. Keep calm. Don't panic too much."

"Don't panic too much is not the answer!" I exclaimed.

"I will go first. You must crawl like this," he said, tightening his fists, demonstrating how to push his body forward using the elbows – a technique he had learned during six months as a conscript in the army after his medical graduation.

"I can't do that!" I said, pointing at my big, dome-shaped stomach. "I can't pull myself along on my stomach."

"Oh, I totally forgot." He looked at my belly. "What can we do?"

"I'll try to pull myself along on my back."

"That won't be easy."

"We have no choice. The children are too frightened by the bullets."

Seeing my determination, he gently opened the children's bedroom door and prepared to crawl.

"I'll go first," he said. "Haseeb, you crawl after me. Then Lida, and then you, understand?

Watching how Kabir pulled his body forward, I made Haseeb lie flat on his stomach and told him to follow his father. He nodded, too scared to utter a word. Haseeb learned well. Lida manoeuvred with difficulty.

Without thinking that I might be hit, I pushed her head down to make sure she stayed as flat as possible. Then I followed on my back, using my feet and legs to propel my body painfully and slowly across the floor. In my imagination the height of my stomach seemed twice as much, easy to be hit by a bullet. Each time a bullet hit a window or a wall, I stayed flat and did not move. My mouth was murmuring, my brain a bomb itself, ready to explode. What I didn't want to do was scream. I didn't want the children to go into a frenzy. I had to clamp my hand over my mouth to stop myself from screaming and further frightening the children when I stopped moving because of bullets or loud explosions.

With difficulty, turning my head, I watched Lida to make sure she did not get up. After reaching the stairwell, Lida found it hard to slide her body down. She stood and I shouted, "Run quick!" I did the same when I reached the stairs at exactly the same moment a shower of bullets hit the wall not far from my head. I screamed, missed a step, lost my balance and almost hit my head on the wall. But I saved myself at the last second by grabbing onto the hand rail.

In the basement we lit candles to try to reduce the children's fear, but we trembled every time there was an explosion. All Kabir and I could do was look at each other helplessly. Since the Mujahideen came to power there was no electricity and because of that we had bought a big stock of candles, keeping them in the basement. But the children were in shock and could not stop their frenzied crying. "Don't cry," we told them, forcing ourselves to remain optimistic and calm the children by telling them that the fighters would soon leave our street and then all would be fine.

I don't know how long we were there because I had left my watch in the bedroom. Kabir and I huddled together with the children, Haseeb, now 6, and Lidam, 3, telling them that the shooting would soon stop and trying to hide our own fear. I wanted to reassure them, but time seemed frozen and I wanted to live in the future, away from the war. I wanted to wake up one day, twenty years older but living in peace.

Haseeb brought me back to reality. "Mother, I am hungry."

"I will give you breakfast, but wait now," I replied.

"It is late afternoon," Kabir protested.

"Afternoon?"

"Yes it is."

"How do you know?"

"I know."

"But there is no bread," I told him.

Every morning before the fighting came to our street, Kabir went to the bakery to bring us freshly baked bread for the day, before going to work. On the days when Kabir had to go to work very early in the morning I would go to the bakery, because then women could still walk in the streets provided they wore *chaderi* covering their faces.

"We can't let them go without food," Kabir said, looking into my eyes and indicating the children.

"Will they eat rice?" I asked

"They'll have to."

Fortunately, there was plenty of rice in the basement and Kabir volunteered to go to the kitchen on the ground floor to fetch the small portable gas cooker we had bought when the electricity supply became irregular. If you think cooking rice is easy, then you are wrong. Afghans are famous for cooking *Kabuli Palaw* with rice, knowing that just one drop of water can be too much, or too little, and I prided myself on my cooking. That day, the rice I prepared was tasteless, yet the children did not complain. The only criticism came from Kabir telling me how expensive rice was those days to be cooking tasteless food.

There were no other ingredients in the house to prepare any dish with meat or even vegetables. We had always bought vegetables twice a week and, unfortunately, the day before the war came to our street, we had finished all the garlic, onions, and tomatoes, which are the main ingredients for Afghan-style cooking.

Going to the toilet on the ground floor was risky, but the children could not wait for long, so we waited until the shooting was less intense and then rushed to the toilet as quickly as possible. By the time night came, Kabir and I went upstairs once each to the living room to fetch something for us to sleep on.

I had encouraged Kabir to rent this apartment because its windows overlooked the street and I liked to watch people. That had been my journalistic background, but now things were different. Now I wished I had chosen an apartment with smaller windows and away from the street.

The fighting continued throughout the night and intensified at daybreak. More rockets were fired from the street with some landing in our neighbourhood. Through these years of civil war, I had become an expert in differentiating between the sounds of weapons. I could tell a DSHK from a Kalashnikov and knew whether the rockets were incoming or outgoing. Sometimes a period of silence gave us hope that maybe the fighting had stopped. Then seconds later we would hear the men shouting *Allahu Akbar*, followed by another barrage, all weapons firing together, making our apartment shake. Both sides called themselves Mujahideen, both sides were Muslims, both sides used *Allahu Akbar*, and both sides killed in the name of Allah – mainly innocent people.

We were fed up eating boiled rice three times a day, especially the children, who refused to eat any more. On the morning of the fourth day, the fighting became less intense and by afternoon it had almost died away. Then we heard people hammering on the steel door of our apartment. The owner had installed a steel entrance door and metal grills on the ground floor windows to protect us from robbery. The banging continued. All we could do was look at each other. Kabir was even more frightened than I because these fighters killed men easily when they became angry, but women had a chance of being spared.

A man with a hoarse voice shouted "Open the door, you son of a whore. Open!"

Kabir moved from where he had been squatting, but stopped. He moved again but seemed undecided and confused.

I held his wrist. "Don't go."

"But they will not give up."

"Open up, you mother fucker, or I will break it down," the man shouted again and continued banging on the door very loudly with what I assumed was the butt of his Kalashnikov. None of us could move. Suddenly the men outside started shooting at the door and the children screamed. However, the steel door was strong and impossible to open with bullets. I imagined from that basement where I was shaking that the door must have many holes in it. Then the shooting stopped.

"I give one last warning. Open the door or we bring a sledgehammer and other tools to open it by force and you know what we'll do after that. We'll kill you all." When the children heard this, they both wailed.

"I must open it, we have no choice," Kabir said.

"No," I shouted.

"If I don't, they will kill us all when they force it open." He shouted very loudly to make sure the men behind the door could hear him. "Don't shoot! I am going to open the door."

"Oh no," I said, but knew we had no choice. I got up and followed Kabir but stayed at the entrance to the basement where I could see the entrance door and the entrance hall but was protected from being hit by bullets. I must save myself for the sake of our children, I thought.

When Kabir opened the door, the first man who came in kicked him in the stomach and knocked him to the ground.

"Please, brothers, don't hit him," I shouted."

"Shut up you *kanchani*, whore," the second man shouted, hitting Kabir in the chest with the butt of his Kalashnikov. Kabir's painful cry made the children scream.

"Please, please, brother," I screamed again, but one of them rushed towards me and slapped my face hard. I nearly fell and my face became numb. The men continued beating Kabir with their fists and with the butt of their Kalashnikovs. I heard his painful cries until he became unconscious.

"Please, brothers, don't kill him. We have done nothing," I pleaded.

"Done nothing, you *kossi*, bitch?" One of them shouted, foaming at the mouth. "Come upstairs all of you! Who else is down there?"

"Only my two small children, brother."

"Bring them all."

We all went to the living room where glass from the shattered windows littered the carpet. They dragged Kabir into the room. His face was covered with blood, his eyes were shut. Was he dead? The children could not stop crying at the sight of their father. One of the men shouted, "Shut up, bastards!" That was enough to shock them into silence.

"These bastards have a house full of food," another of the men shouted from the basement.

"You have a basement full of food and the rest of the people are dying of hunger?" said a man in a dirty oil-stained waistcoat. He looked around at the framed photos on the walls. "Chief! The bastard is a doctor," he shouted to their leader.

The leader focused on the picture of Kabir in a white doctor's coat walking along a corridor of the People's Hospital. "Is it true he is a doctor?" he asked me.

"Yes, brother."

"What kind of doctor?" he asked.

"He is a surgeon."

"Wake the bastard up!" the leader shouted. "We need him for Torab Ali and Kahtam Ali."

Only then did I realise that my husband was alive and probably would not be killed because this Hazara Mujahideen group needed him for their war-injured fighters.

"Now you must prepare a good lunch for all of us," the leader said.

"But I don't have basic ingredients."

"Tell us what you need for *Kabuli Palaw*. You have the rice and the rest we will find for you. All the shops around here now belong to us."

"I need a bigger stove."

"Don't make too many excuses! We'll bring a bigger stove from another house. We are the owners of all the houses in this area too."

"Yes, brother. I will do what you say," I said in a tone to please them in order to save our lives. I took a last look at the lifeless Kabir, praying in my heart that he was still alive, and then took the children with me to the kitchen where they held onto my legs, refusing to let go, making my work difficult. In no time at all the Hazara fighters brought all the ingredients required, including meat, which was very hard to find. Obviously they had confiscated all the meat and vegetables from shopkeepers or, if the shops were closed, broken down the doors and taken what they wanted.

Despite the smashed windows and debris, our neighbourhood was quiet once more. That meant these Hazara fighters had defeated the Panjshiri fighters who had previously controlled our area. The war had taken different shapes: war between communists and Mujahideen and then war between different factions of the Mujahideen becoming war between different ethnic groups – war between bandits in a lawless country.

Our neighbourhood had been controlled by the Panjshiris, the strongest Mujahideen fighters of all, and it puzzled me how the Hazaras could have overwhelmed them. Later I discovered that they'd constructed a 2km-long tunnel from the Jamal Mina, which they controlled, to behind the lines of the Panjshiris. Large numbers of Hazara fighters passed through the tunnel to get behind the Panjshiris. The Hazara group surprised the Panjshiris by appearing like mushrooms from underground, surrounding the Panjshiris and eventually defeating them.

How they calculated the length of the tunnel to where they wanted to resurface was beyond me, but one thing I learned during these years of war was that the Afghan mind is perfect for fighting. Most recently they had defeated the Soviet Union but throughout history they had made the British, the Arabs, the Persians and others run for their lives and never think of invading Afghanistan again. Unfortunately, invaders have short memories and history is repeated. The only people who could defeat Afghans is the Afghans themselves, and they should not be so proud of their achievement in wars against invaders – the biggest destroyers of our country are the Afghans.

I used all the pots and pans we had in our kitchen to cook for about twenty men. The rest of the fighters must have made similar arrangements in other houses and apartments. As soon as I finished cooking, I gave some food to the children and begged them to eat fast before a Hazara fighter appeared. The poor children burned their mouths but they were hungry and had no choice. Even at that age they knew what was going on and why they had to force themselves to eat hot food.

When I told the fighters that the food was ready, they invaded the kitchen and took all the plates and bowls we had, filling them with food. I left them to it, taking the children with me to the living room. To my delight, Kabir was sitting up with his back resting against the wall watching the Hazara fighters eating like animals.

"Fuck, chief. We found treasures," shouted a man with greasy ginger hair and a patchy ginger beard while grease from the oily vegetables dripped from his fingers. "We have a professional cook and a beaten up doctor. Hee, hee, hee."

"Not perfect," the chief said, looking at my stomach. "One has a big dome and can't move her arse fast enough and the other is half dead." He shifted his gaze from me to look at Kabir.

"Chief, I will make the man just as strong as a bull in two days. Leave it to me," said another man. "And for the queen of cooks, I also have a solution. We have many women in our custody in this neighbourhood. They could work under her direction cutting vegetables, preparing salad and they can move the queen's arse if she can't do it herself." They all laughed and continued making crude jokes, happy that they had defeated the strongest Mujahideen group, the Panjshiris.

"Come now! We take you to another place," the leader shouted as soon as they had all finished eating.

Two men supported Kabir, holding him under his arms. I held the hands of Haseeb and Lida with horror. Where were they going to take us? After about ten minutes, we came to a big house where we encountered almost the entire neighbourhood packed into different rooms. Men were separated from women and children accompanied the women. This big house with eight bedrooms and two living rooms became a prison for us, sleeping on the floor next to each other, eating only bread. But the worst thing was having to share the toilets. The house was a modern house with three flush toilets and one dry pit for the servants in the corner of the garden. They were all occupied most of the time – used by more than a hundred captured men and women. No dignity for anyone. Men occupied four bedrooms and the women the other four bedrooms as well as the two living rooms because of the huge number of children.

Cooking twice daily for so many in the Hazara group was painful, regardless of the help I received from other women, some of them very kind, trying their best, and one even volunteering to take my place. But the Hazaras did not agree. As the days passed I didn't know when we were going to be released. The children and I slowly adapted to this situation, accepting one *naan* bread for each of us per day and whenever Lida complained that she wanted to eat something different, Haseeb with his child's voice comforted her: "Soon we go home Lida, don't cry," learning from me. We even managed to sleep better at night in the middle of children crying, sick people coughing. The wife of the owner of the house watched us helplessly as we damaged furniture, broke glasses, dented the walls by moving items to create space to sleep on the floor, making the whole house as dirty as cow barns. None of these actions were deliberate and could not be avoided. The normal neighbourhood politeness had disappeared as all of us fought for space, food and water. In the middle of this struggle I prayed to God, that none of my children got sick, and I was worried about my pregnancy. If we were going to be kept for months, how could I give birth among the crowd?

An old woman among us coughed day and night, her eyes shut because of the pain that kept her awake. Her daughter and granddaughters begged the Hazara group to allow her to be taken to hospital, but the fighters ignored them. Then one day the woman stopped breathing and her family started wailing. Then after a moment, the old woman gasped and began breathing again. The children were scared. I told Haseeb and Lida not to look at the old woman and went out to the fighter who had been appointed to guard the door of our room.

"Brother, please help. An old woman is in urgent need of a doctor. If a doctor doesn't come, she will die."

"Shut up and go inside," he replied. "I don't want to hear any complaints from you lot. If anyone asks for anything, I shoot that person."

"Brother, for Allah's sake! My husband is a doctor. Just bring him here."

He jumped off his chair, raising his hand to slap me. "I told you. Get back to the room, you whore. You want me to put a knife in your big balloon stomach?"

I screamed and slammed the door, hiding among the crowd in the room. To reduce my own mental pain, I avoided looking towards the dying woman but could not stop myself hearing the sobbing relatives. That night I could not sleep and my mind was busy wondering how human beings could become so cruel that they changed into a completely new type of savage animal. Before the Soviet Union invaded, we did not see the ethnic and religious differences among us. I had had Panjshiri and Hazara classmates who were best friends. Then we were all Afghans and our ethnic background did not matter. Now a Muslim woman needing kindness before dying was denied it because of our differences. I stared at the dark ceiling, unable to block the sound of a family's suffering, praying to God to take the soul of the old woman to heaven and release her from such pain and indignity. God heard my prayers that night. In the morning Hazara fighters took the dead woman's body out of the room. Her relatives did not know what would happen to her body, where she was going to be buried, or if she was going to be buried at all.

Every day a Hazara came to the women's part of the house to choose women for work. The women they chose were young and beautiful, so I guessed what was happening to them. Being ashamed and embarrassed, these women never talked about what kind of work they were required to do, and those who were not yet chosen never asked. Obviously, we all knew what was happening and I dreaded that one day it would be me. To this very day I don't know why my turn never came. Was it because of my ordinary looks? Was it because of my pregnancy? In our culture Afghan husbands avoid having sex with their heavily pregnant wives for fear of harming the unborn baby. But these Hazaras were not my husband. Or was it because Kabir was now a very valuable person for these Hazara fighters? Knowing that God listens to my prayers, I prayed to God to release my soul before I was raped – the most dishonourable act of all.

Every day there was a skirmish but nothing like a full-blown war, until one day the sky and earth exploded together. Now, instead of fearing that we might be killed because of the war, we were all hoping that the other group, whoever they were, would defeat the Hazaras and release us. Rockets were fired and grenades exploded in the courtyard, but the building still stood. Among the shooting and explosions, we constantly heard *Allahu Akbar*, God is great, and I cursed them all for using the name of God while continuing to rape and kill fellow Muslims. What kind of Allah were they worshipping?

The intense fighting continued for many days. During those days of fighting no one had brought even that single bread for each one of us. No one could sleep at night. In our hearts, fear and hope were mixed together. "Please God, let the other group win or take our lives together," I prayed.

Then one day a woman, who had gone to the toilet, came back shouting, "Get out, they are gone!"

We all got out of the room but no one dared to leave the house because fighting was still continuing outside, though less intense. No

Hazara fighter was to be seen in the house. Men from the other side of the house came to the women's part and, for the first time, after nearly a month, I saw my husband Kabir among the crowd. He was shouting my name, looking in every direction. How come he cannot see me I thought, shouting his name. Excitement and worries had blinded him and when he finally saw me he rushed towards us, grabbing me so tightly that I felt he was choking me. We sobbed uncontrollably, watching the children who watched us with excited and terrified eyes. Kabir left me and picked up Lida first, kissing her hair, her face, her hands, putting her down and then doing the same to Haseeb.

"Sit. I want to see you all," he said and dried his eyes with the palms of his hands. "I can't believe that we are all alive."

He touched our faces and hair as if to confirm that he was not dreaming and I examined his long hair and beard, seeing his *piraan wa tonbaan* stained with dirt and sweat. It mattered not at all that none of us had been able to change our clothes during all that time.

We were alive.

The iron entrance door to our flat was riddled with bullets. Our bedroom and the corridor were pock-marked by bullet holes. The flat had been wrecked by the Hazara fighters. They had taken money, Kabir's expensive watch, and all my jewellery. There was no food left in the basement and almost everything was damaged. But at that moment I was thinking more about my children's empty stomachs than the state of the apartment.

Having surveyed the apartment, Kabir said: "We have to go to my mother's house."

"How can we get there?" I asked. "All the streets have checkpoints and are controlled by different groups."

"We have no choice," Kabir replied. "The children are very hungry."

"How are they going to walk that distance?" I asked. Taimani was at least a two-hour walk. And even if we were able to walk it, could we make it through those checkpoints? That was not an easy question to answer.

"I can carry one of the children for a while," he said. "And then the other."

"And do you think I will be able to walk in this condition?" I asked, pointing to my stomach. "The baby is on its way."

"I will find a solution," Kabir replied, tugging on his long beard.

"What solution?" I asked.

"Wait for me, I'm going out." He looked towards the damaged door. "Lock the door and wait."

"Please don't go," I shouted. But he just stepped out and disappeared.

Not having a watch or a clock I had no way of knowing how long he was gone. Time seemed frozen and my worries were eating me. It is true that time is relative to the conditions. One day is like a minute if you are happy and one minute is like a day if you are a mother living in a war zone. I sat on the floor, holding my children beside me, looking around and feeling a great pain in my heart to see in the middle of our living room burned and half-burned piles of books. They were more important to me than my jewellery or any other possessions.

Many days passed in my mind but probably it was less than half an hour before Kabir reappeared with a smile on his face and he announced: "I found a way."

"What way?" I asked.

"Come and see."

Outside I saw an old man standing next to the sort of hand-cart used for carrying goods, mainly wood and coal for winter fuel. The surface of the cart was blackened by coal.

"What is this?" I asked, thinking Kabir was making a tasteless joke.

"I couldn't find a taxi but this kind man agreed to carry you and the children because I told him you were pregnant and the children small."

"Taxi?" I questioned. "But we have no money for a taxi or even for this cart."

"I tried to find a taxi to take us to Taimani. I told them that they would be paid when we reached my mother's house. No one agreed, until I met this kind-hearted man."

I didn't know whether I should laugh or cry or do both. War had created a different attitude to life, making us do things we would never have considered before. Who would have thought that one day I, an educated Afghan woman who had worn western clothes and conducted herself in a sophisticated manner, would have to be loaded like coal onto a hand-cart?

"I can't do this, Kabir!" I protested. "First, I'm pregnant – it's impossible for me to climb on that cart. And, anyway, it is embarrassing."

"Please don't argue," Kabir pleaded, "or we will lose this opportunity."

Having no choice, I put on my burka, the now required item of clothing for women since the Mujahideen had taken over. I felt almost blindfolded, never having got used to it. I walked towards the cart with Kabir holding my hand and guiding me like a blind person. Then he put my right foot on the tyre of the cart to help me climb and told the old man to hold the cart steady. With a pounding heart I gripped Kabir's left arm more tightly that I had ever held anything in all my life, fearing that I might fall and injure myself or lose the baby. Kabir was pushing me and the old man was saying helpful things to guide us but to which I paid no attention. With my right foot on the tyre of the cart I pulled myself forward onto the surface of the cart and I felt a pain like an arrow piercing my back. Nevertheless, blinded by the pain and the burka, I managed to sit myself on the cart. Moments later I heard the excited voices of Haseeb and Lida sitting next to me sounding as if they thought the cart was for children to play with. Their happy voices brought a moment of happiness to my heart after such a long time of suffering.

Here was I, a woman on top of a cart pulled by one of the most senior medical doctors of our country, running away from one part of the city to go to another but unable to run away from the war. I could no longer believe in a peaceful past in the modern world that existed when I was at university, mixing with boys and girls in a class where we studied the world's literature, listened to western and eastern music, shared fashion magazines, went together to cinemas and the theatre. What happened to that woman? It seemed like we did not exist anymore as human beings. We were treated just like a commodity.

Despite the burka obstructing my vision, I could see that there were not many people on the street and cars rarely passed. Obviously, no one wanted to risk their life in this lawless country ruled by men who had not been to school or university and thought that just by being able to read the *Quran* made them capable of managing the lives of ordinary Afghan people. These fighters who claimed that they were fighting for Allah did not even understand the meaning of verses from the *Quran* because they could not speak Arabic. Now they governed a country with a Kalashnikov and their Sharia code of conduct derived from their own interpretation of the *Quran*. As I pondered all of these issues, I also prayed for our safe passage.

The cart stopped and the authoritarian voice of a man demanded: "Where are you going?" A Panjshiri fighter was pointing a Kalashnikov at me and my children.

"We are going to my mother's house, brother," Kabir said.

The man laughed. "Going to your mother's house in this Mercedes?"

I heard the laughter of his companions.

"Must be a big party," one of them said.

"Can we go with you?" asked the first man, still pointing his Kalashnikov at us.

"Brother, there is no party. Our apartment has been destroyed by Hazara fighters and we have to go to my mother's house to stay there. We were kept captive for almost two months."

I realised that Kabir was talking about our ordeals in the hand of Hazaras, the enemy of Panjshiris, to attract their kindness and make them to let us pass.

"Come on!" The first man said with giggling voice. "People make up all these stories to cheat us. How do I know that you are not a Hazara yourself?"

"Brother, do I look like a Hazara?"

"Let me see your ID."

"Brother, I tell you the truth. The Hazaras took all my money and threw away my ID. They left nothing for us in our apartment."

"Maybe your wife is a Hazara."

"God curse you, you disrespectful man!" I retorted. "My mother is from Nijrab just next door to Panjshir," I took my burka off. "Do I look like a Hazara? You can ask me anything you like about Nijrab and I can tell you. Or did you just want to see my face? Don't you have a mother or a sister of your own? What would you do if someone treated your sister or wife like this?"

I was in a frenzied state and the fighters were stunned by what I said. Kabir was amazed. "And I am pregnant," I continued, pointing towards my stomach. "Where is your humanity? What kind of Islam do you follow?"

"Don't lecture so much." The Panjshiri lowered his Kalashnikov "Go! Go! And put on your burka now." So saying, he let us pass.

When we reached Taimani it seemed as if it was in a different, peaceful country. There was no trace of war here. Shops were open and people were going about their daily business. Reaching Adai's house, Kabir ran to get his brother Rabi and together they helped me climb down. The family rushed around us. Even Adai, who could hardly walk, seemed to be running as she came out of the house without her headscarf, which, for religious reasons, she would never ordinarily have done.

"Oh my dear son! I thought you were killed," Adai wailed, holding Kabir tight, kissing his face, hair and neck, tears flooding from her eyes. She kept touching his face. "Am I not dreaming, is it you my Kabir, my life?"

Adai spoke in Pashto, which I understand with difficulty because my language is Farsi. I learned Pashto in school, but it was not adequate for conversation. The rest of the family picked up the children, passing them hand to hand, kissing and touching them. Their words to me were kind, but without showing much emotion.

"If you had stayed with us this would never have happened to you," Adai said in Farsi after a long period of holding and kissing Kabir. I wanted to reply that no one could have predicted that our area would be targeted or that their neighbourhood would be safe. This war had no plan and prediction was impossible. I kept quiet, just happy to see that my children and husband were safe.

"We are very hungry," Haseeb said when he was finally released from the kissing and cuddling. "We have not eaten for days."

"Hungry! Oh, my grandson is hungry and I am still alive. I give my life to make sure you are not hungry. Come!" Adai turned towards the house and my sisters-in-law rushed ahead to prepare food.

Kabir interjected loudly. "Please, just bring us some *naan*. We are very hungry and the children can't wait. You can prepare food later."

Quickly they brought the *naan*, which we all tore into pieces and stuffed it in our mouths, just like animals tearing carcases apart. The family watched us and kept talking in Pashto, asking questions. We had no time to answer with our mouths full, grabbing one piece of bread after another. That simple bread to me seemed the most delicious food I had ever had and I remembered a Sufi saying: The most delicious food is the one when you are hungry.

Chapter 13

At the mercy of Adai

I had never wanted to live with Adai as she was a forceful person whose house was her kingdom. With Kabir's support I had avoided that through all the years of our marriage, but it was war that finally forced me to live in my mother-in-law's house. We had no other choice but even Kabir could not adjust to Adai's strict traditional and religious rules. Kabir loved entertaining his friends, organising lunch and dinner parties when men and women mixed and alcohol was served. Nothing like that could happen in Adai's house. When male guests came, unless they were relatives, only the men were allowed to entertain the male guest while the women had to take their food in another room. This was typical behaviour among Pashtuns but I came from a Tajik background, where such rigorous segregation was not practised.

The layout of the house presented another problem for me as it resembled a Pashtun *qila*, consisting of a large courtyard with buildings on three sides. Adai's late husband, who had died many years ago, had built this house so that each of his three sons would have his own part of the house with enough rooms for his family. Kabir's brothers, Jamal and Nawab, had been married to close relatives chosen by Adai. The part intended for Kabir, the only disobedient child who had chosen his own wife and lived apart until now, had been left vacant and used for storage. At first we stayed in Jamal's part of the house with no privacy, although that was nothing in comparison to sharing a space with more than twenty women and children in one room when the Hazara fighters forced us to live together.

We were given three rooms with a bathroom but no kitchen or living room because Adai's husband had built one huge living room so that all family members could sit and eat together. There was also one big kitchen where the women of the family prepared the food together. After my ordeal in the hand of Hazaras I was ready to accept any situation. I was sincerely grateful for what we had. I would have been happier to have had something to my own taste. But we had been unable to bring anything and so all the furniture, carpets, bedcovers and even photo frames were chosen by Adai, including one larger than life photograph of Adai's husband that graced our bedroom. Frankly, I felt as if he might be looking at us when we were making love – a woman's mind must be at ease with her surroundings to feel romantic, to desire sex. Despite discovering the Russian woman's photo in Kabir's pocket and knowing that his late nights were not all related to work, I still desired him and had a very good appetite for sex. I knew that our privacy while living independently had helped me to become a healthy woman with regard to romance.

My father had told us that the mullahs were wrong to say that sex between husband and wife was just creating another human being to worship Allah. Marriage is for joy and there are *hadith* (quotations) of the Prophet Mohammad saying directly that he loved his wives in a romantic way and not just to create another human being. My father read us a verse from the *Quran* which said that husband and wife are like each other's clothes, meaning they can discover their bodies and their souls. The mullahs, though, tell us: "Before having intercourse you must recite 'in the name of Allah', otherwise *shaitan* will enter your wives at the same time and he would be the father of your child, not you. You must finish the act very quickly and soon after that wash your body." Unlike traditional fathers, my father was very open to talking about everything with his children. Maybe it was because of his love for my mother that he hoped his children would have the same joy in marriage – meaning love, romance and sex. Although Kabir was not as caring a husband as my father was to his wife, he was an expert in the field of love-making and because of that I also had a healthy appetite.

One thing I was completely sure about my husband was his love for his work. His profession had saved him from the Mujahideens' punishment and he continued to be a person in great demand, and so our life continued. The Panjshiri Mujahideen Group with all sincerity wanted him to remain safe because he was saving the lives of many of them. Despite Adai's insistence that he should not go to work, Kabir was adamant that he continue with his work in the hospital. I must admit that I admired him for his decision because the life of a person was very valuable and ordinary people also benefited from his treatment. What troubled me was his choice of adviser, his mother. I wished he would consult me about matters but I knew that, from the moment we started sharing a house with Adai, it would be her who would advise and decide. My two brothers-in-law had stopped going to work since the Mujahideen took over. Jamal was an agricultural engineer who worked for the Ministry of Agriculture and Nawab was a school teacher in a very unsafe part of Kabul where schools were not open anyway. Those like the employees of Ministry of Agriculture went to their work at their own risk, going through checkpoints, minefields, explosions, bandits. Kabir was a celebrity doctor, transported in an armoured vehicle with Mujahideen bodyguards. The first time he wanted to go to the hospital after arriving at Adai's, he had to go to the Panjshiri checkpoint nearest us and introduce himself. They sent a messenger to the hospital and the vehicle was sent to collect him. After that the Mujahideen came promptly to collect him from Adai's house and bring him back.

Lunch at Adai's was a community affair. Adai, Jamal with his wife Palwasha and three children, Nawab with his wife Torpikai and their two children, and myself with my two children – thirteen of us all together – the only person missing was Kabir because of his hospital job. I prepared lunch with the help of Palwasha and Torpikai.

"The food tastes better if you perform *namaz*, Deeba," Adai said, taking a piece of bread from the *dastarkhan*, looking at me from where she was sitting, the dominant part of the room.

"I perform my *namaz* – well some of them – when I have time," I said, avoiding eye contact.

"Only some of them?" She put the piece of bread back on the *dastarkhan*, looking at me with very serious eyes. "Do you know the morning *namaz* is the most important one and it is at that time when the doors of heaven are open and our prayers reach Allah."

"I like morning *namaz* but I don't want to disturb Kabir. As you know he sometimes comes home late from work and would not like to be disturbed so early in the morning."

"Well, you must get up gently and come here to pray with us. It is the duty of wives to pray for the health and fortune of their husbands."

Adai was uneducated and had her own interpretation of Islam – such as which *namaz* was the more important, when the doors of heaven would be open, and that husbands should go on sleeping but wives had to wake up and pray for their husbands. Could she even imagine that Kabir did not believe in God?

Living with my in-laws was like living in another Kabul. Apart from the different way I had lived at my parents', I was also living with a family who used the Pashto language, of which I had only a very basic knowledge. Misunderstandings were quite common. On many occasions I made Adai and my sisters-in-law angry when they asked me to do something in a certain way but I did it differently. I could imagine that the reason Adai was mistreating me was because of my sin of marrying her son. She herself had arranged it, not because she wanted it but because Kabir desired me. I took her son away from her. That is what she told me each time she got angry with me: You took my son away. But what I could not understand was the rivalry and dislike of me among my sisters-in-law. Palwasha and Torpikai were good friends but clearly did not like me. I had never felt so lonely as I did among that big group of relatives.

I had to join the rest of them in the living room where the women shared stories, joked, laughed, all in Pashto, not even looking at me. For them I did not exist. If I stayed in our part of the house, Adai would think I was avoiding the family. Adai wanted to show the world that she was pious and virtuous, an obedient follower of Islam. But how could she justify her behaviour towards me? Wasn't she aware that all my siblings and parents were away and I needed company too? When I was living in our apartment, I compensated for my loneliness by reading books, meeting friends or finding some other activities. But here, if I were to read a book, it would have been seen as deliberately avoiding others and taken as a sign of arrogance. Adai organised activities now and that was mainly to tell me: Today you must wash family clothes, or Today you must clean the house, or Today is clothes-ironing time.

One morning after breakfast I was in the living room, listening to the family speaking in Pashto when Adai looked at me and said in Farsi, "Aren't you aware that there is a pile of dirty clothes needing to be washed?"

"Yes, I saw them. I thought Palwasha and Torpikai and I could wash them together."

Both Palwasha and Torpikai looked at me with sharp eyes. Adai fixed her *chador* around her head, a sure sign that she intended a serious conversation. "What!" she exclaimed. "Are you organising the task force here?"

"Well, that is what we normally do, wash clothes, the three of us."

"Madam! I decide whether the three of you wash clothes together or you alone, and today I tell you to wash our clothes before it is too late. Palwasha and Torpikai have other things to do."

"What other things?" I dared to ask with a shaky voice.

"Get out and don't argue with me!" she shouted, pointing towards the living room door. "Someone has to cook for you. Someone has to do the other chores."

I left the room quickly, my whole body trembling. I looked at the mountain of dirty clothes I had to wash, all piled up in a spare room. I sat down and started weeping, hoping no one would see me.

In the evening I was lying down when Kabir came home. My whole body ached. I thought of telling him but decided not to because I did not want to create a rift. Kabir just asked whether I was ill but I told him I was just tired without explaining the cause. When Palwasha's son came to inform us that dinner was ready, I told Kabir that I could not eat. Exhaustion had made me lose my appetite. I was almost asleep when Kabir and the children came back.

"You should not sulk when my mother asks you do something," Kabir said and then walked off into the other room we used for sitting in.

His words surprised me and I immediately followed to talk with him. "I am not sulking, Kabir."

"Why have you decided not to eat?"

Obviously Adai had told him about my work and said that I was sulking. "I am extremely tired and as a doctor you know extreme tiredness stops appetite – at least that is how it affects me."

"Please don't say housework makes you extremely tired. Others do the same and they don't complain."

"I am not complaining, but you know I am pregnant and can easily get tired."

Receiving no support or sympathy from my husband, I went back to the bedroom to rest my aching body.

I could not finish washing all the dirty clothes of fourteen people in one day. The washing must be done, Adai had said, and I was assigned to wash the next day again. I had pain in my back, my wrists and my arms. The day was hot and although I was under the pear tree, I was sweating. To fight the heat, I kept drinking water, but the more I drank the more I became thirsty. Sweat bubbles formed on my forehead and dropped into the washing basin.

The next morning, I saw blood clots and some unusual discharge in my underwear when I went to the toilet. I had abdominal pains too. When I told Kabir, he suggested I see a gynaecologist. The lady gynaecologist was kind and considerate and extra attentive because Kabir was well-known in the medical circle.

After a thorough examination she said, "I am sorry for your loss."

I thought I had heard wrong, so I asked her to tell me what happened. When she explained I felt a python encircling my heart, pressing it so hard that it seemed about to explode. I felt that I was in my dark womb just as dead as my baby, sharing the same coffin. The gynaecologist suggested a dilation and evacuation procedure. I wanted to be dead too.

After the miscarriage I lost my appetite, my weight decreased and my sleep was disturbed. Most of the time I was in bed I was not sleeping but thinking about many things, mainly negatively. I felt that not only would I never become a member of Adai's family but even my children would be treated differently from the rest of her grandchildren. Maybe Adai was waiting for something to happen to me so she could find a new wife for Kabir from her own circle. I envisaged Kabir with a new wife after I was dead, my children treated badly by their stepmother. But if she was so determined not to accept me, why had she come to my parents' house to ask for me to marry her son? Sometimes Adai tried to show sympathy, or pretended to, saying that I was young and would have plenty of children. That only made me feel even worse. To me, what she said meant that the loss of a child was not important for a mother. Did she not know that a mother mourns the loss of a child even if she has had one thousand children? Love is not related to numbers. Mothers love all their children and the loss of one would never be filled by the birth of another.

Previously, Kabir had not found my company more interesting than that of his siblings and their wives but now I had nothing to say, he avoided me. All I wanted was to be left in a corner without being dragged into a conversation.

When I went to my drawers for clean clothes I found none, the laundry having been neglected for some time because of what it had done to me. None of my sisters-in-law came to ask if I had clothes for washing, but I would not have wanted them to touch my clothes in any case. To me they were contributors to my misfortune. Although they ignored me, they fed my children and washed their clothes when I did not join them. I was determined not to cook, which once I had loved, because I could not tolerate the smell. I no longer thought of how to pass a day pleasantly or profitably. I lost any desire for sex but Kabir remained demanding and, according to our culture and religion, I had to accept what he was doing to me and prayed that my coldness would make him leave me alone. However, since the arrival of the Mujahideen had put an end to his nightly drinking with friends, or possibly spending time with a woman, he demanded sex more frequently.

If a fly buzzed around, I watched without interest. If it landed on my cheek, I did not swat it. I had no desire to respond to anything whether outside or inside my body, apart from going to the toilet, which was beyond my control. My will to do anything was near gone.

One lunch time, Haseeb came and sat next to me, putting his head on my shoulder. Running my hand through his hair and noticing how slim he'd become I asked, "Why did you finish your lunch so quickly?"

"Didn't like it much," he replied.

"But why?"

"They cooked the aubergine in a different way – not the way you cook it with garlic and mix it with yogurt after you fry it."

The children pulled me out of that dark well. I felt guilty because of the loss of one child. I had forgotten my other children needed me too.

Since Kabir was the only one working and bringing in money, Adai was careful how she spent money on food, with only one type of vegetable for lunch in order to allow a variety at dinner when Kabir came home. Realising how ignorant I'd become, leaving my children at the mercy of relatives who did not care for them, I asked Kabir that evening when he came home, to buy some books for me because in that house there was not a single book. When he asked what type of book I wanted I snapped at him saying any book would do and also would he buy a cassette player with cassettes of the music I liked. I hated the music my in-laws listened to, which was all in the Pashto language.

My recovery was slow but the best medicine was looking into the shining eyes of my children and responding to their smiles. I had knitted clothes for the baby boy I had lost. Finding them one day and inhaling their smell made me think I was smelling my baby. To say goodbye I wrote a letter to him:

My boy Jamshid,

I call you Jamshid because that is the name I had chosen for you. This time I would not have allowed your father to choose a name. Jamshid, you are my king as it is the name of a great conqueror in Shanama and also the name of a brave man whom I met, a horse rider hero. I knew you were a boy without asking the gynaecologist about your sex. Boys kick hard and you were a hell of a kicker. I loved those kicks even when I felt some pain.

When I lost you, at first, I blamed myself for not being a good mother, not careful enough. But then I came to conclusion that it was the will of God, or perhaps your own will, not to be born in an unhappy country torn by wars and surrounded by relatives who hate instead of love. My sweet kicker, you certainly would have kicked the ball of happiness from one side to the other, shooting away unhappiness and hate before it reached you. That is a continuous struggle in which we can never be sure if we can ever succeed. Perhaps you did not want such a struggle. My own struggle continues without knowing whether I shall see an end to this war, or when my in-laws will accept me.

Now you are in heaven, a place of peace and love, and soon, one day, I will join you. As they say, you were in a hurry to travel the distance and reach your destination.

I will always love you and remember you.

Your mother.

The education of both my sisters-in-law was cut short by their families. In Pashtun families the place of a woman is at home serving her husband and children. In such an environment, showing any sign of interest in politics, or even discussing our ordinary lives, was a mistake. A woman's duty was to cook, clean the house, look after the children, be respectful towards first the Iron Adai, and then her husband. They were proud of what they were and looked down on me for being a career woman. But I was determined to show that an educated woman can be a good wife and useful for family and society, so I decided to help all the children of the family with their school work, including mine, who were not at schooling age yet.

Our area was safe and for that reason Palwasha and Torpikai could send their children to school, but I was horrified to find out what was in their textbooks. The Mujahideen had changed the curriculum, claiming the previous one was un-Islamic. In these new textbooks, every invention in chemistry books was the work of Allah, every discovery in biology was mentioned in the *Quran*, all science channelled through our religion. For example, Nobel invented dynamite after reading the *Quran*, or 2 Guns + 7 Guns = 9 Guns. If one must learn maths, it must be learned by thinking about Kalashnikovs.

Trying to bond with my sisters-in-law, I planned to cook *ashak*, a dish that requires women to participate and not be prepared by a single cook. Unfortunately, neither of them showed any interest. Then, when I served my *ashak* for lunch, Adai said, "You forgot the *daal chini*, a vital ingredient."

"I am sorry, but I could not find it in the kitchen," I admitted.

Typically she replied, "You could've asked someone to buy it for you."

If I told her that we did not have it in our kitchen, I was sure Adai would have said: "Can't you cook without *daal chini*?" So, from that day onward, I gave up attempting to bond, or cook something special. I cooked without interest, which was hard because I loved cooking.

One day Haseeb came to the kitchen where I was cooking, screaming that his cousin Farid, son of Palwasha and much older than him, had beaten him because he was playing with Farid's marbles without Farid's permission. I left my work and went to the courtyard to look for Farid. After finding him, I gently told him that Haseeb was much younger than him. He was his cousin and Farid should protect him, not beat him.

Not much time after I had spoken to Farid, Palwasha came into the kitchen screaming and shouting in both Farsi and Pashto, threatening me that if I ever interfered with what Farid was doing, she would beat me. I tried to explain, but she would not listen, shaking her body, moving her hands, walking up and down. Frankly, I was frightened and thought she would beat me – a woman much taller and stronger than me. She was from a rural area, trained to be physically strong. I am glad that she was swearing in Pashto, which I did not understand.

I had little chance of talking with Kabir. When I did it was mainly listening to him complaining about the rule of the Mujahideen, a monologue. Perhaps he thought I had nothing to say. And yet I did not dare to say that it was the communists who had brought us to this situation. Before the *coup d'état*, which he still referred to as the Saur revolution, Mujahideen had not existed. I was in a house surrounded by his family members in an area completely away from war, while he risked his life daily going to the hospital, moving through life-threatening areas.

Despite my difficulties and lack of respect in the family, I was satisfied that my children were safe and my husband continued to do work that he loved, or so I thought. He surprised me one evening saying that he would not be going to the hospital again.

"But why, what happened?" I asked.

"I can't take it anymore."

I sat next to him, holding his hands, looking into his eyes, searching for the answer.

"They think, I kill their injured ones." He rumpled his untidy hair, which needed cutting.

"What are you talking about? Please explain."

"Today I tried my best to save the life of a man who was the brother of a Mujahideen commander, but his injuries were so severe that he died despite all my efforts. In the corridor, the commander took his gun out and was about to shoot me because, according to him, I did not try hard enough. I was lucky that the head of the hospital was nearby and managed to make the commander put his gun away. This is not the first time. Once before an angry Mujahid slapped my face hard. I can't take this humiliation and risk. When the first incident happened, I thought it was a one-off."

In a way I was glad that he decided not to go to the hospital, even though I sincerely believed that all human beings needed medical attention, even the brutal Mujahideen who themselves never respected the lives of others.

Two days later Kabir was playing cards with his brothers, I was mending some clothes, my sisters-in-law and Adai busy with gossip, when an army Jeep entered our courtyard.

"Can I talk with Dr Kabir?" a man shouted.

I was really worried, thinking the relatives of the dead man had come to punish Kabir, but Kabir recognised the voice. "No panic, it is the head of the hospital," he said, and then asked all the women to leave the living room so the head of hospital and his companions could sit there.

I prepared some tea to be hospitable but also to make those Mujahideen be kind to my husband. Their meeting continued for a long time and we all counted the seconds to find out what it was about. When those men left we all rushed to the living room.

"Why they were here?" Adai asked first

"The head of the hospital requested that I must go back to work."

"Did you agree?" Adai thought it was her right to ask questions first.

"Yes, but I told them I need some time to have a break."

"You don't need to go there if they mistreat you," Adai said.

"Do you think they will leave me alone?"

Although Kabir spent most of his time in the company of his brothers and Adai, I was delighted to see him around making small talk, and praying in my heart that the Mujahideen would leave him alone. He now decided not to work anymore and just wanted to find peace in a country devastated by war. I knew it would not be possible to disappear anywhere within our country because he would soon be identified and punished for what the communist government had done to our people. Days passed very quickly and the day that he would have to go back to work was approaching when he came in from the family living room as I was putting the children to bed.

"I talked to my mother and brothers about my decision," he said and sat on the bed.

I sat next to him, curious to know what they had been talking about. They always talked for a long time in Pashto after I left the living room to put the children to sleep.

"What decision, Kabir?"

"To leave."

"What did you say?"

"To leave Kabul. These idiots will never leave me alone and I am sure, one day, they will either kill me or I will be killed on the way to hospital."

"But where?" I asked. In my heart I was delighted that finally he thought about his own safety. Would it be possible that only he and our children and I would leave without his family?

"It has to be out of Afghanistan."

"We all leave?"

"No, I asked my mother and brothers to come but my mother loves this house and she knows the moment she leaves it empty, the Mujahideen will claim it."

How wonderful, I thought. "But still you have not answered me. Where?"

"There is only one place," he said. "Pakistan."

"That is not bad. Perhaps we will find my family and they will help us settle there."

"Don't raise your hopes. Pakistan is a big country, not a village."

"I think it is a good decision. Your safety is important."

"Yes, that is not bad," he agreed. "Not bad at all. Hurry up, prepare yourself. We will be leaving in four days, before the head of the hospital drags me back. It is an escape."

We had few belongings, so the task of getting ready was easy. Apparently, Adai knew a person from Laghman District, where she'd come from, who helped people escape from Afghanistan to Pakistan for a considerable amount of money. Such a person had to be reliable, not just anyone from the street claiming they could do it. We had heard stories of families being handed over to bandits in exchange for money by such persons. But I wished my husband had talked to me first before making such life-changing decisions, or at least included me in his conversation with his family. Certainly, Adai was delighted, I thought, in making decisions about my life and keeping me away.

Chapter 14

Going to Pakistan

Of all the seasons, I like autumn the most. The massive pear tree at the centre of the courtyard was rich with leaves coloured green and yellow and a deep warm brown. Haseeb was climbing alone in the tree, away from his cousins. I felt his loneliness among the relatives. I felt my own isolation. In my mind I made a list:

1. *This courtyard is bigger than many gardens. Instead of a single, lonely pear tree there could have been a garden with a lawn and roses, carnations, geraniums – to name just a few.*
2. *Adai's family could have been my family if they did not push me away. Were they blind not being able to see I was the only person from my family left in the country? And even if they did not like me at least they could have shown some mercy. Instead they made my life much harder. Was is better to stay in an area where war was going on and accept that one day I would be killed by a bomb or a rocket, or stay here slowly dying because of harsh treatment by Adai's family? Even Kabir, my own husband, was becoming cruel to me.*
3. *This country could have been my paradise. As the proverb says: Every homeland is Kashmir for its natives – the paradise on earth – but instead the Soviet Union invaded and it became Hell.*
4. *I could have become a well-recognised journalist, winning awards, appearing on television, even becoming a minister as there were equal opportunities for women among men in Afghanistan. Instead, like all women, I became a commodity, a piece of furniture, after the Mujahideen took over.*

Several days before the date of our departure, Kabir told me to prepare myself for our journey. Immediately I thought of our luggage and belongings. Kabir said that our journey would be through steep mountains where roads did not exist. It would be impossible to take anything with us – not suitcases nor even a small bag.

Now, when the day of our departure had come, everyone was gathered in that courtyard. A cool breeze susurrated through the leaves on the branches and on the ground, trying to tell me something. Nature and the surroundings spoke to me at that moment, but not my relatives. Even when they did say something to me, I could not understand or did not pay attention. The time for listening and understanding had passed. I felt sad that there was so much bitterness in me. We gathered to say our goodbyes. I heard their cries, their wailing, each person holding part of Kabir's body, kissing his face, his neck, his hands. But I cannot see them clearly, as they cannot see me and have not seen me since my arrival. Instead I see my thoughts. What happened to us here? What will happen when we reach Pakistan and are living among strangers? But I knew one thing – it would be better than living with Adai's family. My children, their father and all the rest of the family were crying. The only person who did not cry was me. I could not fake it. I was honest to my heart and my heart was saying: I am indifferent and perhaps even happy. The war and the treatment I received in Adai's house prepared me to accept a life in exile.

Apart from the family, there was a stout man in a grey *kamis, shalwar* and a grey waistcoat. His white turban was wound tightly around his head. His dress showed that he was from Pakistan, at least until he spoke. This man was called Mullah Mohammad. I wondered how it could be possible that a religious man, a mullah of a mosque, who would have a comfortable life conducting prayers in the mosque, would ever decide to become a guide – a difficult and tiring job, even though guides earned good money. But soon I discovered that he was not a mullah at all, having been given his name by a religious father. Getting to Pakistan was difficult and a reliable guide a necessity. Guides made good money as, by then, Afghanistan had 5 million refugees. Mullah lived in the same village that Adai had come from and could be totally trusted. He travelled frequently to Pakistan accompanying people going into exile. That was reassuring because many people who tried to leave Afghanistan guided by fake guides disappeared. Those guides were either gangsters or, during the communist period, police informants. They either robbed families or handed them to the government in exchange for a reward. He stood in a corner patiently watching the family while we said goodbye. His mannerism showed that he had carried out such an operation a thousand times. It gave me the feeling of being in safe hands.

Our plan had been to leave at six o'clock in the morning, but we finally stepped out of the house about an hour later. No matter how hard Kabir had tried to get away, Adai would not let him go without reminding him that there was a long, dangerous road ahead of us and continually issuing instructions, things she'd been saying time and again ever since Kabir had announced we were leaving.

Finally, though, we were outside where a dark green Russian Army Jeep with a driver wearing a turban was waiting for us. The scene was almost mad enough to make me laugh! Here was the pride of Russia driven by a man who I was sure could not read and write. The Russian designer had not thought his car would be used this way. It was built for a Russian Army officer, but how it ended up in the hands of this turbaned man was beyond my understanding – although, as a journalist, I would have liked to have investigated further.

Mullah Mohammad sat next to the driver and we all squeezed into the back seat. Rockets and bombs had created ditches and potholes in the streets of Kabul, which made the use of the Jeep perfect, although whenever the car went over a pothole it either threw us from one side to the other or made us hit our heads against the roof. The wild driving made the children excited, but I knew both Kabir and I would develop bad headaches. From the window I could see that the streets were almost deserted after we passed Taimani, and it was rare to see any house undamaged. Some were razed to the ground. There were bullet marks everywhere and when we reached the Russian Silo, on a street called Silo, I saw big holes created by guns and rockets in that massive yellow building. The Russian Silo had produced healthy brown bread for thousands of people daily before the Mujahideen came but was now half destroyed. I knew that building very well because I had interviewed its workers and written an article about it. The intensity of fighting in this area had been so high that the streetlights and poles holding cables for the electric buses were either bent or looked beheaded by bullets. A country destroyed by its own people.

I was watching and looking, feeling sorry for my country and its people, when our car stopped at a checkpoint. Remembering what happened to us before in such a place, I grabbed Kabir's arm and looked at his face through the mesh screen of my burka. His face was pale. A Panjshiri man with a Kalashnikov slung on his shoulder approached the driver, but it was Mullah Mohammad who responded.

"Salaam brother. I am a member of Jamiat-e Islami Group and travelling with my family."

"Jamiat?" the man with Kalashnikov asked.

"Yes, and here is my card."

Mullah Mohammad dug his hand into the inside pocket of his grey waistcoat and took out a card. The man with the weapon looked at the card, looked at all the passengers and the driver, and then told Mullah Mohammad to carry on.

"You are a Pashtun. How come you have a card from Jamiat-e Islami?" Kabir asked.

"Do I look like a Pashtun?"

We both looked at Mullah Mohammad as he turned his face towards us. The man could be Pashtun, Tajik, Uzbek or Noorestani. He had a universal face.

"Okay, you look like a Tajik too, but how can you get a card from Jamiat? They must have asked you to produce documents that you are a Tajik."

"I have my connections, Doctor Sahib. This war is more about money than Allah, as you know."

"But it is not just the Jamiat all the way to Pakistan," I said.

"I know. I know and I am a member of all of them."

"How many?" Kabir asked.

"Oh, just ten."

"Ten?"

"Yes and my pockets are full of cards. I have all of them."

Kabir looked at the mesh in my burka searching for my eyes behind it, his eyes full of surprise. I was looking at him, just as puzzled.

"Surely you make a mistake sometimes and you show a card of a rival to a group?" said Kabir.

"There is no room for mistakes in this business. I know exactly where the checkpoints are and to which group they belong. The cards themselves call, 'Take me out, I belong to this group.' I also know which corner of my pocket is a home to which card."

"You have become an expert, Mullah Mohammad."

"You know they say survival of the fittest? I say survival of the streetwise."

"You are amazing," said Kabir.

"Did Adai tell you about my background?"

"No she didn't."

"Perhaps she didn't because she did not want to make you worry," said Mullah Mohammed.

"I don't understand," Kabir said, his face a picture of doubt.

"Don't worry, you can still trust me and your mother has not made a mistake, even though I have some blood on my hands."

Now this was a bombshell. How could Adai leave us in the hands of a murderer?

Mullah Mohammad took a cigarette packet out of his pocket and offered one to his driver and then one to Kabir. To my surprise Kabir, a non-smoker, took one. Was it to get closer to Mullah Mohammad or was he nervous and scared? Mullah Mohammad looked around through the windscreen and side windows shaking his head in disapproval.

"Such a beautiful country but full of mad people. You know, my father was a farmer working on land belonging to your father, Doctor Sahib. That is how Adai knows us. We had almost nothing but we worked with honesty, even after your father died. When the communists took over, land was redistributed, but my father refused to take your land. Such was his loyalty.

"When I reached the age of 22," he continued, "I became a conscript soldier. The communist government made us murderers, telling us to shoot whoever was against the government. So we were forced to go to the villages and shoot farmers – my own people.

"Disillusioned with the communists, I left the army and joined the Mujahideen. I thought now I was fighting for the liberation of my country but, once again, being with the Mujahideen was mainly killing innocent people, besides looting and raping, so I left the Mujahideen too.

"Some years ago, when the communists were still in power, I decided to become a guide or, in other words, a people-smuggler. Believe me, there is much more honesty in this business than being a communist soldier or a Mujahid. At least in this line of work I am not pretending to change the world or fight in the name of Allah. The business is hard but it pays well. I managed to buy this car and some land of my own. To help others, I employed my cousin here, Deen Mohammad, to become my driver. We are both married to two sisters and you know what the proverb says: 'When a brother-in-law meets his brother-in-law, it is like a hungry dog sees a piece of meat.'" They both laughed aloud and made us laugh too.

"No really, we get on well and we are like brothers. No rivalry as it is between brothers-in-law."

After the checkpoint, signs of war were no longer visible, but I could hear the sounds of bullets and rockets being fired. What would happen if a rocket just exploded in front of the car, or our car was hit by bullets? I had heard that those Mujahideen who occupied the hills practised target-shooting at anything moving on the ground. Mullah Mohammad assured us that the roads he took would be safe and our car would not be targeted, which I found an empty promise. Those guns were in the hands of crazy, wild people, and they wanted to shoot anything. No one can be sure about the situation in Afghanistan, even a man like Mullah Mohammad, who probably travelled the country from east to west and from north to south. A place that might seem safe one moment could suddenly become as dangerous as the hottest corner of the Second World War.

The next checkpoint belonged to the Golbudin Hikmatyar Group, the most notorious Islamic party, which killed innocent people claiming that if the man was innocent he would go to heaven anyway and that they had merely speeded up his entry. Its members were particularly against educated people and they could easily find out if someone educated was among the others. The beard that Kabir had sported since the arrival of the Mujahideen and the wearing of dirty clothes helped him to blend in and acted as a camouflage to hide his identity. He had also learned not to carry any letter, any card, or anything written in his pockets. But I knew he was trembling with fear.

"Osman Khan, *stelay mashay*, I hope you are not tired," Mullah Mohammad shouted in Pashto, the language of the group. The Golbudin Group comprised mainly Pashtun people who, apart from fighting other groups, also thought that it was their mission to kill other ethnic groups, mainly Tajiks, to which I belonged – but fortunately they never asked women any questions. For them women did not exist. Osman Khan talked with Mullah Mohammad and asked Kabir some questions in Pashto, which was Kabir's mother tongue, and then let us go. But I knew that our temporary happiness on leaving that place behind was not going to last forever during this long journey. There were murderers at every checkpoint, killing innocent people in the name of Allah. Crossing only two did not mean the end of danger.

The road we'd taken would lead us to Jalalabad, the border town of Afghanistan, beyond which was the Peshawar Province of Pakistan, where millions of Afghan refugees lived since the Russians invaded our country. As we reached Surobi, we heard the sound of firing and explosions nearby. Mullah Mohammad informed us that the fight was between Hezb-e Islami and Harakat-e Islami. These two groups were both predominantly Pashtun and both were fighting in the name of Allah. A little further on, the road was blocked and laden lorries going to Pakistan had stopped, their drivers lying on the road next to their vehicles as if nothing was happening, waiting for the road to open again. Certainly, they'd seen scenes like this many times and had become accustomed to them.

"Only two days ago I was here and nothing was happening," Mullah Mohammad said.

"What are we going to do?" Kabir asked.

"Let me think," Mullah Mohammad scrutinised his surroundings. After a while he got out of the car and we saw him chatting with the other drivers and passengers.

"We have to make a U-turn," Mullah Mohammad said when he came back.

"What?" Kabir asked, close to having a heart attack. "Surely you don't mean that we have to go back to Kabul."

"Oh no, we'll take a diversion and drive off-road."

"Off-road?"

"I've done it before."

We drove back towards Kabul for about 20km, until we reached a village called Maidan where Deen Mohammad turned right, taking a dirt road. Mullah Mohammad told us that this road had been made by the smugglers and only experienced drivers like Deen Mohammad managed to drive on it. We were taking our lives in our hands on a track just wide enough for the two tyres of the car with, on our left, a sheer drop of 100m and on our right a continuous cliff into which this narrow ledge had been hewn. One small mistake and we would all be dead. All I could do was close my eyes. At that moment a thought came to my mind – how many people leaving Kabul to find refuge in Pakistan had instead lost their lives on such a road or been killed by the Mujahideen and other bandits?

I don't know for how long I kept my eyes closed but I heard Kabir say, "Thank God it is over." The mountain on the right was still there but the deep drop was not. We were driving on a plateau. Kabir suggested I remove my burka because there was no sign of any Mujahideen group. I felt so happy that for once my husband was considerate.

The rocky surface of the plateau created a perfect surface for driving and through the left-hand window I saw a magnificent sunset. There was nothing in that lonely and yet peaceful landscape making any noise, apart from this single car moving slowly. I imagined camping there, away from everything, a vast area just for ourselves. Then, when the car crossed a small stream, Mullah Mohammad said, "Doctor Sahib, the evening prayer is the most important prayer and this is a perfect place for it." I remembered Adai saying, "The morning prayer is the most important prayer." These people have made their own rules about Islam, I thought. Any prayer is important.

We all got down. Kabir joined the men for ablutions and I prayed that he could remember how Adai had taught him. I knew his *namaz* would be only to make Mullah Mohammad happy, but I hoped that finally in his heart he had accepted Allah, because submitting to His kingdom would bring peace. I wished I could join in the ablutions and *namaz*, but I could not show my body to men. The children on the other hand were happy to get out, drinking water upstream, away from the men, running after one another. After *namaz*, Mullah Mohammad suggested we spend the night there because driving on a non-existent road in the dark was dangerous. They took their shawls and left the car for us to sleep. They spread their shawls on the ground, made their turbans their pillows and went to sleep. We put the children on the front seats and tried to make ourselves comfortable on the back seat to get some sleep.

The children slept well but Kabir and I slept very little, partly because of the discomfort but also because of worries such as what would happen if a group of Mujahideen or bandits appeared in that place far away from any civilisation? And yet we were both surprised to see Mullah Mohammad and his cousin in deep sleep. Had the war trained them not to worry about anything?

While the men were asleep, I had the opportunity to make my ablutions and then, ready for prayers, I spread my shawl on the ground, faced east from where the sun would kiss the earth with its rays, and stood alone.

Connecting with Allah in that place of solitude away from war I felt that Allah spoke to me in the language that Hafiz, our great poet, spoke:

> *Even after all this time*
> *The sun never says to the earth,*
> *"You owe Me."*
> *Look what happens with*
> *A love like that,*
> *It lights the Whole Sky.*
> *Allah has spoken to me. Almighty was my sun, my rescuer from darkness.*

Just before dawn the two Mohammed men performed morning *namaz*. They had a built-in alarm clock. Before they had left their rock-hard bed, we had heard their loud snoring in that very quiet place.

The sun, the powerful king of the day, was making its slow progress in the blue circle of sky, illuminating with its liquid light the mountain's brow, revealing that we were in an impressive and beautiful place on that rocky plateau. It was too high for grass to grow, there was very little earth, and the place was littered with boulders, but the whole plateau was covered with a thick carpet of butterfly bush. There were countless thousands of them on thick green stems.

After morning *namaz*, Mullah Mohammad and his cousin collected some *butta* to be used as fuel and in no time had lit a fire and put a big fire-blackened kettle upon it. Mullah Mohammad was well equipped for all occasions and, thanks to Adai filling bags and boxes, I had enough food for a long journey. But according to Mullah Mohammad, it would not take more than two days to reach Peshawar. With some difficulty I managed to wake the children and the breakfast we had on that plateau tasted as if it was food from heaven because of the magnificent view and the peace.

We set off again. The car circled, crossed streams, climbed hills and jumped over ditches until finally we reached the road in Tagab District. My burka was on but by then I was used to the garment and through the mesh I could see gardens full of pomegranates as we drove. Afghanistan is famous for the best fruits in the world and during peace time, especially when President Daud was in power, Afghanistan exported large quantities of fresh and dry fruits to Central and South Asian countries. The president even intended to export our fruit all the way to Europe. Such thoughts were interrupted as we approached another checkpoint.

"Oh! There is a new group in charge of this place," Mullah Mohammad said.

"You don't know them?" Kabir asked.

"Not yet, but I will," he replied.

His coolness made me smile under my burka but I could see the sign of worry on Kabir's face. A group of people armed with Kalashnikovs manned the checkpoint. One of them, a man with dirty, dark brown clothes, dusty long hair, and a beard, approached us.

Mullah Mohammad greeted him. "*Salaam alikum.*"

"*Chirta zai,*" replied the man in Pashto. "Where are you going?"

"We are going to Jalalabad, brother," said Mullah Mohammad.

"Who are they?"

"This is my cousin." Mullah Mohammad pointed to the driver. "And at the back are my sister with my brother-in-law and their children."

"You all get out!"

"But why? We must continue. We are attending a relative's funeral."

"Out I said," the man shouted.

I held Kabir's hand tightly, knowing that even experts like Mullah Mohammad cannot guarantee a safe passage for us. At that moment, I remembered our money I'd hidden in my underwear. Usually they only searched men, but of course for some savages there was no respect, no difference, and the man with that beard and hair looked like one. We had no choice but to get out.

The man who resembled someone who'd escaped from a lunatic asylum put all his ten fingers on his scalp, scratched and then between his fingers he showed us the lice that he caught. I nearly vomited.

"Here it is," the man said, taking the lice out of his finger nails one by one. "Open your palms, all of you. I give you one each and you must look after it until I finish your paperwork to give you permission."

He laughed like a mad man and put one louse on each of the palms of Mullah Mohammad, Deen Mohammad and Kabir. Thank God he did not ask me or the children. As soon as he turned his back, the three men threw the lice away. We were standing there watching the rest of the group and other people like us who wanted to cross the checkpoint but were held up as well. They were watching us, not knowing what to do. I was the only woman among men and did not feel comfortable. After a while the man appeared from a direction that none of us knew and this time his hair was even more dusty.

"You know the best way to clean is to roll in dirt." He laughed and I saw his brown teeth affected by snuff, some missing. "The city people wash but Allah said: I created you from dust. Dust is also good for my lice. Now they are happy. Talking about my lice, please return them, I missed them."

"What?" Mullah Mohammad asked in disbelief.

"What do you mean, what?" The mad man rushed towards Mullah Mohammad, lowered his body, focusing on Mullah Mohammad's chin. "I told you to keep it, didn't I?"

"You expected us to keep the lice?" Mullah Mohammad asked. I thought the mad man would pick up a Kalashnikov and kill us all. A mad man confronting another man.

"For me those lice are my treasures. You lost three and each cost you one thousand dollars."

"We don't have three thousand dollars."

"Sarfaraz Khan!" shouted the man with dusty hair. "Come out. The man with the Jeep says he doesn't have the money."

A tall and well-built man in a clean white *piraan wa tonbaan* appeared from the mud hut pushing the ends of his bushy moustache upward with the palms of both hands. He approached us. "Well, either you pay or you leave the car with us."

Mullah Mohammad looked at his cousin whispering something to him and then took some steps forward towards Sarfaraz Khan shouting. "Sarfaraz Khan, son of Gulbaz Khan. I joined the Mujahideen because of you and left them because of you, but never did I think in my life that I would see you stoop so low."

Sarfaraz took a step back, his eyes bulging, his lips trembling with anger, searching for words. "Who are you and how dare you talk to me like that?"

"Sarfaraz Khan, I was in the Communist Army and even among soldiers and officers your fame was well-known. We knew how you fought against the Russians, making them run for their lives. Your photos as the bravest commander appeared everywhere among the Mujahideen and I carried one too. You influenced me to leave the army and join the Mujahideen, hoping to meet you. But when the Russians left and the Mujahideen started fighting each other, I left *jihad*. Now you can kill us all if you want, but we have no money to give you."

Sarfaraz Khan looked at us one by one, stunned by what he heard, not knowing what to do. He turned his back and walked towards his hut.

The mad man followed him. Some minutes later the mad man came and told us, "You are the only people who have not paid for missing lice."

We took our seats in the Jeep and Deen Mohammad drove so fast that when I looked through the rear window I could not see the crowd because of the clouds of dust created by the car.

"That was absolute madness what you did there, Mullah Mohammad," Kabir protested.

"No, it was well-calculated," Mullah Mohammad said and reached for his packet of cigarettes, offering one to the driver and one to Kabir. We encountered some more checkpoints but none of them as dreadful as Tagab with a lice man guarding it.

Just before the border crossing in Jalalabad, Mullah Mohammad asked the driver to stop in his usual place, a restaurant in which he treated his passengers to tea. Framed verses from the *Quran* and photos of the Mujahideen hung on the walls. There was a place for the family where women who were with their husbands and children could sit away from the rest without wearing the burka, drinking or eating. We all enjoyed eating the *kabab* but especially the children, who had only eaten the cold food that my sisters-in-law had prepared for them. The place was called Hadda, which I had previously visited with my family. Some 23,000 Greco-Buddhist sculptures, both clay and plaster, were excavated in Hadda between the 1930s and the 1970s. Buddhists had lived in Hadda in the first century and when the discoveries were made our king, Mohammad Zahir Shah, asked the archaeologists to make it into a living museum. There I had seen magnificent statues of Buddha attached to the walls, as they had been in the first century. I had planned to write an article about it, to make the nation aware of its significance, but now all of that was gone. The Mujahideen had looted everything and sold it for pennies in Pakistan, selling their history and their identity.

Mullah Mohammad assured us that the border town was safe and he and Deen Mohammad left us in a private room to be together while they sat with others in the main part of restaurant. That gave me a chance to take the money I had hidden out of my underwear and give it to Kabir. After we had eaten and were ready to leave, I asked Kabir to bring Mullah Mohammad and his cousin to the private room so that we could thank them.

"I must say I was a bit nervous about this mission," Mullah Mohammad admitted as he sat with us. "But I have the ability to cover my nervousness."

"But why?" Kabir asked.

"You know, Doctor Sahib, because of your background," Mullah Mohammad said with a smile. "You don't know who you will encounter on this road. You have treated many people. So, I am glad it is over."

"Thank you," Kabir said.

"This country is already divided among so many different groups," Mullah Mohammad responded. "But now there is another one emerging calling themselves Taliban. They are students of Madrasas located in Pakistan. But I hope when you cross the border you will find a new life, a peaceful one."

At the border I saw that the men guarding our side wore tattered clothes, had long beards, and carried Kalashnikovs. They looked more like criminals than soldiers. That reminded me how different it was from the elegant and disciplined Afghan soldiers manning our side when we had been there years ago with Father. As we were about to cross the border a man with a long beard and a Kalashnikov slung on his shoulder demanded, "Show me your passports."

Kabir was shocked but Mullah Mohammad took some money from his pocket and put it in the hand of the man. "These are their passports," he said.

The bearded man smiled, showing his brown teeth, "*Safar ba khair*, have a safe journey," he said as he let us pass.

It was late afternoon when we sat next to each other in a Pakistani bus heading towards the city of Peshawar. In my mind were images of Mullah Mohammad, the coolest smuggler.

Chapter 15

Searching for Shah Mahmud: Part 1

We arrived in Peshawar when it was dark. My watch showed it was just after 9 p.m. I had woken up when other passengers started moving around and street-sellers approached the bus trying to sell drinks or snacks. Kabir, Haseeb and Lida were still asleep, exhausted.

I shook Kabir, who was on my right. "Wake up, we've arrived."

"We are in Peshawar?" Kabir asked doubtfully. We were unfamiliar with the distance between the border and the city of Peshawar and the journey had taken a very long time because the roads were in poor condition. Along the way, the bus stopped in many places and each time we hoped it would be our destination.

As soon as Kabir's feet touched the ground, a man grabbed his arm and said in Pashto, "Rickshaw?"

"Yes," he agreed, "we want a rickshaw."

"Very good, come with me." He walked ahead of us, turning from time to time towards us to make sure other drivers did not approach his passengers. I held Haseeb's hand as we walked behind, and Kabir carried Lida, who was still half asleep.

"But wait," Kabir shouted. "We want to go to a cheap hotel."

"I know, I know, come."

"First, tell me how much for the ride," insisted Kabir.

"Oh, come you pay what you like."

Even at that time of night the bus terminus was crowded with travellers, street-sellers, rickshaw-drivers, porters, drivers, conductors, their ceaseless activity creating a deafening noise that filled the terminus.

When we reached the small rickshaw we realised it could just take two passengers in the back and only space for the driver in the front, who looked like a head atop a wooden stick.

"But how can you carry three of us?" I protested, using my school-learned Pashto, trying to convey the sense of what I wanted to say. He understood.

"You speak Farsi?" he asked in my language, surprising me.

"Are you Afghan?"

"Yes, sister. Most of the people who work in this terminus are Afghans, those are the jobs available for refugees." His Farsi had an accent, and I guessed he was a Pashto-speaker from south of my country.

"Tell me how we are all going to get into your rickshaw," Kabir said.

"Oh, brother, don't worry. I have carried many people in my rickshaw."

His solution was to sit Haseeb on my lap with his bottom half sticking out of the rickshaw and his head inside, touching mine. Kabir sat on the other side pressed against the door, which also served as a window, with Lida on his lap. I could only see the city with some difficulty through the door, but Kabir had a better view. From the moment I sat on the bus at the border crossing, I took my burka off and was wearing only a scarf on my head. The tiredness of the journey and late-night arrival made me forget it, and I left the burka on the bus. This was an item of clothing I was not used to and could easily forget.

Unable to see much, I became more aware of the tuk-tuk sound our vehicle made and the potent smell coming from the exhausts of all the other rickshaws rushing alongside or overtaking us. The stink poisoned my nostrils, the fumes choked us, and we all started coughing. Until that evening none of us had seen a rickshaw, let alone travelled in one. Afghanistan was free from them and their pollution.

The driver slowed down and I saw many pedestrians, cars and lorries moving about. We had reached a busy area.

"This is a good and cheap hotel, brother," the rickshaw-driver said after stopping. With difficulty, Kabir got out first with Lida, then Haseeb, and I was last.

"This is the old town. Hotels are good and cheap," the driver said.

I quickly noticed a strong smell of sewage coming from a roadside ditch.

"One hundred rupees, brother," he demanded, forgetting that he had said we could pay him whatever we wanted. "I don't charge people from my country unfairly."

Not knowing the proper price, Kabir paid him only to discover later from another Afghan who was working in the hotel that he had charged him four-times the usual rate. These events taught us that we could not trust anyone as easily as we had, and especially other refugees from my country.

Kabir and I shared a single bed and I listened to the sound of footsteps of the guests coming and going all night long. Shouting continued even past midnight: 'Bring one chai, two chai, three chai; to the first floor, the second floor, the third floor.' Loud music mixed with coughing, snuff-spitting, swearing filled the gaps when the calling for tea stopped. Kabir was fast asleep with his face towards the blue-painted wall. The journey had exhausted him and it was his first night of sleeping soundly. The children were also in a deep sleep on the other single bed next to the window, which opened onto a narrow balcony. The rooms in this three-storey hotel measured 3½m by 2m, had two single beds, each less than 2m long, and with only just enough space between them to walk sideways to reach the entrance. Eventually, I too was overcome by tiredness.

Rays of sun lancing through the un-curtained single window lit up the room and blinded me when I opened my eyes. My first morning in Peshawar. I sat up, next to a sleeping Kabir, and noticed that each time a guest passed our window, he took a long hard look to see who was inside.

My bladder was about to burst, but I didn't dare to leave the room in case someone stole what little we had. I also didn't know if there was a male and female toilet. Not able to hold the call of nature any longer, I finally woke Kabir and walked down the long corridor in search of a toilet. Eventually I found it, not because I saw a sign but because of the smell. Having no other option, I pushed the wooden door to get inside. It didn't open. I pushed hard again and heard someone's fake coughing. The occupant was in no hurry and I was about to shame myself when the door opened and a dark-skinned man with a moustache like shiny black needles walked out. He looked me in the eyes and spat his *naswar*, creating what looked like a map of a country in chicken shit on the door. I had no time to study it and I rushed in. Sunlight coming through a small window enabled me to see the steam coming from fresh excrement heaped on top of old excrement in a Turkish-style toilet. I urinated on them, trying to distract myself by looking at the wall covered by writing and drawings. "Pussy, pussy, pussy." Next to that a half-apple-shaped figure targeted by two massive penises from the right and left. More graphics, of half-apples, different sized penises and circles divided by a line, assaulted my eyes. The erotica and smell of faeces almost overwhelmed me.

Later, the four of us sat on our beds, satisfied that we'd reached a safe country without major incident, knowing that many people escaping from Afghanistan lost their lives at the hands of the Russians or the Mujahideen. Over-sweet *chai* was our first treat of the day. We admired the delicious mixture of tea, milk and cardamom. In comparison, our tea at home was simple – just a tea made with boiled water. From that first moment of drinking *chai*, I knew I was going to become addicted to it.

"God, what a place," Kabir said.

"But you slept well," I replied with half a smile.

"I was talking about other things," Kabir, winked.

"You mean the toilet?"

"Had no choice, had to take the children there."

"Let's skip the details," I said with a gentle voice to avoid describing the ugly things he'd seen that morning, even in code language which the children would not know. Besides, we were lucky to be staying there while we looked for Shah Mahmud.

The man who brought us the *chai* came back to collect the teacups.

"Where are we?" Kabir asked, handing him his cup.

"What do you mean?"

"What is the name of this place?"

"It is Qisakhani Bazaar."

"How magnificent. Storytellers' Bazaar," Kabir said, and we both laughed. "A writer spending her first night in the storytelling bazaar of a foreign country," he added.

"Let's go out and meet the storytellers," I suggested with excitement.

Kabir carried Lida and I held Haseeb's hand as we walked in the street. What we discovered in that overcrowded bazaar was anything but storytellers, yet every scene told its own story. Maybe that is what it was, I thought. You saw the stories instead of hearing them. Waves of people moved aimlessly. In a big open pot, carcasses of chickens floated in a soup made yellow by turmeric. A customer approached the seller and, after a brief conversation, the seller took a transparent plastic bag and filled it with the soup.

"How is he going to carry that bag full of soup in this busy place without bursting the bag?" I asked.

"That would be funny," replied Kabir. "A stream of soup flowing on the street, but I am sure he has done it before."

The street smells were a mixture of food – kebabs fanned on charcoal grills – and the stench coming from the road drains, blocked by people dumping rubbish in them. Even a dead dog. Sellers of fabric, shoes, cheap jewellery and toys were shouting for customers, competing with men who fanned kebabs inviting the hungry to come and eat. It was only 11 a.m., but restaurants expected their customers.

"Watch out!" Kabir screamed when a lorry almost hit me. Cars and lorries pushed their way through without paying any attention to the safety of pedestrians. The only warning the lorries gave was to honk loudly with their deafening air horns, making walkers jump for their lives. Street-sellers blocked the whole of the pedestrians' pavement, so we had no choice but to walk, like others, in the road.

"Make sure you don't get hurt and don't get lost," Kabir raised his voice to both Haseeb and me, ensuring we could hear him.

Over the noises of the bazaar, of people shouting, laughing, arguing, negotiating, came the sound of music, a sort of wild drumming. I noticed that some people pointed up at the balconies above the shops and shouted. I stopped and looked. On one of the balconies several women wearing bright green, red and yellow saris looked down at the crowds, waving their hands, shouting and laughing.

"What are you looking at?" Kabir asked, turning back and pulling on my arm.

"Look at those women."

The women, not veiled, were wearing dramatic makeup and dancing to the loud music, waving their hair and beckoning to people like us who had stopped to look at them.

"How odd," Kabir observed, tugging at my arm and examining the crowds around us, "I didn't know women were so liberal here."

"That's incredible!" I said. "Women on the street are completely covered in big *chador* and they're, well... they must be different."

"What is going on?"

"I think they maybe *hijras*," I said.

"Why are they called *hijra*?" Kabir asked still staring at the women on the balconies. "Are they migrants? I can't believe women like that are on a pilgrimage!"

"Not *Hijrah*, but *hijra*, which I think means they belong to a community of eunuchs," I explained, still watching the women.

"Eunuchs?" Kabir scoffed, as if he doubted my sanity.

"I read somewhere about them." I wasn't about to admit that I had no more understanding than he, but felt I ought to explain what little I did know. "In India they have a sort of special status – they aren't really men or women."

Kabir continued to watch the women. "But why they are doing that?"

Then I realised that it was we who were drawing attention, and not simply because of our fascination with the *hijras* but because of me. We had been observing the old city and its people like tourists. Although I was wearing a modest, all-body covering, *piran wa tonbaan*, with a scarf to cover my head, the few other women around us were under big *chador*.

"We must get out of this place now!" Kabir announced, pulling my arm. "I think those *hijras* are prostitutes looking for customers."

When an empty rickshaw appeared we all jumped in without delay, instructing the driver to take us to our destination – the parking area for lorries used for export and import, where we could find Shah Mahmud.

After reaching our destination, we were lost again among lorries and lorry drivers in an area larger than where I had grown up. Rows of parked lorries created deep alleyways – the drivers, all wearing *pato* shawls and *pakol* hats – congregated in different parts, smoking cigarettes, chewing tobacco, having conversations. But when they saw us they all stared in our direction. I guessed what made us look like aliens was me in that dress. No woman had any business being there, but we did not know that until we had entered the place.

"Salaam," Kabir addressed a group of drivers in Pashto, standing in front of a truck's bonnet. "Do you know Shah Mahmud from Laghman Province of Afghanistan? He owns trucks here."

"Shah Mahmud." One of them repeated the name, holding his chin, thinking but looking at me instead of Kabir, making me uncomfortable, and I knew Kabir felt even worse.

"Yes, Shah Mahmud," Kabir said, ignoring his rude observation, noticing that all the others were also examining me. "He uses his trucks for export and import." The man who answered Kabir continued thinking and then faced his colleagues.

"Have you heard of Shah Mahmud?" They all moved their heads sideways, clicking their tongues.

We walked away from that group and when I turned to look back at them, they had followed us with their eyes. Other groups reacted the same way, making me silently pray that we might leave that place as soon as we could discover the whereabouts of Shah Mahmud.

"How the hell we are going to find this man?" I asked Kabir, embarrassed and angry.

"I don't know."

"But your mother said if we ask anyone about Shah Mahmud, the people would know him. Peshawar is not a village and has a larger population than the whole of Afghanistan," I said, and I was almost right, I'd seen nowhere in Afghanistan as heavily populated.

We continued going from one group of drivers to another, asking the same question. Some drivers seemed to know him, raising our hopes, but in the end none of them was certain.

The children were tired, thirsty and hungry. We managed to find water and some street food for them, praying that they would not get sick as there was very little regard for hygiene. Flies buzzed around and no matter where we went the foul smell continued to follow us. Kabir and I were very hungry too but did not dare try what was available. However, the children could not wait. We were grateful that they did not ask us to go back to the hotel. I dragged poor Haseeb and sometimes Kabir had no choice but to make Lida walk a little as he'd become too tired to carry her.

Sunset approached. We were mentally tired too, thinking that our money would not last much longer if we could not find Shah Mahmud. The exchange rate was poor, the Pakistani rupee valued twenty-times more than our money. Besides, Peshawar was much more expensive than Kabul. Knowing that our money was worthless, Adai had exchanged our money to dollars in Kabul. Kabir was now exchanging his dollars to Pakistani rupee. I knew it was not much because I had carried it in my underwear until we reached Pakistan but never counted how much we had. Our hope was to find Shah Mahmud so that he would help us, or that is how Adai thought of him, and then he would arrange for someone to bring money from Adai in Kabul to us in Peshawar. Adai was a rich woman with a lot of farmland in Laghman. The income from that alone was enough for her extended family to live comfortably, and yet it was her greed that made her sons share the cost of living in her house. What I discovered later was that after the arrival of the Mujahideen, Kabir kept his money with his mother because the banks were not operating. Apparently, Adai knew well how to hide money even if her house was robbed. Not like us who had lost everything.

Despite all these worries, I asked Kabir to buy me a *chador* as big as a bedsheet to cover myself from head to foot. I could not bear men looking at me as if I was a prostitute. I had noticed that if women moved about at all in Peshawar, they covered themselves either in a big *chador* or a burka. In a *chador* one could only see their eyes. It was not the best garment for a hot place like Peshawar but nevertheless, much better than a burka. I believed before that I would spend my life free of any burka or *chador*, but now I was asking my husband to buy the biggest *chador* for me. My body would be in a cage but I would never allow anyone to imprison my mind. With my mind I fly above the clouds, to freedom and justice for women.

The following morning, I found myself lacking energy. The disappointments of the previous day disturbed my sleep, and worries made me less enthusiastic to go out searching for Shah Mahmud, fearing that if he was really such a well-known person we would have found him already. Nevertheless, I drew some comfort from the thought that the parking place for lorries was so massive that we should continue with our search.

We started again from where we left off the previous day, though not as confident as we had been then, and we experienced the same reactions to our questions. Hope dissipated fast, making us conclude that perhaps the information about Shah Mahmud's whereabouts had not been correct and my mother-in-law must have been wrong. We continued our search with little enthusiasm. In the late afternoon, we reached a group of drivers standing beside a pot over a fire making *chai* for themselves. During all this time Kabir and I had only had our morning *chai*, having gone without breakfast or lunch. They stared at us as we approached them.

"Salaam. We are looking for a man by the name of Shah Mahmud who has some trucks here," Kabir asked when we neared a group of drivers.

"Who?" One of them in dark brown *pato* shawl and grey *kamis-shalwar* asked.

"Shah Mahmud."

"Aha, my friend, there are many Shah Mahmud's here," a young man with a stubble beard said in Farsi, puffing on his hashish-filled cigarette and handing it to one of his friends to have his turn.

"Shah Mahmud from Laghman?" the first man asked again in Farsi.

"Yes, yes, that one," Kabir jumped into the conversation with excitement.

"He operated here some years back." My heart sank and I read the signs of despair in Kabir's eyes. What do we do now? I thought.

"Do you know where he lives?" Kabir asked, still hopeful.

"I am not sure if he is still there, but he lived in a place called *Qaed Abad*. I saw his house because one of his drivers was my friend."

"Do you have his address?"

"I don't know the name of the street and the house number, but I know where it is," said the stranger.

"Brother, please come with us to that place," I begged, knowing that men would respond kindly to a woman.

"But I am waiting for someone right now. Come back in two hours and then I will go with you."

"Allah reward you in heaven, brother. We take a rickshaw for you to go there, and the same rickshaw will bring you back." I continued, realising that I was getting through to the truck driver.

"Okay, come back later."

"We wait nearby, brother," I said.

"If you wish."

We turned around and squatted on the ground just far enough away from and yet be able to keep an eye on the man.

I continually prayed we would find this man who could save our lives. "*Khodaia komak kon*, God help us," I whispered repeatedly, while Kabir kept looking at the drivers. Time stretched slowly, torturing us. If I'd had the power, I would have grabbed the hand of the man who said he knew where Shah Mahmud lived and asked him to take us there without delay. How indifferent could this man can be? Did he not realise our lives depended on Shah Mahmud? And, of course, that kind-hearted man knew nothing about our suffering. He could have just said he didn't want to come with us, not leave his friends, not sacrifice his relaxation time. But eventually, after what I thought was an eternity, he came towards us.

Kabir hired two rickshaws, one just for the man and another for the four of us. The man suggested that we let Haseeb travel with him, but Kabir politely declined saying Haseeb was uncomfortable with strangers. Our rickshaw followed the one occupied by the truck driver.

After about half an hour we reached *Qaed Abad* where the streets were paved and houses, most of them three-storey buildings, were constructed with concrete. The absence of noise and smell indicated that we were in a neighbourhood where well-to-do people lived. When we reached our destination, Kabir paid for both rickshaws while Qasem, the truck driver, stood in front of a well-painted light-brown iron door and pressed the bell. A bare-headed man in *kamis* and *shalwar* appeared. We thought he was Shah Mahmud and immediately said salaam.

"Is Shah Mahmud at home?" Qasem asked.

"Who?"

"Shah Mahmud."

"There is no one here by the name of Shah Mahmud."

"But he lived here. Shah Mahmud from Afghanistan."

"Nobody is from Afghanistan here."

We were stunned, and none of us knew what to do next. The man in the doorway stood there, surprised that Qasem was so sure Shah Mahmud lived there. Another man appeared from the street.

"What is happening?" asked the man.

"Sir, I am sure Shah Mahmud from Afghanistan lived here," Qasem replied.

"Yes, he did," the man street said.

"Where is he?"

"I don't know. I bought this house from him three years ago. This is my servant you were talking to. He doesn't know about this."

What the man said was a hammer to my head. What now? I thought.

"Do you know where he lives now?" Qasem asked, not losing his composure.

"Not me, but I think my next-door neighbour was his friend. He might know about him." After that the man and his servant went inside.

Instead of disappearing, Qasem still wanted to help us. He pressed the bell of the neighbour's house and we were glad to see an old man appear at the door.

"Salaam. We are looking for an Afghan man called Shah Mahmud who lived next door," he said and, pointing to us, continued. "These guys are his relatives and they've come from Afghanistan. They are desperate to find him."

"But he left this place years ago," said the old man.

"Yes, we found that out but perhaps you know where he lives now."

"I don't know where he lives. He is a friend of my son and my son is in Lahore."

"When will he be back?" Qasem asked.

"Sometimes he goes for a long time, but sometimes he returns in a week or two. It depends on his business and he seldom phones. You see, he is a single man and he doesn't want to be in touch with his old father." The man smiled.

Suddenly, Kabir squatted, unable to keep standing. I could hardly hold myself upright either.

Chapter 16

Searching for Shah Mahmud: Part 2

People involved in construction work, villagers seeking low-paid jobs and lorry drivers from Lahore and Karachi used the hotel as a temporary accommodation. No doubt the hotel was one of the cheapest in Peshawar but no matter how cheap it was, we could not afford to stay there for long. Every evening at the hotel Kabir counted our money and calculated our daily expenses.

"How well do you know Shah Mahmud?" I asked.

"He is a distant relative," Kabir replied. "When we moved to Kabul, Shah Mahmud remained in Laghman but came to Kabul at least three or four times, staying in our house. About five years ago he emigrated to Peshawar. Even then, though, he came once or twice to visit us. He was very successful in his business here and gained Pakistani citizenship. If anyone can help it will be Shah Mahmud, because he is both Afghan and Pakistani."

"What will happen if we can't find him?" I asked.

"We must believe that we find him as we have no other option."

We had made it safely to Peshawar but Kabir and Adai had not calculated that something like this would happen – almost sure that we would meet this man as soon as we arrived – our only clue was he had a truck and was involved in export and import. My mind became torturous, especially at night, not allowing me to sleep, thinking of the worse. And the worse was that we would be forced to go back to Kabul. But did we have the money for that after waiting for Shah Mahmud? Pakistan was not cheap. And what would happen if we miraculously reached Kabul? Would the Mujahideen let Kabir live after what he did, escaping from Kabul, leaving his post, not saving the lives of those fighters?

"Even if we find Shah Mahmud, we cannot stay with him forever," Kabir said.

"No, of course not," I agreed.

"But he can help us receive money from my mother in Kabul. He knows men who go to Kabul delivering goods, just like those truck drivers we saw."

"Except his business has changed and we don't know what he is doing now," I said, unable to make a positive contribution to the conversation.

"Then pray that we find him," Kabir retorted.

"I have one more possibility to buy us some time."

"What is that?" Kabir asked.

"This." I extended my right hand, showing the ring on my finger.

"Oh no, Deeba," Kabir protested.

"It is not my wedding ring!" I exclaimed. "I kept that tied on the drawstring of my *tunban* while we travelled.

Kabir didn't know what I had kept in my *tunban* because it had been a very long time since we had made love. There had been no privacy since and at night we slept fully dressed.

On my ring finger I wore a 2-carat diamond set in a silver ring, a precious present from Kabir. I did not like gold much and had asked Kabir to set the stone in silver, my favourite metal. The result was a very unusual combination such that no one would suspect the ring of having much value, believing it was unlikely even to be silver and the stone just an imitation in glass. I was sure that if we sold the ring we could survive for a very long time, but that was the last thing I wanted to do.

I dreamed of food all the time in those days. There had been nothing to eat during our journey, and now the smell of kebabs cooking on charcoal in the bazaar, the aroma of rice and spices, made my knees weak. Sometimes I slowed my walking just to inhale the smoke coming from the *chabli* kebabs sizzling on the grill, producing sparks when fat dripped onto the fire, releasing the aroma of burnt meat marinated in spices and, strongest of all, garlic. But Kabir only bought boiled eggs, cheap over-ripe bananas with black skins, milk with *naan* for us to eat, and then not all of them together. If lunch was milk with *naan*, dinner was a boiled egg with bread and breakfast a rotten banana with *chai*.

Kabir went three times a week to Qaed Abad to ask for Shah Mahmud, but there was no sign of his friend. He travelled there by bus, not wasting our money on rickshaws and one day he even walked all the way to Qaed Abad from the hotel, which took about two hours.

The worst way to spend the day was sitting on our beds in the tiny hotel room, so we went out to explore Peshawar. This was, after all, our first trip to a foreign country and for me just as fascinating as being on the moon, because on my previous travels, discovering my own country, how happy I felt when I worked as a journalist.

Now I was wearing a big *chador*, my appearance drew little attention and we were able to walk around freely, not only discovering Peshawar but also the suffering of our own people who wandered the streets, searching for jobs, looking for an opportunity to get out of poverty. How easily they had become aimless without even noticing it, just like us. Where were we going? Nowhere!

"Look, Uzbek *naan*," said Kabir, pointing to something in the crowded street.

"Where, where?" I asked, not believing him. In Peshawar it was not possible to find bread made in Afghanistan.

"On that tray on the head of the boy in front of us."

Because of the crowds, it took me some time to see what Kabir was trying to show me, but finally there it was – our delicious Uzbek *naan* on a big metal tray on the head of a teenager.

"If it takes the last coin in my pocket, I must buy this bread for us," Kabir said, looking at me for my reaction.

"Oh, I love the smell, the taste, the way it looks," I said encouragingly.

He rushed forward. "Wait, wait we want to buy."

The boy turned around on hearing Kabir and stepped to the side of the street, putting his tray down in front of us. We all looked at the bread and its aroma delighted our nostrils. Only Uzbek bakeries in

Kabul baked this *naan* in tandoors. Thick, flat circular loaves about 10cm in diameter with crispy crusts and soft insides, nigella seeds spread on top and brushed with butter outside – it was a delicacy.

I was focusing on the tray loaded with bread when the boy said, "Salaam, Deeba jan," attracting my attention.

"What?" I asked in shock, not believing someone had called me by name.

"It is me, Hashmat."

I looked at the boy from his head to toe while Kabir also watched both of us, also astonished.

"Hashmat?" Finally, I shouted with excitement. I could not believe it. The teenager selling Uzbek bread was my neighbour from Kabul who had left with his family when the communists took over.

"Yes, it is me."

"Hashmat, what are you doing here?" I asked.

"Selling *naan*," Hashmat said with a sad smile. "What are *you* doing here?" He asked humorously.

We both realised how silly our questions were, because 4 million Afghans out of a population of about 20 million had taken refuge in Pakistan – so it was quite possible to meet people we knew.

"How long have you been here, Hashmat?"

"About four years."

Seeing Hashmat there selling *naan* made me sad. I knew he would also be embarrassed because in Kabul his family had a good life. Then, the communists put his father, a civil servant, in prison because they thought he was anti-government. Just some months after his capture the family disappeared and now they were here.

"Any news about your father?" I asked.

"Come to see us. We will tell you everything."

"How is Mahbooba?" I could not stop asking questions.

"Come tomorrow and find out."

Hashmat gave his address and a clear landmark in case we got lost. We bought four *naans* and no matter how hard Hashmat refused to take the money, we insisted and Kabir shoved the money in his pocket. I wanted to ask him more question about his life in Pakistan but did not want to distract him from his business.

We found a small, quiet park to eat our Uzbek *naan* but, for me, it tasted of sadness seeing Hashmat in those old unwashed clothes.

The following evening we went to where Hashmat and his family lived. In Kabul, Mahbooba and I went to the same primary school and became classmates, but our paths diverged when we continued our secondary education in different schools.

We found their apartment in Thakal, along the main road connecting Afghanistan to Pakistan. This was the way we'd come after entering Peshawar. From what I saw on the streets in that neighbourhood, Afghan refugees occupied many of these run-down apartments. A small grocery shop owned by an Afghan at the beginning of the street was the landmark that Hashmat had given, and the owner directed us to their apartment. We took a narrow stairwell, trying not to miss a step because it was dark even during the day, and it smelled of different aromas coming from those apartments – a mix of Afghan and Pakistani food. I knocked on the door of their third-floor flat. A man of about my age with a face full of beard opened the door.

"Salaam, Deeba jan!" Jamshid, Mahbooba's eldest brother greeted us and shouted for Mahbooba. I heard fast steps from the corridor and then Mahbooba appeared. Without saying a word she opened her arms and embraced me tightly, kissing my cheeks, and I responded the same. She picked up the children, knowing they were my children, and kissed them all over. Again she hugged me tighter and our cheeks pressed against each other, warm tears flowed from both our eyes. I felt the rhythm of her heart. I was in ecstacy. It was not just the fear of the uncertain life refugee that made this meeting so precious to me, but also the length of my loneliness since my family left. It became worse after the Mujahideen took over. At last I had found someone I knew well and it felt as though I had been looking for her ever since she left Afghanistan, missing her.

They were all there in that two-room apartment. We sat in one room on a folding *toshak*, which I assumed was also used for sleeping on. Unpainted plastered walls made the room seem dark. Aunt Habiba, lost in her thoughts, looked much older than the last time I'd seen her, but both Hashmat and Mahbooba kept smiling, happy to see us.

Mahbooba had married a man called Wakil, who she met at the university, and when Mahbooba's family decided to leave Kabul, he also joined them for two reasons: Firstly for Mahbooba to be close to her family; and secondly because, like many others, he was worried about his safety. But here in this apartment I could not see any sign of him and their children if they'd any.

"Where is Wakil?" I could not stop myself asking.

"He is in Gulf," Mahbooba said.

"Gulf?"

"Yes, he is working on a construction project."

"How did he go?"

"You know he is a civil engineer and here he was working as a foreman for a very low salary. Someone told him if he gave him 30,000 Pakistani rupees, he would help him to reach Gulf. So whatever savings we had, we gave it to that man because we heard how people became rich working in Gulf. It is now more than four months since Wakil left for Gulf and we haven't heard anything about him. He is supposed to get us out of this situation, but now we are worried about his safety."

We talked and talked and I asked about my family, if they'd seen them. But the response was that most Afghans who could afford to went to places like Islamabad, Rawalpindi, Lahore or even Karachi, where cities were more liberal for the women and there was no threat from the Mujahideen or Pakistani fundamentalists. I also found out that Uncle Asif, Mahbooba's father, had been executed in prison by the communists for speaking against the Russian invasion. None of them was aware that my own husband was a communist because they were my childhood neighbours and didn't know who I married. They thought to emigrate to the US because one of Mahbooba's cousins lived in California. Occasionally that same cousin sent money to them, but there was never enough. So Mahbooba baked Uzbek *naan* in a neighbour's tandoor for Hashmat to sell on the street. I genuinely felt sorry for the family and nearly cried because first the father was killed and now Mahbooba's husband has disappeared.

We tried not to stay for dinner, but Mahbooba and the rest of the family would not permit us to leave. In Kabul we had often eaten in each other's houses without being invited, just like close relatives. The simple *Kachaloo* stew prepared by Mahbooba tasted heavenly and during that time of being together I realised how much I had missed her. Her smile warmed my heart. At least I had found someone in this alien country whom I loved as a friend.

Worry robbed me of sleep and many questions circled in my mind during the night. Since coming to Peshawar, it had become my habit to discuss our situation in the morning.

"Where the hell is this Shah Mahmud?" I said in frustration.

"Sorry, what did you say?" asked my husband.

"I didn't know finding the man would be so difficult."

"Yes, I agree. And I think I should have planned it better with my mother."

"I was thinking last night, when I could not sleep, and I have an idea."

"What idea?"

"You should go back to Mahbooba's house right now before Hashmat leaves and tell them we are looking for Shah Mahmud. Either they will give you a clue or they may know someone who can help us."

"You are right," he said. "We must use any contact, and so far we have only one. And that is thanks to you."

After Kabir left, I tried to keep the children busy in that small room with nothing but two single beds and bedsheets that had not been changed since our arrival. I asked Haseeb to sit next to me and

I put Lida on my lap. "I will tell you a story, my little children," I said, looking into their eyes.

"Oh yes, yes. You have not told us a story for a long time, ever since we left Kabul," Haseeb said. He jumped off the bed and stood in front of me, Lida followed.

"Yes tell, tell, please," she said.

"Okay, but now you must both go to where you were sitting," I said and started:

"There was and there wasn't. Under the blue sky there was a man riding his donkey, while his son walked behind. A passer-by saw them and made a comment, cruel man riding his donkey while this small child walked. The man felt embarrassed, so he got off the donkey and put his son on the donkey's back. Then another passer-by appeared saying, the old man is walking but the son is riding the donkey. No respect for the father. Hearing that the, father and son both climbed up and sat on the back of the donkey, but they'd not gone far when a man said, oh God, what cruelty. Two people riding this poor donkey. The father heard that and they both got down. Now the donkey was walking without anyone on it. A man saw that and told the father, where is your brain? You both walk and no one is riding the donkey. At that moment the father lost his patience and shouted: it is my donkey and I will do what I want to do with it. He can even ride me if I wished."

I made the children laugh and seeing them laughing after a long time made me happy too. About three hours later Kabir came with a hopeful news.

"I talked to the family. They bake bread for an Afghan restaurant frequented by well-to-do Afghans. Hashmat knows the owner well and he said that here in Peshawar, the people from rural areas, especially those who have businesses, know each other. The owner of the restaurant is from Laghman Province, like Shah Mahmud and he knows his customers by name. So I went there and to my surprise he confirmed that he knows Shah Mahmud and he comes to his restaurant on average three times a week. I left a note with the owner to give it to Shah Mahmud. In the note I have written the name and the address of our hotel."

I jumped off the bed and kissed Kabir's forehead. There was hope at last.

Chapter 17

Living with Shah Mahmud

It didn't take long to get used to the city but it quickly became boring and repetitive. What can poor refugees with no money expect, roaming around, looking for a man who could save their lives? When you are at the bottom of the ladder, any sign of kindness means a life-saver. All Shah Mahmud could do for us, if we found him, would be to allow us to live in his house until money from Kabul arrived for us.

We preferred to stay in the small room at the hotel, despite it looking like a prison cell, to avoid the heat, pollution and noise of the streets. But it was very hard for the children. One evening we went to a small area of green where the children could run and play, Kabir carrying Lida and I holding Haseeb's hand. As they played we watched them in silence, afraid that if we talked we might say something that would depress us, like talking about the good life in Kabul before the Mujahideen took over or what we could do if we never found Shah Mahmud. Going back would be suicide for Kabir. The Mujahideen would not forgive him this time. The first time they had forgiven him because he was valuable to them and could save their lives. But now they knew he was unreliable.

When we got back to our hotel after taking the children to the green, the hotel receptionist told us that a man by the name of Shah Mahmud had been there looking for us and that he said he would return. We regretted that we had been out and had to ask the receptionist to repeat the message in case we had not heard it correctly the first time.

It was almost the children's bedtime when there was a knock on the door. When we opened it the man introduced himself as Shah Mahmud. He was a tall, well-built man wearing a light blue Pakistani *kamis shalwar*. He had brown skin, a bushy moustache and thick hair that fell onto his forehead. He was constantly smiling, trying to put us at our ease. He insisted that we should leave the hotel immediately and go with him to his house.

Shah Mahmud's house was a two-storey building built in the Pakistani style with a courtyard at the centre into which its windows opened. There were no windows towards the street, which served a double purpose – creating complete privacy and also protection from the torturous sunshine and subsequent unbearable heat. I never imagined that a country could become so hot in the summer until I went to Pakistan. Most days the temperature was above 40°C. Just inside the entrance was a big room Pakistanis refer to as *baitak*, a guest room built specifically for male guests. In Peshawar, male and female guests never mixed. The male guests were taken to *baitak* and the female guests, the wives of the male visitors, were taken to *zanana*, the women's quarters.

Shah Mahmud had given us and our children a big room. When we awoke the next morning, we could barely believe our good fortune and the children, who had got up very early, were excited, jumping on us, waking us up and using the good-sized room like a playground. Over breakfast of *dudh pati*, a mix of tea with milk and some spices, fried eggs and cheese, we talked about our luck and the generosity of this wonderful man. For once I could see the usefulness of Adai and I sincerely praised her for what she'd done to make sure we should reach Peshawar safely and find refuge with Shah Mahmud.

After breakfast, Shah Mahmud took Kabir to see a *saraf*, a moneychanger who would facilitate the transfer of money from Adai to Kabir. Shah Mahmud included a tour of Peshawar in his brown Toyota Corolla, a much better way to discover a new city than we did before, wandering around under the hot sun with two hungry and thirsty children. When Kabir left I was asked to join the rest of Shah Mahmud's family in *zanana*. There I met Shah Mahmud's first wife Arifa, who was somewhere between 45 and 50 years old, and his second wife Sabri, about 25. Her marriage to Shah Mahmud had been arranged when she was 16, and she had three sons. Arifa was a very fat woman, hardly capable of moving, and had one married grown-up daughter living in Laghman. Her adult son was married to a Pakistani living in Jamrud Road, an area occupied by well-to-do families. This showed that Shah Mahmud had done well and, because of his wealth, Sabri's father, a peasant from Laghman, had arranged for Shah Mahmud to marry her, a girl with the wild beauty of the rural areas. Our children were quickly accepted and I could see satisfaction in their eyes, their smiles and their laughter. We were now living in a peaceful country and I was grateful to Kabir for finally having decided to leave the hell created by wars in Afghanistan.

Quite soon I also discovered that Shah Mahmud was not really in the import and export business but he smuggled Afghan *lapis lazuli* to Hong Kong. With his wealth he made friends among influential politicians to keep the government quiet and the borders open, and for that he shared his profits with them. Shah Mahmud was a big fish. He was a proper smuggler – and that worried me. I hoped that, despite his kindness and generosity, we would find somewhere of our own to live. But a month passed and Kabir was getting used to the comfort of living as a guest in Shah Mahmud's house and was reluctant to go anywhere else, especially as there was no pressure for us to leave.

Despite the kindness we received, I was not comfortable staying longer. There was not a single book in the house and both Sabri and Arifa were illiterate. I liked them, especially Sabri because of her innocence. She was still like a teenage girl, smiling and laughing easily watching comedies on television, which she and Arifa were both hooked on. The television was on all day long and, instead of going to my room, I watched programmes in Pashto, improving my knowledge of the language. But there was no Adai to force everyone to speak Pashto and both women spoke to me in Persian.

Nevertheless, I thought we were stretching their hospitality and was shocked when Kabir said, "You know Shah Mahmud has said that we can stay in his house for as long as we want in exchange for helping him with his business."

"Oh no," I protested. "Surely you don't want to become a smuggler?"

"No, not smuggling, just handling his accounts. He is not surrounded by many educated people."

"You would be handling the accounts of a smuggler," I whispered.

"You must stop interfering! In my society women never interfere with what husbands do. These two women don't even know what Shah Mahmud is involved with."

"It is not necessary to mention the difference between Tajik and Pashtun households," I replied. "I am concerned about your safety. What would happen to us, God forbid, if you were caught?"

"Caught?" He jumped up from where he was sitting and glared at me. "Shah Mahmud has been in this business for many years and he has not encountered a single problem."

Regarding him fearfully, but still unable to stop myself, I said, "Please try to find a job. You are a good doctor and this is against your principles. You wanted to change our country and that is why you joined the Communist Party."

"Okay! I'll try to find a job. But so far, what enquiries I have made point to the fact that I am not a qualified doctor in this country for two reasons. First, I don't speak English. To them anyone who is educated must speak English. And the other reason is they do not recognise my Afghan degree."

The growing friendship between Kabir and Shah Mahmud worried me. We were running from war to a place where the life of my husband and the rest of his family could be in danger because of this smuggling business. I knew that Kabir was willing to be involved in Shah Mahmud's business because we did not have unlimited financial support and because of the exchange rate and the high prices in Pakistan. We would not have been able to sustain our livelihood. But my hope was still that Kabir would get a job as a doctor in this country. And I was not sure to what extent Kabir would be helping Shah Mahmud – was it just accounting or more? They'd become drinking partners too and came home late. Kabir was excited meeting affluent and influential people in Peshawar, sometimes meeting even a minister. Occasionally they went to Lahore, Islamabad and other major cities. Kabir seemed satisfied with life but I could see danger associated with such a business.

I could suggest to Kabir that he borrow some money from Shah Mahmud to go to Gulf to find a job as a doctor but didn't because I would be left alone. Also, there was no guarantee that he would find a job as Gulf might be just like Pakistan and not recognise his medical qualifications. It seemed that private companies in Pakistan and Gulf employed construction engineers after testing them on site. But the hospitals never offered jobs to Afghan doctors.

When Kabir was away with Shah Mahmud, I went to see Mahbooba. I was delighted when she informed me that she had learned her husband Wakil was alive. In fact, he had sent her many letters but made the mistake of putting some banknotes in each envelope, not knowing that the postmen knew about Afghans abroad sending money in letters. They opened those they suspected contained money, and so his letters never arrived. Wakil had been annoyed when no one responded to his letters but now Mahbooba did not have to bake bread any more and Hashmat did not have to go around under the hot sun selling it.

Being with Mahbooba and her family in that poor apartment made me very happy because of their kindness and hospitality. Mahbooba also needed someone to visit to relieve her boredom. Like me she sat in the apartment from morning until evening with no purpose in life but was at least able to occupy herself with books and magazines that Hashmat bought for her. It was in her apartment that I saw a magazine called *Future*, which was edited by my professor from the Faculty of Journalism, Professor Jamil Abawi. I borrowed the magazine and some books before leaving her.

I suspected that my husband was more than just a person who handled Shah Mahmud's accounts. I realised it was greed that made

Kabir do such work. He'd become a communist not to save his country from poverty but to gain power. He had continued to work as the head of hospital for the respect that position brought. Now he'd become a smuggler. These days I thought about my mother and her choice of husband for me, but the poor woman did not know Kabir. I wished I was not married to a man who could so easily change his personality. I started to dislike Shah Mahmud. We were in the house of a man who bought everything with illegal money – wives, houses, cars, trucks, politicians, government officials, even my husband. I was powerless, unable to make Kabir realise how dangerous our association with Shah Mahmud was.

By March we had been in Shah Mahmud's house for more than six months and our children were happy making friends with Sabri's children, but there was no sign that Kabir wanted to find a new home for us. He kept saying we could save on our expenses by living in Shah Mahmud's house and one day be able to pay a human smuggler to get us to Europe or the US. Shah Mahmud, he said, would help us to find a reliable smuggler. But one day he shocked me. We were sitting in our room, just the two of us, our children were with Sabri's children playing. Kabir was in a very good mood, talking about many things, which was unusual because he rarely talked with me this way.

"Do you know why I am so happy today?" he said joyfully.

I went to sit next to him. "You must have found a job," I said.

"Well, yes but not exactly the type of job you are thinking of."

"What do you mean?"

"Shah Mahmud has asked me to go to Hong Kong on business."

"Business?" I jumped up and confronted him. "You mean you will be going there with a consignment of *lapis lazuli*?"

"Calm down," he replied, surprised by my reaction. "It's just business."

"It is a dangerous business, Kabir. Very dangerous. What happens if they catch you?"

"Catch me? He has done it a million times with no problems. Besides, I will see a new country and he will pay me good money for it."

I pleaded with him. "Please, please Kabir, don't go."

Without saying anything further he stormed out of the room. After Kabir left, I held my head in my hands and covered my eyes. In darkness I imagined the nightmare of Kabir going to prison – my children without their father in a country I knew nothing about. Would I be begging on the street to support my children? The pain in my heart would be incurable unless circumstances changed. In Adai's house, Kabir spent most of his time with his mother and siblings leaving me alone with the children – now Adai had been replaced by Shah Mahmud.

I don't know for how long I sat there. Finally, I got up and looked for a pen and paper on a shelf where Haseeb kept his notebooks and pens. I sat down and started to write a letter:

My dear brother Hanif,

I hope you are well wherever you are. It has been a long time since I have written anything. After the arrival of the Mujahideen, I was only a housewife but, despite losing my contacts with the intellectual world, I still accepted my life. I suppose if I was just an ignorant and uneducated woman, my life would have been easier after the Mujahideen took over. But education had opened my eyes and I could differentiate between light and darkness. Unfortunately, women with no education cannot see that. But once you have seen the light and are then forced to live in darkness, life becomes suffering. My suffering continues, it just takes different forms.

In Adai's house I felt very isolated because she and her relatives thought of me as a complete outsider. When Kabir decided to leave Kabul, I was delighted because of the prospect of finding you and the rest of the family, despite knowing that Pakistan is a huge country with a population ten times more than ours. I also felt that emigration would give me a chance to escape the mistreatment I received from Adai and her family. Now my life is in even bigger danger. My husband, the one who joined the Communist Party to change our country for the better, has become a smuggler, a criminal.

Our mother thought that, by marrying me to Kabir, I would have a happy and prosperous life and even I believed that Mother would not be wrong. Initially I was very proud of my husband, until I realised that his joining the Communist Party had been to gain power and a leisurely life of spending nights with friends drinking. He enjoyed the power that he gained, travelling to Moscow and meeting Russian women. Now he is going to Hong Kong for the same purpose of having fun, seeing the country, enjoying intimacy with women. But he forgets that if he gets caught there will be no one to look after his wife and children.

Now I think that our mother made a mistake. I don't hold a grudge against her. No one can predict the future, know how a person will change. Just as all bad people have the potential to become good, all good people can become bad if one day they forget the goodness in their hearts.

I miss you my brother Hanif. God keep you safe.

Your unhappy sister,

Deeba

After writing the letter I read it to myself. Tears came to my eyes. I ripped the page out of the notebook and tore it to pieces so that Kabir should not read it.

Chapter 18

Without Kabir

Kabir had left for Hong Kong less than a week before. I was waking much earlier these days, partly because I was feeling the bug of loneliness under my skin when I opened my eyes in the morning, and partly because of the loud voice of a mullah preaching to the faithful through a loudspeaker. I went to the window and looked at the clear sky of the dawn. The courtyard paved with concrete was empty of flowers or a single tree. In a way it also conveyed its own solitude and, like Adai's house, it would never give me a feeling of being at home regardless of how long I spent there. Mullahs here in Peshawar did not leave people to rest at night. Well before dawn they started preaching. Even with my poor Pashto I could understand the gist of their preaching, which most of the time seemed to be addressing meaningless matters. After morning prayers again the mullah would continue preaching, showing his own dedication to religion but ignorant of how irritating it was to me, a person who was also religious.

I listened to the sound of Haseeb's light snoring. He is my man now, I thought, although just a small boy of only 7. I am his mother and teacher and he is my protector. Since the day we arrived in Pakistan I continued to teach both of my children, rather than send them to the schools for Afghan children in the huge tented refugee camps. Life for people in the camp was unbearable. Mahbooba had told me about life for women without their husbands because of the continuous wars. Women who lost their husbands were at the mercy of the Pakistani government, living with their children under a single UNHCR tent, very hot in summer and very cold in the winter, receiving a monthly ration if they were lucky. The unlucky women had to offer their bodies to the Pakistani officials who distributed the rations for refugees. These officials knew which women had no husband or protector, making them easy prey for sexual predators. Women had no option but to accept such an undignified life for the sake of their children. Mothers will do anything to make sure their children have food. Would I have to suffer the same fate if Kabir was caught and put in prison? What he had done seemed very selfish to me. I believed that he was thinking only of himself.

In huge contrast to Adai and my sisters-in-law, both Sabri and Arifa were very kind and hospitable. They were Pashtun too but not all Pashtuns are unkind. From Day One they had given us breakfast, lunch and dinner with a variety of food and I could see the beneficial impact of their food on Haseeb and Lida. In the morning after breakfast I taught the children primary school subjects from memory, the lessons I myself had learned as a child at school. I wanted to interest them in learning by making them believe that the lessons were a sort of play. Teaching the children was self-help for me because I was engaged with them and that diverted my attention from feeling sad and lonely. In the afternoon, Haseeb and Lida played with Sabri's children after they had come back from their private school.

One afternoon after the children had gone to play with Sabri's children, I heard a knocking on the door. Thinking it must be Arifa or Sabri, I shouted come in but, to my surprise, Shah Mahmud appeared.

"Salaam, Shah Mahmud," I said immediately when he entered. Fearing something had gone wrong with Kabir's handling of smuggling goods. I asked: "Is everything all right? Have you heard from Kabir?"

He smiled. "Don't worry, Deeba. I have done this work thousands of times. Your husband is fine." He came closer and sat next to me on the cushion. I smelled alcohol on his breath and felt uncomfortable being in such close proximity to him.

"Don't worry! Kabir is in a nice hotel right now in Hong Kong," he said, moving even closer to me.

What he was doing was so unexpected and confusing that I did not know whether to move away or sit still. Perhaps, I thought, he was there to tell me something especially important.

When he spoke, it was with a slurred voice. "I am so happy that you are here, Deeba. You see, I married two women from villages but now I see the difference between a woman from Kabul and a woman from a village. You city ladies never get married to a man like me because I am from a village and because I never finished secondary school. I have only nine years of schooling."

"But you have very nice and kind wives, Shah Mahmud," I said and moved a little away from him.

He pulled himself towards me. "Yes, but they know nothing about passion, how to be a woman. Once I tried to marry a girl from Kabul but her family refused bluntly." He put his hand on my shoulder and looked into my eyes. "What can education give? There are many educated people here but still Afghanistan dies of hunger."

I tried to move away but he held my right arm and pulled me towards him. His hand was so strong I feared he would bruise my arm.

"Let me go, Shah Mahmud, I think you are drunk."

"I am not drunk, wait."

"Haseeb, Lida come!" I screamed, louder than I had ever done, louder even than when I was a child and suffered some sudden injury. "I must change your clothes."

My scream shocked Shah Mahmud and he let me go. I ran to the door and shouted again for my children to come to our room. Shah Mahmud rushed past me and out of the house. When the children came, they sat on both sides of me waiting for their clothes to be changed, but I had no energy to do so. Their clothes were not dirty anyway.

Now I could see the true personality of this man who I had thought kind because he had given us a shelter. I began imagining the man had involved Kabir in his smuggling just to get him caught and that I would then have to become his sex slave. Even if he did not plan it that way, Kabir getting caught would also mean him losing the goods and, consequently, money. Or maybe he would definitely make sure that I would became a member of his unofficial harem by finding me cheap accommodation and providing food for me and my children in exchange for sex, just what was happening to other Afghan women refugees who had lost their husbands. Like them I would not know how to return to my country or how to earn a living and live a decent life. He could easily mastermind the demise of Kabir by employing a hitman – a bullet in unsafe Peshawar, full of lawless smugglers and Mujahideen, all carrying guns.

What happened that day made me keep the children with me all the time as protection from Shah Mahmud's advances. That was not easy for the children because they loved playing with Sabri's children in the courtyard. But if they were with me, the chances were that Shah Mahmud would not enter the room. When it became impossible to keep the children with me, I joined them in company with Shah Mahmud's family, which was not easy because they spent the whole day watching silly television shows or, when they talked to me, it was about matters that did not interest me. There was a world of difference between my upbringing and theirs. I also thought of Kabir, praying that he was safe and would soon return to Peshawar. I feared he would prefer to indulge in his pleasure of drinking and womanising, forgetting he needed to be with his family. What kind of husband did I have if he spent time in pleasure while leaving his own family vulnerable?

Counting the days until Kabir would return, I thought about how to tell him what happened between me and Shah Mahmud. If I did not tell him, there would be a possibility that Shah Mahmud would do the same again, and might even rape me. But if I told him, it could be even worse. No man in our society can tolerate it if another man undermines his honour. Trying to have sex with his wife is disrespecting him. Kabir would probably challenge Shah Mahmud and the result would be a fight, serious injury or even death. But Shah Mahmud was a criminal – someone who carried guns – someone who had connections with government and politicians. He could easily gun down Kabir and yet walk away free.

Therefore, the day Kabir returned was the happiest day of my life. He was alive and free and I hoped that we were now safe. I was surprised that he didn't tell me about what he had done in Hong Kong until after several days later. When he did, he said, "You are right, this business is not safe."

"Yes I told you, smuggling *lapis lazuli* is dangerous."

"I wish it was just *lapis lazuli*."

I did not understand. "What do you mean?"

"Shah Mahmud sends heroin concealed in *lapis lazuli* shipments."

"No, it can't be true." Whatever I thought of Shah Mahmud, I did not want this to be true.

"It is absolutely true," Kabir insisted. "And we must get out of this place as soon as we can. I have been looking for somewhere to rent."

Chapter 19

Searching for work

I was extremely glad that Kabir had realised he was dealing with a man in a very dangerous business. I was glad for three reasons: because of Kabir's decision not to work with Shah Mahmud; because he was determined to find a place for us as a family; and because I would not have to tell him anything about what happened that day between Shah Mahmud and myself.

Within days Kabir found a two-roomed first-floor apartment with a small toilet in which we could wash using buckets, but no kitchen. The owner suggested we use the small balcony for cooking. The balcony had a solid wall instead of a railing, giving me enough privacy to cook there as it faced a cornfield. Kabir bought a small portable gas stove with one hob and three *charpai*, a simple construction of four strong vertical wooden posts connected by four horizontal members. The natural-fibre webbing was made out of date-palm leaves and we bought mattresses to put on them. The design made them self-levelling and they were comfortable to sit on as well as sleep on. That was our furniture.

Wazir Abad, where Akbar found this tiny apartment, was on the outskirts of Peshawar City, somewhere between town and country. On one side of our apartment we could see cornfields and on the other a busy street full of traffic and with shops on two sides. The cornfield was a good place to walk with the children – if Kabir was in the mood. For me the place was perfect, not because it was comfortable accommodation but because it gave me peace of mind. Regardless of its ugliness and poor construction it felt like home, unlike the beautifully constructed houses of Adai and Shah Mahmud, a place without the harassment of a criminal.

The air in this semi-rural area was better than the city polluted by cars and rickshaws. It would have been good for the children to go and play in a park, but Kabir told me there were no parks in Peshawar. Nevertheless, I thought what mattered most was Kabir's safety and there was no threat of being raped by Shah Mahmud.

As soon as we were settled once more Kabir started looking for a job, this time any kind of job as long as it was not hard labour. Every day, after a very early breakfast of bread and tea, Kabir took a bus into the city and came back in the evening, exhausted, ate a single vegetable dish, the cheapest in the market, and would fall asleep next to me on a *charpai* only big enough for one person.

One day he came back only half an hour after he had left the apartment. Thinking he had probably forgotten something I asked: "What happened?"

"The police," he said, and sat on our *charpai*.

"What?" I asked, thinking I had misheard him.

"The police stopped me."

Immediately I thought of his trip to Hong Kong and the prospect of him in a Pakistani prison where it was worse than capital punishment.

"But why?" I asked.

"To take money from me."

"I don't understand. Please explain."

"On my way to the bus stop two policemen stopped me. I don't know how they recognised that I was an Afghan refugee. They asked me questions like where was I going and then started searching my pockets, saying I was carrying hashish."

"That's absurd!"

"Yes. But you know what? They found hashish in my pocket."

"Really? You were carrying hashish?"

"Noooo, Deeba, don't be stupid. One of them planted the drug in my pocket while searching, and then took it out telling me I had hashish in my pocket. I protested and they both started slapping my face and head. The worst thing was the crowd of the people. They dragged me by my wrist to take me to a police station, but when there was no other person around, just the three of us, they said there were two options: either take me to the station where I would face the possibility of prison, or I give them all the money I had in my pocket. I had no choice but to give them the money."

For some days Kabir did not go out but I knew he could not afford to give up. The money from Adai was not going to last for ever. We could not return to Afghanistan and Kabir was not going to work for Shah Mahmud. The only option was for me to try and find work. What I was hoping for, apart from Kabir getting a job, was that his experience of living as a refugee might humble him and make him realise what the communists did in Afghanistan was a mistake and the suffering of refugees was a consequence of that.

One day after Kabir had finished his breakfast, I said: "Can I try finding a job instead of you, Kabir?"

"Now that is a joke."

"I believe in miracles, Kabir."

"You and your miracles!" he scoffed. "Look what religion has done to us. If only those idiots begging in Pakistan or getting themselves killed as the *jihadis* of Allah had come to their senses we would not have had to fight. No one would have had to lose their lives and no one would have become a refugee."

I realised that Kabir blamed others, not the communists, for our misfortune, but I was not letting go of my desire to work. "Just trying would do no harm," I said pleadingly.

"And who is going to look after the children?"

"You've worked very hard all the time we've been together – perhaps it is my turn to help you. You could look after the children and relax at home."

Immediately he accused me: "You have already planned everything in your mind."

"Just give me your blessing," I insisted.

"Fine! But I will not allow you to work as a domestic servant in strangers' houses. You'd be a potential sexual target."

My husband was a jealous man worried about strangers but blind to a criminal like Shah Mahmud who could not be trusted with his wife. "No, I am not thinking of that kind of job," I replied.

My plan was to go and see Professor Abawi about working for *Future Magazine*. I gave the address of the magazine's office to the rickshaw driver and in about thirty minutes the rickshaw dropped me in front of a modern two-storey building in University Town. It was a fairly expensive looking house that was both Professor Abawi's home and his office. I told the watchman who I was, saying I was an ex-student of the professor and hoping he would remember me. The watchman told me that Professor Abawai was not yet there but took me to the ground floor office where a team of journalists, four men and one woman, were busily working, typing, writing and reading. No one paid any attention to me, which I thought must be quite normal because they probably had frequent visitors. I was offered a seat and someone brought me a glass of water.

The office walls were decorated with large framed photographs of the Bamyan Buddhas, Wakhan Natural Park, the Afghan Snow Leopard, and a larger framed photograph of our former King Mohammad Zahir Shah. I gazed at his handsome face, not having seen it since the communists took over. The Mujahideen did not like him either and would not allow his photograph to be shown in public. A wave of nostalgia swept over me, taking me back to the time when Zahir Shah was our king and we had lived in peace. Certainly, in the time of the king, officials were corrupt – but they made no secret of doing something in exchange for money. That was honest corruption – unlike the hypocritical communists and Mujahideen who pretended to be God-fearing and to care about the welfare of the people they promised to protect and then went about robbing and killing them.

I had drunk half of my water when Professor Abawi appeared. "Well, well, you are here too?"

"You remember me, Professor?"

Professor Abawi had studied in France and for some years had taught in Lyon University but then decided to come to Afghanistan to teach in Kabul University as he thought he was needed there more than in France.

"Come on, Deeba. How could I forget a student with such a beautiful mind and face?"

"I am glad you've not lost your sense of humour," I replied. "I was hoping that you might employ me as a journalist here, Professor," I said sipping the water.

"Oh Deeba, you were one of the best students I ever had and one of our country's best journalists. I wish you'd come to me when I was establishing this office. Now, however, I only have funds enough to support the employment of my current staff. I can't do anything." He looked around at his staff and whispered to me: "It would not be fair if I dismissed one of them to make way for you. They also have families to feed."

I sat there listening to stories the professor told, each one very attractive, good for a journalist to write about. He spoke about his meetings with people in France while campaigning for the return of the king. About help he gave to French journalists who were going to Afghanistan to report on the war. Stories about the hard life of refugees in Pakistan. He told me because of his contacts, his funds came from France and he also produced *Future Magazine* in French and another quarterly publication called *Afghanistan Today*. The king, also a graduate of a French university, had great support in France and Professor Abawi thought the only way to get Afghanistan out of misery was to reinstate the former king, who lived in Italy with his family. Regardless of how popular the king was in France or how many reliable contacts he had, more funds were not on the horizon to expand and employ more people.

I was about to leave when the professor said, "Wait! I've just thought of something that might interest you."

"What?"

"I have a contact with Serve NGO, an organisation helping the most vulnerable Afghan women. It is a fairly big NGO. I'll write to my friend Trudy and ask her if she has a position for you. I know it is not journalism, but in such circumstances, we do not have many choices."

"Anything, Professor. Anything," I said with a smile, despair in my heart.

"It is not guaranteed, Deeba."

"I have to try it."

"Wait while I write a note to Trudy. The Serve offices are not far. They are just a little way along this road. You can go there after you leave here."

Less than ten minutes after leaving the professor I found myself in front of the offices of the Serve NGO. It was a big two-storey western-style building with a lush green lawn in front. A watchman was sitting in the shade of a neem tree by the gate in the metal-barred fence. It was a very inviting building. An image came to my mind of myself saying good morning to the gate keeper and walking on the stone path that divided the lawn, and entering a freezing-cold air-conditioned office. I introduced myself to the gate man, explaining the purpose of my visit, and he reluctantly took me to see the receptionist sitting behind a clean oak desk. She told me that Miss Trudy was not in. I would have to come back the following day.

My disappointment increased when I reached home, having to listen to Kabir telling me that in Peshawar women stayed at home and it was impossible for women to get a job. I told him that there was a woman working for Professor Abawi, so it was not completely impossible. Fortunately, he did not stop me from going to Serve's offices the next day, but I knew that would be my last chance. So, the next morning, after preparing breakfast for Kabir, I was sitting in a van, a little more expensive kind of public transport than the bus but much cheaper than the rickshaw, whispering the ninety-nine names of Allah and praying for success at getting any kind of job with Serve.

After reaching Serve's offices I had to wait probably between ten to fifteen minutes – but it felt like an eternity. The previous night I had dreamed of working for a humanitarian organisation helping my own people. Such a job seemed to me even more precious than being a journalist. It would save my family's life. Then a woman with white hair, a zig-zag-creased face, thin lips and thick glasses entered the reception room.

"Salaam. So you were a student of Professor Abwai," she said in perfect Persian but with a western accent, holding the note that I had given to the receptionist to pass on.

"Yes, madam," I said politely. I thought she would ask me to come to her office but she kept looking me up and down, from head to toe, as if she was buying something from a market but was not sure about the price.

"You have come at the right time," she said with a smile. "Zarmina's application for immigration to the US has been approved. She is one of our staffers and will be leaving soon with her family. You could fill her position. Presently she gives health advice to refugee women but we are hoping to distribute food in the refugee camps in future."

"I see," I said, delighted but frightened. I had never done such work before and thought that giving health advice was the work of a doctor.

"I trust Professor Abawi's recommendation," she continued. "Are you good at dealing with people – especially vulnerable women?"

"I try my best."

"Good. The job is simple but we need an educated woman. Zarmina learned on the job and we provided training for her. We will do the same for you. Initially you will accompany Zarmina to learn what she is doing. In that period you will not be paid and I am sorry. Our budget is not very big and donors these days have cut some support as the war in Afghanistan has continued for a long time."

"Madam, I am so grateful. You have helped a family by giving me a job."

"Call me Trudy, everyone does. I hope we also benefit from your employment. Do you speak English."

"No, Trudy." An icy hand gripped my guts.

"Well, Zarmina does. But don't worry, we'll take care of that as well. We provide English language courses for our employees and also schooling for their children." She laughed. "You seem very bright. I am sure you will learn quickly."

Chapter 20

Almost six years later

Five Springs have passed since I came to Peshawar. I am sitting under a maple tree in Serve's beautiful garden. Amjad Khan from Peshawar, the gardener, is the only Pakistani employee. The rest of us are either Afghans, Americans or Europeans. I prefer to use the back garden as my morning office before I leave for the refugee camps. Abdul Salam, our watchman, makes an excellent *dudh pati* before he opens the gate, and I always arrive early to have the pleasure of his *dudh pati chai* in the quietness of the early morning. It is not only for the sake of *dudh pati* that I like Abdul Salam, I also respect him for his decision to give up fighting. He had been a Mujahideen commander in Shomali, where he comes from, fighting against the communists. When, after the communists, the Mujahideen started fighting each other, he chose to stop fighting and got this job to support his family. He knew, like I did, what would happen to the women of husbands killed during the war.

Spring and autumn are the best seasons in Peshawar while winters are cold and summers unbearably hot. I learned how to make the most of the good weather when the leaves seem clean and shiny, the roses on their way to full blossom, the birds are singing. My new friend, a brown-, yellow- and white-feathered nightingale, is up there in one of the branches and will not leave until he has delivered all his new compositions. Beside all the delights of the day I have a letter from Mahbooba that arrived yesterday, but I have not yet read it because I love the waiting, the anticipation, the guesses. She has been living in California for the past two years, a place all Afghan refugees dream about.

Yesterday I went to the Naser Bagh Refugee Camp to teach Afghan women about hygiene and baby delivery. Serve provided me with a year-long course here in Peshawar to become a midwife, as well as handling other duties. When I got there, I saw a long line of refugees queuing for their monthly ration provided by the UNHCR and distributed by the Pakistan government. Through my research I had found that at least half of what is provided for the Afghan refugees is taken by the Pakistani officials distributing the rations, filling their own pockets. Although a spring day, the sun in a clear blue sky makes the camp hot and I can imagine that the women under their burkas carrying their children in their arms must be boiling. There were some young children too in tattered clothes holding their ration cards. Trying to torture the refugees with a long wait, the Pakistani officer holding the keys, surrounded by police, was not opening the door of the storage container. When he finally opened it, the line of the queue broke as every single refugee rushed to reach the door, some falling with others trampling on them. I heard the cries of women and children but was unable to help any of them. Instead of helping those who were injured in the crowd, among them pregnant women, the Pakistani police started hitting people with canes to disperse them. I saw one teenage boy with blood running down his forehead. The refugees dispersed and after a short while the official closed the door of the storage. Refugees' loud cries filled the camp, begging the man to continue distributing. But the man left in his official Jeep, leaving desperate people to starve. When I returned from the camp I wrote a letter in English to UNHCR, describing what had happened and demanding that they should assign at least one officer from UNHCR to be present when rations are distributed. My colleagues say that I've learned English very well and I cannot thank Serve enough for providing English courses to employees as well as in-house schooling for their children.

Since I came to Pakistan many things have happened in my life that made me think positively despite being a refugee. In fact, my situation is much better than when I was in Kabul under Mujahideen rule. Thank God there is no Adai here. Her house, the place I hated, is completely destroyed by rockets fired from the mountains. She now lives in Laghman Province, where she is from and has a big farm there. We received that news through the *saraf,* the money exchanger, the one who used to bring us money from Adai at the beginning. We don't need money from Kabul any longer.

I am the bread-winner of the family and have relieved Kabir of the burden of looking after the children because both Haseeb and Lida spend their day in the school run by Serve for the children of its employees. The children speak perfect English. My boy is almost a man. Or that is how I look at him – grown up, a tall teenager, polite and my king. They both go to Sunday bible studies and I don't mind that they learn about Christianity. There is only one God anyway. They also benefit from learning better English on Sundays. Even I go there sometimes.

This is the day that the Lord has made
We will rejoice and be glad in it.

This message is the same in our religion. I also talk to my colleagues about my own faith, Islam.

I have a third child named Fariba, but that is the last since I now know how to prevent unwanted pregnancies, learning that from my work place. While I am in the field my baby is looked after in a creche that I can afford to pay for. Kabir has given up looking for a job and seems satisfied with life, meeting with Rashid, one of his communist friends who immigrated to Pakistan after the fall of the communists. They drink together in Rashid's apartment or at ours when I am not at home. I have told Kabir that I cannot tolerate his drinking in front of the children. I am sure he would not have accepted what I told him but now I am earning he has to be flexible. Once I found an earring in our bedroom and when I challenged Kabir about bringing women to the house when I am not at home, he beat me. Occasionally he slaps my face hard, especially when he comes home drunk, to remind me that he is the husband and I am the wife. Once or twice a month he goes to Lahore Province with his friend Rashid. Having been a journalist, I investigated and found out that there are plenty of dancing girls and prostitutes in Hira Mandi, a most attractive place for men looking for pleasure.

I became the programme manager after Trudy died. I miss Trudy, that kind American lady with a golden heart. I also miss Professor Abawi who was killed by Golbudin Hikmatyar's group because of his support for the former king of Afghanistan. So, I have lost two people who changed my life for the better and allow us now to live in a much nicer apartment than the one we lived in after leaving Shah Mahmud. He is now dead, but that is a loss of life about which I do not care. Shah Mahmud was run down by a truck on the road. He was not killed at first, but when the truck driver saw him trying to get up, he reversed his truck over him. I heard many reasons for his killing, but Abdul Salam, who always gossips with me, said that the truck driver, an honourable Afghan man, had heard that Shah Mahmud was going from camp to camp finding vulnerable young women to provide sex for his Pakistani government friends. He had killed him to protect the honour of Afghan women. This is the explanation I like more than any of the others. There is also a new development in the life of Afghans – the Taliban. This most cruel and brutal group has taken power in Afghanistan. They kill women they suspect of adultery or flog them just because they wear white socks. It is forbidden for women to wear white socks because they think it provokes men sexually.

"Tell me, little bird, shall I read my letter with your music in the background?" I called to the nightingale with a smile on my lips. The answer was yes. So I opened dear Mahbooba's letter. She is working in a posh bakery in Fremont, California, until her husband finishes his Master's Degree in civil engineering.

My dear Deeba jan,

I want you to be hopeful but not excessively because, as you know, crushing hope is heart-breaking.

Yesterday, during the funeral of one of my distant relatives, I talked with the deceased's daughter about our lives as refugees in Pakistan. Like us, she also spent some dark years there. I talked about you, your loneliness, and your quest for finding your parents and siblings, describing your family.

My friend, who lives in Los Angeles, told me that she'd met some Afghans at a social gathering in Los Angeles who talked about one member of their family, a married woman, they had left in Kabul, and she remembers vaguely in which part of Los Angeles they live. I made a note of that place and I am going to send my husband there to search for the family. You might think it is like finding a needle in a haystack – but finding an Afghan in California is very easy. One just goes to the mosque the Afghans use and describes the person sought to the Afghan mullah and other worshippers. No one can avoid the mosque here even if they don't go to prayers. Funerals and other social events are arranged in the mosque and our community all know each other.

This is a very short note just to let you know. In two weeks, my husband will be on his way to where my relative mentioned. Unfortunately, he cannot go immediately because of his university exam.

I pray that this family is yours. I love you more than my sister and remember you almost every day. May Allah brings everlasting peace and happiness to you and your family.

Your friend,

Mahbooba.

I could no longer hear my Bulbul, the name I'd given to the nightingale. There was complete silence. But my thoughts moved into territories I had forbidden it to. After extensive searching in Pakistan, I had given up looking for my family and whenever Mahbooba talked about it when she was in Peshawar, I stopped her. It was not necessary to raise my hopes, knowing that the next letter would disappoint me. The US is not like Taimani where I grew up, easy for people to find each other on the streets or in mosques. For all I knew my family could be anywhere in the world, including Pakistan. But I also knew that the majority of educated people who had money either paid smugglers to get them to the US or arranged it themselves by contacting friends or relatives. All they had to do if someone sponsored them was to buy their plane ticket. There was a third category too. Those who worked for the US government or the US embassy in Kabul were eligible to emigrate to the US. My father, an engineer, had worked as a contractor in Helmand on a project where the US government built dams and irrigation canals, changing a barren land into agricultural farms, making Afghanistan self-sufficient in producing wheat. It would be silly to think that the Americans would honour a contribution from an independent contractor to such a project. And how could my father prove that he had participated in the Helmand Project? He had left the country in such a hurry without his documents and job certificates.

Despite all the odds, that night I could not sleep, imagining that Mahbooba's friend might have been right about meeting my family. But as the days passed I became calmer, believing the news was simply raising and crushing hopes. More than a month passed without any news and my belief grew stronger. Then, one day after I returned from fieldwork, our receptionist informed me that there had been a phone call from my brother Hanif. She said that my brother had left a number and asked me to call him at any time. Was this real?

I looked at the note and realised it was a US number. My body started trembling, my knees could not support my body, my hands started shaking, and I slumped onto a chair in front of the receptionist's desk. I only became aware of my surroundings when Fatima, our receptionist, put a glass of water in front of me. I drank it in one go. Just a minute later I asked our driver Rajab to take me to the nearest shop where people could phone abroad. These kinds of shops had become very popular because of the Afghan refugees calling their friends and relatives in foreign lands. I dialled the number not knowing it was the middle of the night in California. Immediately it was picked up.

I heard the voice of my beloved brother Hanif. "Deeba jan, is that you?"

Tears came to my eyes, flowing down my cheeks. I could not speak.

"Is that you? Please talk."

Again, I could not speak, pressing the receiver to my ears, holding it tight.

"I can't hear you."

"No, no, no! Don't hang up, it is me," I said and started wailing. The customers and the shopkeeper looked at me with surprise but I could not stop.

Hanif would be flying in in two days. He was going to leave for Peshawar immediately after our conversation but I told him not to risk his job and to get permission from his employers first. I said I had been waiting to see him for such a long time that another two days longer would make no difference. But I talked to him and the rest of the family every day and for a very long time. I didn't care how much it cost. If money connects hearts, it is well spent. My father told me that that little connection, the contract job in Helmand, had helped him to get to the US with the rest of the family. He had a friend in the US who had worked on the same project for the US government. He provided the necessary documents to enable my family to immigrate.

They also became aware of my ordeals caused by war, my in-laws and Kabir. Hanif told me that he had applied for my immigration to the US a long time ago and had been waiting for me to be found. He had twice been to Kabul since the fall of the Mujahideen and the Taliban's strict control of the country had made it safe to travel. He had been unable to find me in Kabul through the place where I had worked and the only other reference was Adai's house, which no longer even existed and he didn't know where Adai had gone.

The last conversation ended with Hanif saying: "Deeba, I think it will take less than a year for you and the children to come to the US but we have cancelled Kabir's application. I know how to bring you to the US without him. He loves going to places for pleasure alone, you said. That would be the time. I shall come and stay in Pakistan for a while after your application has been approved. Then I'll wait for Kabir to go to Lahore. In fact, I shall encourage him."

Chapter 21

Fremont, Freedom, California

I have been in California for the past ten years with my children, away from Kabir for the first time, experiencing both the joy and the trouble of being alone. The joy was that I had no one now to interfere with my life, no one to trouble me physically or mentally. But I still faced challenges of how to live as a single mother. Overall, being my own master gave me the confidence that the future would be what I make of it. Apart from wondering how to provide for my family, I had to look after the children, making sure they learned English and that they do well at school. And they ARE excellent students, because playing with mobiles and watching television is limited.

There have also been some significant changes in Afghanistan. The US helped to topple the Taliban regime and I hear wonderful news that the UN has been surprised by the thirst among boys and girls to go to school. UNICEF predicted that 1.5 million children would go to school immediately in spring after the fall of the Taliban, but attendance had been three times more and there's a significant shortage of teaching material, schools and teachers. On television I see images of girls smiling, studying under the tents. The Taliban destroyed schools and banned girls from formal education. Now the west has provided the ground for girls to go to school.

I watched an interview with a middle-aged man from Hazara region, taking his girls to school, walking all the way for about one and half hours there and back. He'd decided not to work for three hours every day to make sure his daughters were educated. The future for the people of my country will be bright because all we needed was peace and support. Now the west has provided peace and support, the children can be the leaders of their own country one day. One good example is my own children. They are the best in their classes.

It was 5 a.m., I finished my *Fajr namaz*, praying for my family. There was no time to go back to sleep. I went to where my son Haseeb was sleeping and looked at him. Youth sleep is very deep and I could see his chest expanding and contracting. My mind travelled back to Afghanistan and Pakistan and I pictured those horrible times when I was abused by my in-laws, and my own husband, who swore to protect me. A time that should have been invested in love, not torture. A time of my husband's indifference towards me and his children. A time he preferred to be with other women. Two of us had to sacrifice our lives for the rest of the family: Haseeb and I.

My brother had his own problems and family and the cost of living was too high for him to support us. Now I had to work and Haseeb had to do the same, so that the rest of the family could study.

I found a job with Jack in the Box fast food and he worked there with me, washing dishes. Then, early in the morning, he had to do another job, which was better paid, working as a taxi driver in San Francisco. The car, bought in instalments, worked well and he was very proud when he came home in the evening, putting all of his earnings in front of me.

"Look, Mother. I earned so much today. Some people even gave me large tips. I tell you, women are very generous."

I keep all of our earnings to make sure we have enough money to pay for the rent, utilities, food and drink.

When *Nawrooz* came, which is our new year, I invited Nooria, who has become my good friend, to our small two-bedroomed apartment to celebrate the new year with us. She is married to a wonderful man who works in the construction business. She came with her two children, her husband and her brother, a man who was married to an American but now divorced. We had a wonderful time eating *haft miwa* and a few days later she paid me a surprise visit.

"Deeba, it must be hard for you to cope with family here," she said while making tea.

"Yes it is, Nooria."

"Don't you think it is the right time?"

"What do you mean, Nooria?" I said taking the cup of tea that she held out towards me.

"Tariq, my brother, has been divorced for many years and has been looking for the right person to marry."

"I think it is a good idea."

"He is scared of getting involved with another American woman. You know our culture is different."

"So find him an Afghan wife," I said laughing.

"I found one."

"Great," I said and sat next to her. "Where does she live?" I asked, as if I knew all of the places in the US.

"She lives here."

"Here?"

"He loves you, you silly friend."

"But I am married, Nooria."

"How can you still be married to that man?" Nooria asked looking at my eyes. "He tortured you."

"He is the father of my children. If I marry any other man, my children would be angry and disappointed."

"Deeba, they are in the US now, and they know what is right for you."

"Please stop this," I said sharply, and put my cup down without drinking.

Since then Nooria has not bothered me. I am not sure I didn't want to marry again because of my children or because I'd had enough of men, thinking the next person would be the same as the last.

California has given unlimited freedom to Afghans. Coming from a poor country, most weekends are dedicated to dinner parties in which lavish food is cooked and alcohol served for men. I have seen women also drink in secret while they were in the kitchen pretending to prepare the food. I was invited to these parties and I don't mind seeing women and men drink, but I stay away from it. I must admit that I like dancing with guests after dinner.

Sharifa has enough money available to her because her husband works as an estate agent and there is a property boom. She often organises dinner parties, to show us the American way of life. She invites some native Americans too, the people she and her husband go to night clubs and casinos with. It was in her house one evening that I felt the happiest and without being shy I danced and danced. Men watched me with wide eyes and admired my dancing, especially Jamal, who left his seat to come and sit next to me, making conversation, admiring my dancing, admiring my clothes. While I believed him that my dancing was probably good, his comment about my clothes was nonsense. They were bought from a cheap clothes shop.

One Monday about a week after the dinner at Sharifa's, the doorbell rang. No one was at home apart from me, so I went to open the door.

"Do you want a guest?" To my surprise Jamal was on the other side of the door, using the Afghan expression of a guest who comes to visit without being invited.

"Uninvited guests are guests of God." I also used an Afghani saying.

"I knew you would be at home on a Monday," he said. I thought he must have found out that Monday was my only day off.

"Don't just stand there, please come in," I said. Frankly, I was embarrassed to let him in because the living room was untidy. To escape my embarrassment, I went to the kitchen to make tea. There was further embarrassment in the kitchen because I had no *shirpira* or *noqul* to serve the tea with. All of my children have a sweet tooth and even if I were to dig a hole in a secret place to bury my sweets, they would find them.

"It is so different from Afghanistan, Deeba jan," Jamal said by way of starting a conversation.

"Oh yes. We cannot compare Afghanistan to the US."

"Every woman has a chance to work here. Not like back home where even finding a job for a man was difficult."

"Yes, this is the most important thing I like."

"It must be hard for a woman to work and look after the children."

I knew where this conversation was heading, so I said, "But you have no idea what I went through before coming here. The hardship of this country is like a holiday for me."

"Your holiday can become even nicer," he said.

I looked at his handsome, clean-shaven face. He was at least five years younger than me and looking for someone to have a good time with. But still I ignored the advance. I did not want to get things wrong.

"But I don't understand," I said.

"I would love to look after you," he replied.

"I see." For a moment I remained quiet and stared at the pattern on the cheap carpet on the floor, pretending I was thinking about the offer.

"I hope you permit me that happiness." He adjusted himself on his seat and I knew that my answer would matter a lot.

"Jamal jan, you are a handsome and kind man. But I really want to look after my children by myself. I love the freedom of being alone."

The conversation continued with Jamal pleading, but I would not sway. Eventually he left and he never came to my apartment again.

The unlimited freedom in California had confused my society. Women under economical pressure had no choice but to find an Afghan, or any nationality, for financial support. Some were married but their husbands were either in refugee camps in Pakistan or at home in Afghanistan, waiting for their applications to be accepted as a refugee in the US.

The rate of divorce among Afghans in America was much higher than other nations. Women who were mistreated in Afghanistan had the chance to divorce and find someone they loved. As they all could work, they were not dependent on their husband's income. Afghan men saw women like me as easy prey, because I was alone and without a man. This freedom also affected Afghan children. Teenagers experimented with sex and drugs, which alarmed me. So I had to be vigilant and make sure none of my children became addicted. If I had to choose another man, it meant I must spend time with that man and not be able to check on my children. But in my heart, I wished that the husband I already had was a nice man and that he was here raising the children with me. He was a medical doctor and he could help with the children's studies and also help to teach them how to behave.

Men like Jamal did not prevent me from going to dinner parties and dances. I'd become braver since rejecting him and rejecting others was not difficult. Apart from loving dancing, I enjoyed long walks whenever I had time. Going to Victoria Park, which has a small lake in the middle, after a brisk walk, I often open my thermos to pour tea for myself, and then I write, sitting on a bench facing the lake where ducks swim around, like ships without sails.

Fremont has another name among the Afghans. They call it 'Deh Afghanan', which means 'Afghan village' because of the concentration of Afghans living here. Two bakeries, numerous shops and four restaurants owned by Afghans makes the place very Afghani. They also have their own mosque and I have seen women and men wearing Afghani traditional dress, which I have never worn outside the house, walking on the street going to or coming away from the mosque. They don't go there just for worship. Gossiping is also part of going to the mosque, especially among women, who watch every movement of other Afghans. They gossip about who is getting divorced, who is getting married again, and whose daughter was spotted going to a bar with a black man. The Afghans can be racist too, and seeing an Afghan girl with a black man is shameful.

As for me, as long as my daughter Lida graduates from Berkeley, where she wants to go, I do not care who she marries, so long as he is kind and respectful. She is very ambitious and wants to live in England after her graduation, where my brother is.

"I want to get out of this Afghan Village," she says and I laugh.

I do not wear Afghan traditional clothes but nor do I wear miniskirts. My clothes are more or less the same as they were in Kabul before the Russians invaded our country.

In the streets I see Afghan men with long beards, in traditional clothes, walking about. If you look at their passports, they are all born on the first day of the first month of different years, and their wives too. They do not speak English and this is the best way they can remember their new birthdays, given by someone who completed their immigration application in English.

Going to Afghan dinner parties is not enough for me. I also try to be a little more American, and for that reason I have joined the library. It was there that I found out about a writers' group that meets twice a month. Fortunately, the group agreed to accept me as a member and being with them has given me the motivation to write. Now I write poetry instead of articles for newspapers. Poetry heals my heart and is like a meditation. I read Rumi every morning after my *fajr namaz*.

"Oh my, you sound like Rumi, Deeba," Melisa, a Chinese lady, says who has read Rumi, while I read in the group. But I know I am not Rumi and Melisa has not read Rumi in depth.

When I go to work or to the public library I take a bus but sometimes I venture further. Bay Area is my favourite place, or Coyote Hills. One sunny spring day when I climbed onto a bus and was scanning my bus card, I heard a voice.

"Sit down, you bitch!"

I was very scared and rushed to the back of the bus. Then I noticed a big black man sitting on a seat just behind the driver, arguing with the empty seat next to him. People in California don't use buses often so the only passengers were him and me. I was terrified that the man would stop fighting with the empty seat and come to me for an argument, but after a few stops he got off. I feel bad when I see people like that man, ignored by society. We all have the potential of becoming mad. In my case if I did not have the support and love of my brother, I probably would have gone mad with what my husband did to me.

Work, looking after the children, going for walks, meeting my writing group members, it all keeps me away from thinking about intimacy. But at night, when I am in bed, loneliness gets in beside me and for a while I am unable to sleep. At the beginning of my marriage both my husband and I were passionate for sex. But it became less relevant when we moved to Adai's house and again when we went to Pakistan. Kabir discovered prostitutes. Despite all of this, I did feel secure lying next to a body I once loved, and the warm feeling helped me to sleep.

Sitting close to Haseeb's bed, I opened my Rumi book and started reading as I did most mornings after *Fajr namaz*.

> *Don't listen to them!*
> *They seem to protect,*
> *But they imprison.*
> *They are your worst enemies.*
> *They make you afraid*
> *Of living in emptiness.*

I discovered this poem some time back and put a marker on the page to remind me of Kabir's failed protection.

At about 5:30 a.m. the alarm clock rang and continued ringing until Haseeb opened his eyes. Seeing me there, he smiled and turned the alarm off. Of course, I can make Haseeb get up but I am training him to be responsible for his timing.

"Good morning, Mother," he said, rubbing his eyes.

"Good morning. Go and wash and then come to breakfast. I will prepare it while you are in the bathroom."

I taught my children to take a shower every morning before leaving the house because I don't want anyone calling them dirty immigrants. Not all people are tolerant of immigrants and we must follow the American way of life. Besides, Islam says that cleanliness is half faith. By the time Haseeb finished his shower, breakfast was on the table. His favourite, two fried eggs with Afghanis *naan*. We were still having our breakfast when I heard an envelope being dropped through the door, but none of us moved because it was most likely only a bill. When we were about to leave, I was surprised to see a letter from Afghanistan addressed to Haseeb.

"A letter from Afghanistan?" I asked showing my surprise.

"Yes!"

"Who is it from?"

"I will tell you this evening," he said. "We don't have time now. You have to go to Jack in the Box and I must rush to pick up passengers."

"Please tell me, Haseeb."

"Later, this evening."

And he disappeared, making me wonder why he could not at least mention the name of the sender.

At work I could not stop wondering who the sender of the letter was. In the evening, despite being impatient to know, I prepared dinner. When we finished, during tea, which is an Afghan custom, I said to Haseeb, "You did not tell me who the sender of the letter was."

"It is from my father," he said after a long pause.

"You've been in touch with your father?" I asked

"Yes, Mother. I could not resist it. He is our father."

"You could have at least told me."

"I was not aware, Mother, but when I went to the mosque one Friday, a man who was a classmate of my father at the university approached me and he said our father is desperate to be in touch with us."

"Desperate?" I put my tea on the table and squinted my eyes.

"Mother, we all know what he did to you. But he is our father."

"When was he ever a real father to you all?" I screeched.

"I know he did some horrible things to you. But he is seriously ill and I thought getting in touch with him would not be a big deal. He is not here after all. His letter doesn't say anything bad about you," he continued, taking the letter out of his pocket. "Here it is, you can read it."

"You are a big man now," I said, smiling at him and pushing the letter back. "People are writing to you."

My own mother taught me about forgiveness and told me not to hold grudges, so I calmed down thinking, *Let the children be in touch with him.* But for me, my marriage was over and yet I was not looking for another man.

Chapter 22

Children's success and demand

Before leaving the apartment, I prepare a big healthy lunch for me and for my children to take to school. During dinner we eat small amounts, and we eat between 6 p.m. and 7 p.m. That way none of us suffers from indigestion. We also drink plenty of water and water by itself keeps us from feeling hungry because our stomachs are full. My colleagues at work joke with me suggesting that I should be a nutrition consultant, and I wish I had a qualification for that. I would have loved that kind of job but the reason I did not study for it was because I always had to work to provide for my children in order for them to continue with their studies. Their success is my success. Preventing my children from having fast and unhealthy food does not stop me from celebrating their success by going to my favourite Papa's Papaya Thai Restaurant, and I love the spicy papaya salad. While we all share what we have ordered, I am the one who finishes off the papaya salad. The children know how much I love that salad, so they let me be selfish. When Lida informed me that she had been accepted at Berkeley, I took the children to that restaurant to celebrate and I told them that I did not care if they had three portions. I could not hide my delight, telling every single person at work that my daughter Lida had been admitted at Berkeley University. When she told me, I could not sleep that night. How is it possible that a daughter of a refugee who had nothing in Pakistan managed to gain entrance to Berkeley? But miracles happen or, in other words, we make our own miracles. God says, "You move, I grant you success." No one has a better life sitting on their backside.

I always keep fast during Ramadan and I would like to advise anyone who is worried about their weight to try some short fasting. The philosophy of fasting for me is not to lose weight. I have remained slim and after a month of fasting I give *zakat*, money, to poor people and one of the people who deserve it is Khalil, my cousin. Here in Fremont it is fashionable to go to *haj* when you have money. It is like a competition to have the title of *Haji* in front of your name, but I know it is not the way that Islam preaches. It says you must make sure that your family and relatives are not suffering from extreme poverty and hunger and when you have provided for them, only then you can go to *haj*.

My cousin Khalil has thirteen children and I blame the large number of children in his household on the war. Before the war, we had a family planning clinic in which husband and wife were advised how to control birth by either taking pills or using condoms. After the Soviet Union's invasion, such clinics disappeared as doctors were required to treat the war-injured.

Even families with fewer children struggle, and I am sure Khalil, with the tiny land he has in Nijrab District, is not capable of feeding his children.

Sometimes I talk to the moon and the moon in California is just as bright as the moon in Kabul, surrounded by stars. The moon tells me about the rollercoaster of life. How it changes and how unpredictable it is. One day you are at peace in a country that you love but overnight it changes, thanks to things like the invasion from the Soviet Union. Was it life itself following its course, or was it me trying to change my life for the better? I remember the story of Alexander the Great again when after reading his palm, a fortune teller informed him that his life would be short. Alexander took a knife and extended the short lifeline on his palm and made it much longer. Are we the master of our own destiny? Maybe a bit of both. The great emperor Alexander could not make his life longer and, for me, the changes to happiness did not happen overnight. Now that I am happy and surrounded by the love of my children, in a beautiful and peaceful country, there is no guarantee that life will remain the same. Or perhaps it is me who has gone through so much in life, knowing life could change in a minute. I ask the moon questions about my country in poems:

Are they still there?
The mountains and rivers of ten thousand years ago
And the dream twenty years old
All are drowned in the rain.

When I arrived home one day, I was surprised to see Haseeb there. His presence worried me. I thought he might have had an accident while driving his taxi. But his smile calmed me.

"Let me make you tea," he said. "I have brought mouth-melting *shirpira* full of pistachio." He went to the kitchen to prepare the tea while I talked to the other children.

"I want to tell you something, Mother," Haseeb said after placing the tea on the coffee table.

"What is it?"

"I will tell you when we go to your favourite Papa's Papaya."

"It must be something amazing if you are taking us there," Fariba chipped in.

"Yes it is, and I will pay for it," Haseeb said with excitement.

I liked this American voice in my children. In my culture no one from the same house says "I will pay for it." We *all* pay for it as a family. The US has encouraged them to be individuals.

After tea we went to the restaurant. We joked, laughed and relaxed, but I could hardly wait to hear what Haseeb had to tell me. When dessert came he said, "I am going to Afghanistan," and I thought I had heard him wrong.

"What?"

"I am going to work for the US Marines as an interpreter, in Bagram Airport.

"Are you out of your mind?" I put my spoon down.

"No, Mother. I cannot let you work in Jack in the Box for ever."

"What is wrong with my job?" I looked at his eyes, waving my right hand. "Are you embarrassed that I am a low-paid worker?"

"No, Mother. I am embarrassed that I have been working as a taxi driver while my sisters go to university. Working with the US Marines is my only chance to get a job I like, and to progress. I would only work for one year in the safest part of Afghanistan, and there is a good chance that I will continue with them when I return. Kabul is safe, and I would be in the army compound."

The news took the taste of good food away from my tongue. It was true that Kabul was safe now, but to let my son go thousands of miles away without me was beyond comprehension.

"You're sure your motivation is not to see your father?" I asked.

"No, Mother. My motivation is my future."

Haseeb was right. I did not want him to be a taxi driver for the rest of his life and I knew once he was in Kabul he would meet his father. That is the most natural thing for a child to do. His father only did wrong things to me, not to him. But one day, before his flight, once again I had an argument with him, trying to prevent him leaving. And yet I knew if he did not go I would be accused of preventing him from progressing and at least getting one good year's salary. On the day of his flight I gave him my blessing, and we all went to the airport to say goodbye to him.

There in Kabul, Haseeb became in charge of his life, choosing a wife for himself and he wrote to me about his father, that he was very sick and was sorry for what he'd done to me. I knew Haseeb would try to bring him to the US for treatment and Kabir would be living with us again. But now I am different. I am an American woman who knows her rights.

And of course, I went to Kabul to arrange my son's engagement. No Afghan mother allows herself not to be the person to organise her son's engagement. But you heard of this at the beginning when I started to tell you my story. Funny, my beginning was the end, the end of suffering, and the beginning of happiness.

Just days before leaving Kabul to come back to California, the Taliban once again took Afghanistan. But I managed to escape. Maybe I am Peshak-e Haft Jan, the cat with nine lives.